BEATING
THE DOW

Books by John Downes

DICTIONARY OF FINANCE AND INVESTMENT TERMS

THE BARRON'S FINANCE AND INVESTMENT HANDBOOK

BEATING THE DOW

A HIGH-RETURN, LOW-RISK METHOD FOR INVESTING IN THE DOW JONES INDUSTRIAL STOCKS WITH AS LITTLE AS $5,000

MICHAEL O'HIGGINS

WITH

JOHN DOWNES

HarperBusiness
A Division of HarperCollinsPublishers

This revised edition uses material previously published in the *Beating the Dow* newsletter published by the Hirsch Organization, River Vale, N.J. 07675

The charts in chapter 5 used with permission. © M.C. Horsey & Company, Inc., (410) 742-3700, P.O. Box 2597, Salisbury, MD 21802. All rights reserved.

HarperCollins books may be purchased for educational, business, or sales promotional use.
For information please write: Special Markets Department, HarperCollins Publishers Inc., 10 East 53rd Street, New York, NY 10022.

FIRST EDITION

Designed by Pagesetters, Inc.

Printed on acid-free paper

Library of Congress Cataloging-in-Publication Data has been applied for.

ISBN 0-06-662047-3

00 01 02 03 04   RRD   10 9 8 7 6 5 4 3 2 1

TO

Mimi and Dad for the gift of curiosity,
and to Donna, Mark, Brendan, Colin, and Sean,
whose loving presence helps smooth
out the vicissitudes of investment life

—Michael O'Higgins

Contents

Preface

WHEN *Beating the Dow* was first published ten years ago, I knew its simple and obvious strategy, based on the resilience of temporarily out-of-favor Dow stocks, would win converts. As a money manager, I had used high dividend yield as a contrarian strategy in all kinds of markets, and its record of consistently outperforming the Dow and most mutual funds was impressive.

At the same time, I expected the simplicity of the strategy would meet with skepticism in a financial community addicted to the notion that anything as important as managing money had to be complicated. There was also the simple fact that contrarianism—buying when others were selling—runs against human nature. And even if individuals could be persuaded that Dow stocks had more resilience than risk, the full-service brokerage establishment would certainly be inhospitable to a formula system that rendered its advisory services unnecessary.

To my own astonishment, and to the credit of my colleagues in the professional financial community, *Beating the Dow* became the investment discovery of the nineties:

- Average investors moved in droves into a system that featured household names like General Electric and Eastman Kodak. Books and articles began appearing that embraced the system and expanded the underlying research.
- Enterprising financial web sites took the idea and added their own variations.
- A consortium of leading brokerage firms, adapting a legal vehicle traditionally associated with municipal bonds,

created the first equity unit investment trusts. Called defined asset funds, they began by holding *Beating the Dow* portfolios. Then they expanded on the concept, using foreign stock indexes and other portfolios comprising high-capitalization stocks not in the Dow. Equity unit trusts have now become an important industry, led by companies like Merrill Lynch and Nike Securities L.P., with its First Trust products for regional brokers nationwide.

- Mutual funds also began appearing, combining *Beating the Dow* portfolios with other investments such as SPDRS and zero-coupon bonds.
- The popular newsletter *Beating the Dow* was a direct outgrowth of the book.
- *Barron's,* the Dow Jones business and financial weekly newspaper, began following the system on a regular basis, popularizing the term "Dogs of the Dow."

Ironically, 1990, the year *Beating the Dow* was first released, became the first year in our twenty-six-year research period that the system had a significant negative return. Saddam Hussein's invasion of Kuwait and the prospect of war in the Persian Gulf caused a temporary market plunge affecting cyclical stocks in particular. But the following year, 1991, was the second best year in the system's history, led by a 61.9 percent total return for the *Beating the Dow* Five-stock portfolio.

It is equally ironic that as this revision is about to go to press nearly a decade after the first edition, the system seems headed for its second significant off-year. The problem is not too much popularity. Overly widespread use of the system would cause the *Beating the Dow* stocks to move as a group and there is no evidence this has happened. In 1998, for example, three of the *Beating the Dow* five stocks outperformed the Dow, one significantly underperformed and another had a negative return. The reason for a lackluster 1999 is that a superannuated bull market, supported by steady economic growth and low inflation, has relegated "value stocks" to the sidelines while high-capitalization growth stocks, especially those in computer technology, have been bid up to dangerously overpriced levels.

Prolonged bull markets breed complacency, spawn "new era" theories that support overvaluation, and make value stocks— stocks that are temporarily depressed because of cyclical earnings or other problems—less attractive than stocks with momentum.

Beginning in 1995, we have been witness to a two-tiered market. The "blue chip" indexes and averages, especially the price-weighted Dow, have been elevated to unprecedented heights by a handful of overpriced and unduly risky stocks, while the rest, on average, have underperformed.

In 1998, for example, the Dow Jones Industrial Average had a total return of 17.9 percent, led by four stocks: IBM, with a closing price of $185, gained 77 percent. Merck closed at $147 and gained 41 percent. General Electric, priced at $102, gained 40 percent. Wal-Mart, at $89, gained 107 percent. Those four stocks had price-earnings ratios of 30, 36, 38, and 44, respectively. The Dow's historical price-earnings ratio prior to this bull market was 15.

Another bull market phenomenon has made it more difficult to identify out-of-favor stocks using the high-yield criterion. Combined with the lower long-term capital gains rates provided by the Taxpayer Relief Act of 1997, the extended bull market has made it tax efficient for companies to remunerate shareholders by repurchasing their own stock. With earnings per share spread over a reduced number of shares, share prices rise on the wave of the bull market, giving shareholders favorably taxed capital gains instead of fully taxable dividends.

The effect of stock repurchases has been to reduce dividend yields and force them into a tighter range. This has made the dividend itself a less important part of the total return, and with stocks differentiated by fractional differences in dividend yield, it has become harder to separate the companies that are out of favor from those that may be using their cash in other ways.

Actual stock repurchases under formalized stock-buyback programs can be treated as dividend equivalents, but not all stock buybacks are designed to compensate shareholders and considerable analysis is often required to quantify those that are.

Finally, the Dow itself has become more growth stock–oriented. In November 1999 we saw the deletion of four yield stocks—Chevron, Goodyear, Sears, and Union Carbide—and the substitution of one, SBC Communications, Inc. Of the other three substitutions, Microsoft, pays no dividend and Home Depot and Intel Corp. have a nominal payout. This makes the overall Dow harder to beat with dividend paying stocks.

So for all the above reasons, what has been a simple way of beating the Dow over many years has temporarily become less clear-cut. But the operative word is *temporarily.*

Dividends will be back. They are a corporation's way of competing for equity capital and will be paid again when companies run out of excess stock to buy and when the end of this remarkable bull run makes capital gains harder to come by.

Value stocks will be back in vogue when complacent investors are reminded that high price-to-earnings ratios represent unacceptable risk. As this is being written, Janus Funds, one of the most successful mutual fund groups in the last few years, has just announced two new value funds.

And in the constant evolving of the business environment, which is reflected in the Dow, growth stocks become mature companies, cyclical companies diversify, and diversified companies return to basics, becoming cyclicals again and even growth companies.

Floyd Norris of the *New York Times* has always been a wise observer of the markets. In September 1999, he wrote a piece titled "1968 Redux: New Issues Are Hot, Value Stocks Are Not," which is particularly relevant. Here's part of it:

Over the last 18 months, an investor who carefully went through the stock market and chose a portfolio that was balanced among sectors and focused on the 10 percent of stocks with the lowest ratios of prices to earnings—in other words, a value investor—would have lost money.

But somebody who took the opposite strategy, buying only the stocks that were losing money or had the highest ratios of prices to earnings—in other words, the kind of companies that seem overpriced to begin with—would have a portfolio that rose 34 percent. . . . The only other time that value stocks trailed by so much was in the 18 months that ended in June 1968.

There are differences between now and 1968. Then inflation was rising, and the Vietnam quagmire was worsening. In the stock market, the expensive stocks that were flying high were generally smaller technology stocks with no profits but lots of hype. . . .

But the similarities may be more significant. In 1968 the stock market had been rising, with only minor interruptions, for two decades, and the last recession, in 1961, was a distant memory. Many hot initial public offerings doubled the first day they traded. American households had a record 23.7 percent of their assets in stocks—a figure not exceeded until 1998, when it hit 24.3 percent.

The lesson is that long bull markets and prolonged expansions breed complacency. In 1968, there was talk that central bankers could "fine tune" the economy to prevent recessions indefinitely. Now there is a "new paradigm" in which technological progress assures inflationless growth.

Those who profited in 1968 were destined to suffer later, as the leading stocks of that market crumbled. The laggards of that era held up better, but virtually every stock was devastated in the 1973–74 bear market.

It is tempting to note that in 1973–74, when the Dow was down 36.2 percent, the *Beating the Dow* Five-stock portfolio gained 15.8 percent.

Beating the Dow is based on simple logic that will produce exceptional returns in any rational market and until excessive popularity turns contrarianism into conventional wisdom. The most effective preventative of that unlikely oxymoron is an occasional off year, like the one we're now putting behind us.

Michael B. O'Higgins
John Downes

Introduction

I ENTERED the investment business in 1971 as an institutional research salesman for Spencer Trask and Company, one of Wall Street's oldest and most prestigious "research boutiques." My job was to convince banks, insurance companies, and other institutional investors that our research analysts, by virtue of their experience, analysis and insight, could help them beat the Dow. If they liked my pitch, we signed them up for our highly regarded research service at a price of over $50,000 a year.

In 1973 we were in the middle of a bear market. One day I sat talking with a bank investment manager I knew to be something of a market guru. Spread out in front of him was his bank's "approved list," a lengthy roster of top-quality common stocks that had received his investment committee's blessing as suitable for an institution entrusted with public funds.

An approved list is hardly where you'd go looking for excitement, but this respected professional had written something in the margin that made me intensely curious. Reading upside-down, my eye caught a little square box he had drawn in black ink. In it, he had jotted some numbers. Sure I must be onto something, I crossed my fingers and asked him for just a hint. What arcane investment wisdom did that mysterious box contain? His answer, given without hesitation, changed the course of my professional life.

The little black box, he explained almost apologetically, contained nothing mysterious at all; quite the contrary. It listed 30 of the most widely held and popularly followed stocks in the world—the 30 companies making up the Dow Jones Industrial Average.

"If it were up to me," I can still hear him saying, "I would throw out the rest of the list and stick just with the 30 Dow Industrials."

This seasoned veteran of the investment wars, over a period encompassing many market cycles, had determined that it wasn't necessary to attempt, as most professional investors do, to follow hundreds of stocks in order to outperform the averages. Rather, by concentrating on these 30 very important companies, higher, steadier returns were available with relatively little risk and minimal effort.

Being a newcomer to the complex and often intimidating world of investments, the idea that an approach so simple and so safe could result in superior investment returns intrigued me. In any given period there would be Dow stocks that doubled and Dow stocks that went down, I reasoned, so why couldn't I look at the outperformers as a group, figure out what they had in common, and translate that into an investment strategy that beat the market as a whole—the goal of every money manager?

I started spending nights and weekends on research. Eventually I concluded that by periodically applying a few simple criteria to this small group of 30 top blue chips, I could achieve better results with less risk than the majority of independent money managers and mutual funds with their complex investment strategies.

And the idea that it could all be kept simple suited me just fine.

EARLY IN my career I made an observation about human nature and money—that *people tend to complicate something in direct proportion to its importance.* I'm sure I'm not the first person to observe this, but it's been such an important part of my life that as a private joke I call it O'Higgins' Law.

O'Higgins' Law helps explain why over two-thirds of professional investors fail to beat the market averages even though they spend heavily on research, employ economists, follow hundreds of companies, have sophisticated computer models and use techniques like program trading to try to enhance returns and limit losses.

In fairness to my fellow money managers, handling large corporate and institutional portfolios inevitably requires more complicated strategies than personal investing with smaller amounts of money. But most people, professionals included, make it more complicated than it has to be, which usually means making it more expensive and less profitable.

Investing *can* be too complicated. There are more economic variables and other imponderables involved in forecasting corporate earnings (which ultimately determine relative stock prices) and in anticipating market conditions (which move prices in general up and down) than analysts can possibly process with accuracy and consistency. Yet as long as there are computers, professionals will try to anticipate prices and markets. Some will succeed, most will fail, and that's enough to guarantee investment opportunities for personal investors who can see the forest for the trees.

Beating the Dow will show you how to see the forest for the trees.

I'm a contrarian. That means I look at how the majority is thinking. Then I do the opposite. In a market influenced by psychological factors, I usually win. When everybody moves to one side of the boat, I don't spend a lot of time trying to figure out what they're looking at; I know to move to the other side to keep dry.

What I'm saying would be simplistic rather than just simple if it weren't for the following premises basic to *Beating the Dow:*

1. Common stocks are the smartest investment alternative.
2. The Dow stocks are solid blue chip companies of enormous economic importance. All are good long-term investments.
3. A portfolio of out-of-favor Dow stocks has outperformed the Dow Jones Industrial Average on an annual basis, an achievement that has eluded the majority of professional money managers.

In later chapters I will show you step-by-step how to structure and manage your own portfolio of five or ten out-of-favor stocks.

Because they are Dow stocks, both portfolios are conservative, but a ten-stock portfolio offers greater safety. For the more adventuresome, I will also describe a one-stock strategy.

I am also going to prove that these portfolios have outperformed the Dow on an annual basis by margins that are not only impressive but often amazing.

The stock selection methods we'll use are time-tested, take only minutes, and cost the price of a newspaper.

Fair enough?

Method of Calculating Total Returns

UNLESS OTHERWISE specified, annual returns for the Dow components and the Dow Jones Industrial Average were calculated by taking period-end prices, subtracting them from the prices at the end of the following period (adjusting for any stock splits that might have occurred during the year) and adding dividends received for the period.

Historical total returns thus represent actual stocks and real time; they are the results you would have obtained had you been invested in those stocks in those years (as opposed to a retroactive reflection or back test of existing Dow components).

Total returns are compounded annually. (Quarterly compounding would have produced even higher returns.)

All returns are expressed before commissions and taxes.

PART I

INTRODUCING THE DOW STOCK SYSTEM

CHAPTER 1

Keep It Simple!

IN 1985 Texaco, America's third largest oil company, was ordered to pay Pennzoil Company a huge $10.3 billion judgment. In 1987 Texaco filed for bankruptcy. Its stock plunged 28 percent to $27 a share. In 1989, with the legal claim settled, a postbankruptcy share of a restructured Texaco sold at nearly $60, a new all-time high. Although it would be deleted from the Dow in 1997, Texaco was selling ten years later at more than twice that value, and that was after a two-for-one stock split!

When deadly gas leaked from a pesticide plant in Bhopal, India, in 1984, killing over 3,300 people and injuring thousands more, Union Carbide Corporation, America's third largest chemical company and owner of 51 percent of the plant, was sued for over $3 billion. Its stock sank 21 percent to $11, but it bounced back in 1985. In 1989, the Bhopal litigation settled. Union Carbide shares hit an adjusted all-time high of $33. A decade later, having spun off its industrial gases division in a transaction that gave shareholders a 70 percent return in 1992, a significantly downsized Union Carbide, since acquired by Dow Chemical (no relation to Dow Jones) and dropped from the Dow Jones Industrial Average, was trading at over $60.

Early in 1989 the tanker *Exxon Valdez,* owned by America's third largest industrial corporation, ran aground in the pristine waters of Alaska's Prince William Sound. In a tragedy that inspired T-shirts reading "Tanker from Hell," it spilled enough crude oil to cover the state of Rhode Island. Exxon stock dropped 7 percent on the news but quickly rebounded to over $40. In mid-1999, on the eve of its merger with Mobil and after splitting two-for-one in 1997, Exxon was selling at over $80.

I've made three long stories short, but these anecdotes—and I could cite many more—have a common lesson:

By virtue of sheer size and strength—call it raw staying power—blue chip companies tend to be survivors. The old adage "the bigger they are, the harder they fall" doesn't hold when you're talking about corporate giants. Blue chip stocks are usually safer investments than other kinds of stocks.

The investing public invariably overreacts to unfavorable developments. This creates special opportunities when you're dealing with blue chips: bad news is good news because it makes strong stocks cheap.

Here's another fact about today's financial markets:

Contrary to popular belief, large institutional investors, who dominate market volume and cause sharp volatility through program trading, have created more opportunities than disadvantages for personal investors.

Many individual investors turn to mutual funds as a solution to volatility, but the funds are actually part of the problem. Seventy-five percent of them fail to match, much less beat, the Dow and other market indexes. Their flexibility is seriously constrained by size, competitive pressures, liquidity responsibilities and diversification requirements. Together, these factors lower investment returns, increase transaction costs and necessitate trading practices that cause wide price swings, many of which are merely technical.

You can use the flexibility you have and that the mutual funds and institutional investors lack to actually capitalize on the volatility they create. *Beating the Dow* will show how you can outperform the pros, simply and conservatively, with your own portfolio of common stocks.

When it comes to accumulating wealth, common stocks historically have been unrivaled by any other investment alternative, including real estate and gold.

The uniquely simple system revealed in *Beating the Dow* has with remarkable consistency outperformed the Dow Jones Industrial Average (DJIA). I make the 30 Dow industrial stocks—all leading blue chips—your total investment universe, and I identify the laggards and potential winners within it.

My approach to common stock investing is so simple anybody can use it and have fun doing it. It is a direct outgrowth of my personal philosophy, which I learned as a young broker before I became a professional money manager—keep it simple.

Within the small Dow stock universe there are dramatic profit opportunities for individual investors. The key is that *in relation to each other,* there are always Dow stocks that are doubling, moving sideways, or going down. *Beating the Dow* shows how to identify the winners when they are out-of-favor and can be bought at bargain prices.

The companies that make up the Dow are household names that are among the most publicized, analyzed, and widely held stocks. Their immense asset values, financial resources, and economic importance give them strength, adaptability and resilience. As a group, they include the most viable business enterprises on earth.

Part II of *Beating the Dow* includes profiles of the individual Dow stocks, showing how each has adapted to the modern economy and how each is positioned with reference to the megatrends evident currently. Although all of the Dow stocks are solid long-term investments, *Beating the Dow* does not involve a "buy and hold" strategy. As John Maynard Keynes once said, "In the long-term we're all dead." I don't know about you, but I prefer a shorter investment horizon.

Part IV of *Beating the Dow* provides a step-by-step guide to structuring a portfolio of either one, five, or ten Dow stocks (depending on your preference). Your individual portfolio can be self-managed with a minimum of time and expense and has an amazing history of beating the Dow Jones Industrial Average on an annual return basis.

My Beating the Dow–Basic Method incorporates my strategy in its simplest form. Requiring minimal investment, these income-producing portfolios have outperformed the Dow year in and year out. Even in 1987, when October's Black Monday saw a 508-point drop in the Dow Jones Industrial Average, an all-time record in percentage terms, the Beating the Dow–Basic Method made money for the year with an annual return nearly double that of the average as a whole.

My Beating the Dow–Advanced Method is designed for personal investors with a yen for more than vanilla. It covers more sophisticated strategies and shows the results of combining different selection tools with seasonal market timing techniques to produce outperforming returns, often with reduced risk.

Keep it simple—and make a bundle with *Beating the Dow*!

CHAPTER 2

Why Common Stocks
Are the Best Investment
for Accumulating Wealth

BUSINESS IS about risks and rewards. Since stocks represent shares of ownership in a business, you, as a shareholder, share those risks—and those rewards. But business is also about growth. Profitable companies, by retaining what they don't pay out in dividends, grow bigger. With more capital, they are able to generate increased sales and profits. Over time, the value of shares grows as the business grows. This is just as true of General Motors as it is of a smaller business. It's easy to forget that the world's major corporations, with their mind-boggling size and diversity, are businesses.

For these simple reasons, equities—stocks—have historically far outperformed bonds and other fixed-income securities.

One hundred dollars invested in common stocks (as represented by Standard & Poor's index of 500 stocks) in 1925 would have returned $234,989. Invested in riskier small stocks, it would have grown by $511,565. The same investment in United States government bonds would have earned $4,318 and in Treasury bills (an indication of what a money market fund would have yielded) $1,394. Inflation alone would have increased the value to $814.

With an annual inflation rate averaging 3 percent and an annual total return on the S&P 500 of 12 percent the resultant real return of 9 percent (before income taxes) is impressive evidence of the value of common stocks as a long-term inflation hedge.

7

A particular stock is as risky as a particular business, but even as most of the best stocks trend upward, they fluctuate in value. The word for that, of course, is volatility, and if you buy high and sell low you can lose money. Combine chronic bad corporate management with bad luck and stocks can become worthless.

STOCKS VS. BONDS AND TREASURY SECURITIES

A given company's bonds carry less risk than that same company's stock. I put it that way rather than categorically because it's safer to own General Motors stock than Fly-By-Night Bahamian Airline's junk bonds.

Whereas stock represents ownership and the risks that go with it, bondholders are creditors. If a company goes out of business and sells or otherwise liquidates its assets, it first repays its creditors, then the stockholders get whatever, if anything, is left over.

Stockholders, if they receive income at all, get dividends paid out of surplus earnings. Bondholders get interest, which is a contractual obligation of the company.

Bonds are subject to market risk, like stocks but to a more limited extent. General interest rate levels are always changing; the market prices of fixed-income securities go up or down to adjust the yield (the interest rate as a percentage of the market price) to market rate levels. Bond prices are also affected by supply and demand and by changes in credit quality. But, assuming the issuer is solvent, bonds repay their face value at maturity.

So bonds are generally *safer* than stocks, but in terms of total return—capital gains plus income—the wealth-building potential of stocks is infinitely greater.

INFLATION

Inflation is a major argument for owning stocks. Severe enough inflation can cause stocks to lose value, but over the long haul equities have outpaced the inflation rate. Having reached double-digit levels in the 1970s and early 1980s, inflation has been brought under control and currently exists at a nominal rate. Some economists think we could even see a period of deflation. While serious deflation would reduce output and employment and be bad for stocks, a small amount of deflation can actually benefit stocks. That's because wages tend to remain stable and translate into more spending as prices for goods and services decline.

Bonds and Treasury bills, once issued, do not gain value with inflation. Although inflation expectations are taken into account when the rate of interest is originally determined, these investments become vulnerable to erosion of the dollar's purchasing power if inflation exceeds expectations. Conversely, marked deflation would benefit bondholders.

REAL ESTATE AND GOLD

Real estate and gold have traditionally been viewed as inflation protection—"inflation-sensitive" is the buzzword—and are frequently touted as investments offering superior returns to common stocks.

Let's take real estate first. There are numerous ways to invest in it, from owning it physically to limited partnerships, to real estate investment trusts, to ordinary common stock in companies with real estate activities of various sorts.

I'm not going to say there's anything inherently wrong with investing in real estate. Immense fortunes have been made (and lost) in real estate. It can be an excellent place to put money if you know what you're doing and understand the tax ramifications of owning real estate in different ways.

But the charts and graphs you see around that show total returns of real estate investments outperforming common stock deserve another look. They have a special credibility because so many of us are sitting with homes we bought in the 1960s and 1970s that have increased manyfold. What the promoters of real estate investments understandably don't point out is that the 30 years between the 1960s and the 1990s were an aberration; the major factor in the real estate boom has been the baby boom.

The baby boom has moved through our economic system like a beach ball swallowed by a snake. The "baby boom babies" James Taylor sings about were born after World War II and married and formed families in the sixties and seventies, which is when the real estate boom started. As they gained upward mobility and upgraded their homes during the 1970s to mid-1980s, the boom escalated to a peak. As the nineties got underway, they were midfortyish and starting to think in terms of retirement planning. That this bulging population chose stocks with their record of outperforming other investment alternatives has been the driving force behind the record bull market that is still going strong as the twentieth century draws to a close.

Real estate, continuing a historical pattern, underperformed common stocks between 1960 and the early 1970s, then outperformed common stocks until the late 1980s when the traditional relationships resumed.

Real estate is *not* a better long-term investment than common stocks.

Gold has always been a popular doomsday hedge, the theory being that it is a store of absolute value whereas securities and currencies have relative value and are subject to loss. It has been true historically that when inflation or other anxieties have dominated market psychology, the price of gold has risen.

Like real estate, gold can be held in various physical forms, as well as by way of mutual funds and other securities.

The performance of gold was most dramatic in January 1980,

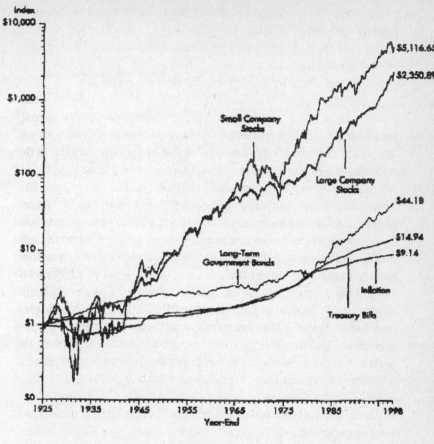

FIGURE 1

when high international inflation led by rising oil prices, tension surrounding the American hostage crisis in Iran and civil disorder in oil-rich Saudi Arabia combined to drive the price per ounce to $887.50 before calmer times returned and gold stabilized at lower levels. It was a memorable lesson in how volatile this store of value can be.

In terms of total return compared with common stocks, however, forget it. Gold, including the common stocks of gold mining companies, has not provided total returns anywhere near those of general common stocks.

SHOULD *YOU* OWN COMMON STOCKS?

No other investment alternative rivals common stocks as a way of accumulating wealth. Unless you're flat broke, reading this from your death bed, and have no heirs, there will be a time in your life when it will make sense to hold common stocks.

How much of your money should you put in stocks? I suggest putting yourself to the lifestyle test. *You shouldn't invest any more in common stocks than you can afford to forgo without significantly changing your lifestyle.* I don't mean to imply that putting money in stocks—particularly in Dow stocks—necessarily means risking a permanent and total loss of capital. All I'm saying is that stocks can go down as well as up, particularly in the short term, and some patience may be required at times to recoup losses. If that means you might need to do something as drastic as giving up your paramour, you might be better off in a money market fund or another investment that offers lower return and more short-term safety.

Beating the Dow assumes you have at least $5,000 to set aside for common stocks.

CHAPTER 3

Why Invest
in the Dow Industrials?

FOR MOST of the last decade, the Dow Jones Industrial Average
and the Standard & Poor's 500 stock index, both dominated by
large companies and driven by burgeoning mutual fund investment, have led the overall market and outperformed indexes of
smaller stocks by a wide margin. Today's institution-dominated
marketplace favors blue chip, high-capitalization stocks, and the
Dow is the purest and most prominent blue chip index.

As the most popular indicator of market activity, the Dow is
itself an influential barometer of market and economic conditions.
Individually, the 30 stocks that make up the Dow industrials are
among the most widely held, widely analyzed, and widely publicized in the world. They are also among the biggest and the
strongest. Combined, the 30 Dow components have assets of
around 2.5 trillion dollars, nearly five million employees, and
sales that exceed the gross national products of every country in
the world except China, Germany, India, Japan, and the United
States.

These prime companies may gain, lose, spin off, acquire,
merge, rename themselves, reorganize, even drop out of the Dow,
but they are an integral and vital part of our economic system, and
in one form or another they are here to stay.

The Dow companies and their products and services are household names to most people. Here is the present list, with some
recent name changes noted:

Aluminum Company of America (Alcoa)
American Express Company
American Telephone & Telegraph Company (AT&T)
The Boeing Company
Caterpillar, Inc.
Citigroup (formerly Travelers Group
The Coca-Cola Company
The Walt Disney Company
E.I. du Pont de Nemours and Company
Eastman Kodak Company
Exxon/Mobil
General Electric Company
General Motors Corporation
Hewlett-Packard
Home Depot, Inc.
Honeywell International (formerly AlliedSignal)
Intel Corp.
International Business Machines Corporation (IBM)
International Paper Company
Johnson & Johnson
McDonald's Corporation
Merck & Co., Inc.
Microsoft Corp.
Minnesota Mining and Manufacturing Company (3M)
J.P. Morgan & Co. Incorporated
Philip Morris Companies
Procter & Gamble Company
SBC Communications, Inc.
United Technologies Corporation
Wal-Mart

As we will see in Part II of *Beating the Dow,* the individual Dow companies have evolved in response to an ever-changing business environment. Their internal dynamism, together with mergers and substitutions, have made the current Dow Jones Industrial Average representative of virtually all important sectors of the American economy.

Multinational without exception, the Dow companies in their different ways are positioned to benefit from current mega-trends—globalization of markets; cleaning up the environment; repairing the infrastructure; depletion of energy sources; revival of manufacturing; increased literacy rate; aging of the population; expansion of the free world.

Most important, however, our discussions of the individual companies will examine the kinds of problems these stalwart companies have encountered over the years—and solved. That even major corporations make mistakes and suffer from unforeseen adversity is a fact of life and always will be. That the investing public will always overreact to bad news is just as certain. The resilience the Dow companies have because of their immense financial, legal and human resources makes a portfolio of Dow stocks a conservative investment risk.

With companies of Dow stock caliber, there is more opportunity than risk. Bad news is usually good news because it makes strong stocks cheap.

FINDING BARGAINS IN THE DOW

Although I keep an eye on fundamentals, which is easy when you're holding stocks that Wall Street is constantly watching and that are in the news every day, as a contrarian I look for Dow stocks that are out of favor and selling at bargain prices.

Sooner rather than later, stocks that are "victims" of overreaction, whether to a news development or a business cycle, will regain a value appropriately reflecting their actual risk. Cyclical stocks, by definition, are subject to good news and bad news and, by the same definition, to times when they're cheap and times when they're expensive.

In Part III, you'll learn how to identify Dow stocks when they are out of favor and most likely to outperform the average as a whole. Buy cheap, sell dear. Same old story, but this time with a twist in your favor. We're not dealing here with obscure, neglected, or emerging companies. These stocks are in the limelight all the time.

Which begins to answer some questions you were probably about to ask.

What if the stocks are cheap because the companies have real problems? Can't actual risks be important, even with Dow stocks?

The answer is yes, but because the Dow stocks are so highly visible and widely analyzed, the possibility of major adverse financial developments coming as a surprise is minimal. Even surprises with financial implications—Union Carbide's Bhopal disaster or Exxon's *Valdez* oil spill, to cite recent examples—were taken in stride financially (although the stocks dropped temporarily, providing an opportunity for contrarians).

In a worst-case scenario, such as a bankruptcy or near-bankruptcy, Dow stocks historically have become "turnaround situations," ultimately rewarding their holders with handsome, sometimes astonishing gains.

Have there been some exceptions? Yes, but they are very few and far between and more than offset by the diversification provided by the Dow portfolio. We'll be looking at actual cases in later chapters.

WHY HASN'T the world caught on to something this obvious? Won't the music stop once this book gets around? I asked these questions when *Beating the Dow* was first published, and my answer ten years later is basically the same, despite the book's great success and the widespread popularity the system has enjoyed.

My colleague owns a Saab 900, which were advertised as the "most intelligent cars ever built." When you open the hood and stand to the side, the oil stick, which in most cars is down among the belts and hoses, is located smack front and center and attached to a cap that is three inches in diameter, bright red in color, and marked (in English) "Motor Oil." He tells me that 100 miles outside the New York metropolitan area, the chances are better than even a station attendant will come around to say he can't for the life of him find the oil stick. The car may be intelligent, and so, no doubt, is the guy pumping gas. But the oil stick is too obvious to be seen.

The anomaly that there is more opportunity than risk in the Dow universe is partly explained, I am convinced, by the fact that it is so obvious it is overlooked or so simple it is suspect. And don't forget who it is that dominates the stock market. It is the large mutual funds with huge pools of money, and as we have seen they are forced by liquidity and diversification requirements to operate in a larger universe than the Dow stocks provide. And if that weren't enough, the temptation to reach beyond the 30 Dow industrials for greater returns would be irresistible anyway to most professionals because of egos, competitive pressures and the need to legitimize fees.

The significance of this for you and other individual investors is that although they can and do hold DJIA stocks, institutional managers have different agendas. Their large portfolios require special strategies and involve special trading dictates.

The simple and relatively safe Dow portfolio is a luxury available to individual investors and not available to mutual funds. And even if everybody who reads this book went out and acted at once, it's unlikely you could eliminate the profit opportunities in the Dow universe. Not when you're outgunned three to one by institutions. I am flattered when I read that an estimated $40 billion was invested in my system by the late 1990s. That's a big number, but it is a very small part of a total investment measured in trillions.

I've had an exceptional record as an investor because I've trained myself to think against the grain. Maybe you can train yourself to think in reverse too, but that isn't necessary to beat the market. All you have to do is learn to recognize the symptoms of opportunity and then have the courage to act against conventional wisdom. The courage should come easily when you see the results my simple approach has produced.

George Soros, who with Warren Buffett, Peter Lynch and a few others is one of the investment world's living legends, has said: "Investors operate with limited funds and limited intelligence. They do not need to know everything. As long as they understand something better than others, they have an edge."

I don't even go that far. I say if you can find the oil stick in a Saab 900 you can beat the Dow. In an investment world addicted to complexity, it can almost be said that keeping it simple is in itself a form of contrarianism. It can certainly be said that for a system like mine to become too popular to work, contrarianism would have to become conventional wisdom. That would mean turning human nature on its head.

CHAPTER 4

How the Pros Try to Beat the Market—and Why Most Don't Succeed

MOST PROFESSIONAL money managers, 95 percent by some estimates, fail to beat the market averages. This fact startles most people, until they consider that the professionals we are talking about *are* the market. Their decisions account for three-quarters of all trading activity and determine which way the Dow and other major indexes move.

To understand why this is true and why keeping it simple can actually give you an edge over the pros, let's take a quick look at some basic approaches to portfolio management.

HOW THE PROS
TRY TO BEAT THE MARKET

Every professional manager of common stock ("equity") portfolios tries to outperform the market—to achieve increases in a portfolio's value that exceed those of the market as a whole. Market ups and downs are measured by various stock indexes and averages composed of representative groups of stocks. The measure most widely followed is the DJIA of 30 stocks. A manager who can beat the Dow has had a successful year.

Independent investment advisers, mutual fund managers, bank

trust departments, and other professional investors follow hundreds of companies, employ staffs of analysts and economists, and use elaborate computerized trading techniques to try to beat the Dow performance—and most of them fail.

For example, *Barron's*/Lipper Mutual Funds Quarterly report published in *Barron's* in January 1999 shows the total reinvested (monthly) cumulative performance of different categories of mutual funds for the decade ended December 31, 1998.

The category most fairly compared to the Dow stocks, Growth and Income Funds, which are made up of dividend-paying common stocks, had a total return of 332.10 percent. The comparable return of the Dow Jones Industrial Average for the same period was 461.86 percent. The funds underperformed the Dow by 28.1 percent.

The average of 39 categories of equity funds was only 249.19 percent, over 200 percentage points lower than the Dow. (The comparable return on the S&P 500 was 480.08 percent.)

The message is clear: If you buy a mutual fund the chances are you will do significantly worse than the Dow.

Whatever their success, managers use variations of four basic investment approaches:

- The *fundamental approach,* a form of what is called value investing, analyzes companies, industries, and the economic and market environments to identify stocks that are undervalued at their current market prices.
- The *growth stock approach* tries to identify companies with high-growth potential before that potential is reflected in their market price.
- The *contrarian approach* identifies established companies that are temporarily unpopular, selling at bargain prices and due to rebound. Contrarians are value investors by definition.
- The *market timing approach* holds that when the market goes up, most stocks go up, and when the market goes down, most stocks go down. It uses various indicators to anticipate market movements.

All these approaches work, although some are inherently more difficult to implement than others and each can get as complicated as one chooses to make it.

A fundamental investor, for example, would examine the daylights out of a company's financial statements and evaluate its earnings prospects in the context of its industry. That way, he or she would try to get an idea of the stock's real worth. If that is significantly above the stock's market value, the investor concludes the stock has no real downside risk and will eventually rise to its proper market value. The legendary Warren Buffett holds the all-time record as a value investor. Of course, it also helps that Mr. Buffett is a genius and doesn't have clients breathing down his neck.

Growth stock managers are fundamental investors who seek out companies expected to enjoy rapid growth whose shares, based on that anticipated growth, are undervalued. These are usually, although not always, younger, smaller firms in emerging industries that carry a higher degree of risk than established companies. They usually do not pay big dividends, since their earnings are reinvested to finance their rapid growth.

Growth investing has its Houdini in the form of Peter Lynch, formerly of Fidelity's Magellan Fund, who garnered gains of 29 percent compounded over a ten-year period. When Lynch retired, he stated publicly that he had been working seven days a week and was afraid he was going to drop dead at 46 if he didn't quit. Enough said?

Growth companies require meticulous and constant analysis. To be sure, there are dramatic gains to be made in some growth stocks but risk, generally speaking, equals return.

And although smaller stocks as a group have outperformed blue chips in alternating cycles historically, it's been the spectacular winners—the fledgling Microsofts—that have tended to lift the growth stocks as a group. Growth stock investors in general have had the same experience relative to the market as value investors.

* * *

BEFORE I touch on contrarian investing and market timing, which are more up my alley, I want to emphasize that nothing in this business is pure. For example, there are growth companies that are among the most highly capitalized and long-established firms around. American Express, to cite a current case in point, is one of the oldest and richest of the blue chips. Amex was a yield stock with erratic earnings in the early to mid-1990s. Then it decided to stop trying to be a financial supermarket and to concentrate on building market share in its core business of international travel-related services. Earnings began a steady climb and the stock went from $30 to $140 between 1995 and mid-1999. And it's a Dow stock to boot.

Nor can any prudent investor afford to ignore fundamentals completely. If I heard hamburger was going to be declared illegal and immoral in addition to fattening, I'd sell my McDonald's.

Want to know what I'd really do? Knowing it would take a lot more than that to sink McDonald's (a Dow stock, after all), I'd sell it short. The market would kill it (not the company, the stock). I'd buy it for next to nothing. Then when the Big Mac came back in some edible and marketable reincarnation, I'd be on my way to the bank. But that's getting ahead of my story.

A CONTRARIAN, by definition, goes the opposite way the crowds do. When the light turns red, the contrarian steps on it (an imperfect metaphor since professional contrarian investors are quite sane and largely law-abiding). Contrarians capitalize on the part of market behavior that is psychological, but that is not to say there isn't a financially logical reason for going against the crowd.

Stock prices follow the laws of supply and demand. As real value becomes more widely recognized, demand increases and the price rises. And vice versa. But in the stock market there is only so much stock and so much money. Therefore, as more investors act on their anticipation that a stock is going up, the more purchasing power is exhausted, which means the market for that stock is closer to its peak. Conversely, when most investors sell, there is a liberation of cash to create upward pressure on a stock representing opportunity.

That's the theoretical rationale for contrarianism. In practice, real value only partly explains why stocks are bid up or bid down.

To the contrarian, just as axiomatic as the fact that the crowd always buys dear and sells cheap is the fact that it almost invariably overreacts to news, both good and bad. *The difference between real and perceived risk is opportunity.* This is an essential part of my Dow stock strategy, and we'll be talking a lot more about it.

How do contrarians stack up against fundamental value and growth investors?

There are contrarians and then there are *contrarians.* Everybody is trying to buy low and sell high, but the actions a true contrarian takes run contrary to conventional wisdom. That's really to say we have to act against our own human nature. Most people, *investment professionals included,* cannot do this.

The majority of professional contrarians take their cue from more courageous contrarians and wind up simply following a different crowd. In practical terms, that means they buy somewhere along the way up and sell somewhere along the way down. In other words, professional contrarian investors as a group are no exception to our rule. Most of them don't beat the market. *But the real ones do!*

MARKET TIMERS use technical analysis of historical price performance to try to predict future movements. In effect, they say: "To hell with the facts, show me the charts." They use statistics and are guided by historical chart patterns, known by such picturesque names as "head and shoulders," "double tops," "triangles," "gaps," and "rising bottoms." (They daydream a lot, those folks.)

Cycles of various sorts have been a fact of market life throughout history. There are also seasonal and other historical market patterns that have a logical basis and recur with phenomenal consistency. But the past isn't necessarily prologue and history rarely repeats itself exactly. Investors who use a market timing approach exclusively have about the same record of beating the averages as other professionals.

Many market timing techniques nonetheless do have well-documented validity. The investor who doesn't make a point of becoming familiar with them is missing out on an opportunity to enhance returns.

In the way of a subtotal, I want to emphasize that to under-perform the market is not necessarily to lose money. In fairness to my fellow professionals, most managers of equity portfolios who have applied a consistent approach—whatever that approach is— with discipline have made money for their clients over the long term even when they haven't beaten the averages. As indeed they should have, since the market has risen over the long term.

Although there will be years, inevitably, when stock portfolios show losses rather than gains, the importance of avoiding losses— and the professionals who cause them—can't be over-stressed. Imagine making money for a few years, then seeing it wiped out because somebody did something stupid. It is an arresting fact that to overcome a 50 percent portfolio loss, you need a 100 percent portfolio gain. Think about that! So try to avoid losing money.

IT'S A simple fact that unless you're Ivan Boesky (Mr. Boesky, you will remember, learned the hard way that insider trading meant trading pinstriped suits for striped pajamas), it's impossible to predict with certainty what a stock—or the stock market—is going to do in the short run. That's why discipline and patience are essential ingredients for successful investing.

But there are additional reasons why the majority of money managers fail to match, let alone beat the Dow or the S&P 500, and they are worth looking at because there are traps you as an individual investor can avoid.

One of them is the short-term focus that most investment professionals have developed in the last 20 years. Deregulation of the financial markets, rising personal incomes, a long-running bull market, IRAs and other tax legislation—these and many other factors worked to change the investment marketplace in two fundamental ways.

The first was to bring personal investing, formerly the province of the wealthy, within the reach of average people. That was, to be sure, a welcome development, but it vastly increased the market for investment services.

The second was a result of the first—the spawning of a financial services industry in which a dizzying assortment of investment professionals, including mutual funds, independent money managers, banks, insurance companies, financial planners and stockbrokers (some of whom have been renamed financial consultants), began competing for the investor's hard-earned dollar.

It's hardly surprising that the name of the competitive game has not been, "Who provides the best long-term investment returns through patience and discipline?" Instead, it has turned into, "Who outperformed the rest last quarter?" Speaking of the pressures the marketplace puts on mutual funds to produce quarterly performance, somebody has said it's as though they all worked for George Steinbrenner. The result, more often than not, has been short-term portfolio profits at the expense of higher long-term returns. That and a self-defeating attempt by investors to go with the hottest fund or money manager, thereby making buying high and selling low a virtual certainty (Peter Lynch and his miraculous Magellan Fund excepted).

Another important factor contributing to a short-term focus has been the need to provide liquidity. A mutual fund, for example, must be able to meet shareholder redemptions if necessary, possibly in big numbers should the market decline or the fund's performance turn sour for other reasons. This requires flexibility, which means holding stocks that can be gotten in and out of with relative ease—namely, the largest companies with the largest number of shares outstanding. Not only do these high-cap stocks tend in general to be mature companies with less potential for sales-driven growth than younger, smaller-cap firms (there are exceptions, of course), but when a lot of huge institutional investors jam into relatively few large stocks, the result is less flexibility, not more. You can't just dump a whole position in GM, for example, on the market. It has to be done over time. This lack of flexibility has its effect in lower returns.

The problem a quarterly mentality brings to stock investing is not a lack of short-term opportunities, which exist in abundance even among the largest stocks. The problem is that investors forced into such a tight time frame are forced to take short-term losses along with their short-term gains and often have to forgo better returns that could be had by following a disciplined approach.

As a personal investor free of institutional investors' constrictions, you have the best of both worlds—the opportunity to capitalize on relatively short-term price increases and the ability to follow a system that automatically ensures you will be buying low and selling high.

Professionals who actively trade and follow a lot of stocks also have high overhead. In addition to management fees (1 percent, typically), transaction costs, custodial fees, and other legal and administrative expenses all take their toll, so that even those portfolios that match the market in terms of pure performance produce underperforming net returns to clients.

THERE IS one other reason most professionals underperform. It's my favorite so I've saved it for last: *They make the process too complicated.*

In fairness, part of the reason they make it complicated is that they have to. Either they are required by law to be widely diversified, as with mutual funds, or they feel extensive diversification is necessary to avoid criticism—or even lawsuits, should one of their heavy positions take a beating. I prefer to keep all my eggs in a few baskets and then keep a close eye on the baskets.

But no small part of the problem has to do with other stuff.

Like egos. How can you look like a genius if what you're doing isn't complicated?

Then there's the simple need to justify fees. How can an investment manager accept a percentage of the assets unless he or she looks busy?

And still another part of it is, I'm convinced, human nature. Remember O'Higgins' Law? If it's important—and money always is—we can't resist making it complicated. We're brought up that way.

PASSIVE "INDEX" INVESTING

Since most mutual funds and independent money managers fail to beat the averages, one way of outperforming the pros is to buy the averages. If you can't beat 'em, join 'em. This is done by buying one of a number of mutual funds that replicate indexes, such as the Dow, the S&P 500, the New York Stock Exchange (NYSE) Composite Index, or the Value Line Composite Index.

These funds simply buy and hold the stocks making up the index or a representative sampling thereof. An example of an index fund replicating the S&P 500 is the no-load Vanguard 500, which has no management fee and a very low expense ratio. Other index funds have nominal management fees.

Although expenses, however minimal, cause stock index funds slightly to underperform the market as they represent it, they nonetheless outperform some 75 percent of all general stock funds and money managers.

The most persuasive apologists for such "passive investing" are advocates of the so-called efficient market hypothesis, also known as the random walk theory. Its practitioners contend that past, present and future stock prices over a broad spectrum simply reflect information coming into the market at random. Thus while there may be for relatively short periods investors who over-achieve and others who underachieve, over the long pull there is no knowledge or judgment an investor can add beyond what has already been perceived and reflected in prices.

In the words of Burton Malkiel, whose *A Random Walk Down Wall Street* advocates passive investing, "A blindfolded chimpanzee throwing darts at *The Wall Street Journal* can perform as well as the experts." Hence money spent on active portfolio management, including management fees and transaction costs, is money ultimately wasted, and the relatively small cost of passive investing is well justified.

The efficient market hypothesis has its staunch supporters and many detractors. The fact that the S&P 500 significantly *underperformed* active managers during the period from the mid-1970s through 1982 is cited as hard evidence by those, mainly investment professionals, who consider the theory academic nonsense. Proponents argue that the market's information-processing and pricing mechanisms were less efficient in the 1970s than in the 1980s, when computers became more widely used in a securities marketplace dominated by large institutions.

I'm a strong believer that no matter what people put into computers, stock prices reflect consensus, consensus means average and average means mediocrity. I've *beaten* the market and so can you.

As for indexing, it seems to me the most effective argument against it is that while you do no worse than the market, you do no better, either. Let's not forget you can do as well as the market and still go broke.

Between 1972 and 1974 the market lost 47 percent of its value. I'm not sure how consoled I would have been by the fact that my index fund had done as well as the market. Incidentally, my system produced positive returns for that period, as you will see later on.

Beating the Dow shows you how to *outperform* the market *and avoid losses* by managing your own *simple* portfolio of top-quality stocks. One of the benefits of self-management is that it eliminates the risk of getting involved with the wrong professional.

CHAPTER 5

The Dow Jones
Industrial Average

HISTORY

Late in 1989 *The Wall Street Journal,* publisher of the Dow Jones Industrial Average, put out a special centennial edition to mark the anniversary of its founding. One part, titled "On the Average: How DJ Indicator Evolved," describes what times were like back in 1884 when Charles H. Dow first published the indicator of stock market profits that would become the DJIA. Wall Street was then about seven blocks of lower Manhattan. Offices had working fireplaces, but unlike the one Citigroup Co-CEO Sanford Weill had installed in the 1980s when he was head of Shearson Lehman (a few megamergers ago), the chimneys weren't poking through the towers of a World Trade Center.

The New York Stock Exchange listed just a few dozen companies (today it lists more than 3,000), and a 300,000-share day was big volume (today 750 million is a moderate day). Instead of computers, news services and disclosure requirements were gossip, inside information, and, according to the *Journal* article, "pools of financiers and plungers who would manipulate stocks up or down, leaving outsiders like shorn lambs. . . . A breath of rumor would bring riches or ruin." (That has a familiar ring, doesn't it?)

Charles Dow brought out his "index of active stocks" in a year that started well but ended in what became known as the Railway Panic of 1884. The first part of the year saw a blossoming of new enterprises and growing investor optimism. But as the months went on, rate wars between railroads, the exposure of some fraudulent market practices, and a sharp drop in Union Pacific shares caused disenchantment and loss of confidence on the part of investors. Eighteen eighty-four ended with bank failures and a market collapse.

Until then, it had been the practice of most investors to focus on individual companies rather than the overall market. Dow was one of the first to see that all boats rise and fall with the tides, and that the market as a whole was influenced by such factors as interest rates and changes affecting trade or agriculture. A man after my own heart, 32-year-old Charles Dow had an analytical bent combined with a love of simplicity. He set about trying to devise what the *Journal* described as "a systematic indicator that would isolate daily ripples from the waves, and the waves from the tide."

A New England farmboy, Dow had a talent for writing and was an avid reader of Horatio Alger's novels about young men who realized the American dream of rags to riches. He brought with him the sense of humor requisite to a Wall Street-related career, revealed in a piece he had written for the Providence and Stonington Steamship Company. After 84 years of excursions, he noted, "there was, proportionately, the same number of elderly ladies who constantly expected an explosion [and] of young people who sought the uppermost parts of the boat and sat quite unnecessarily close together, considering the amount of room there was to spare . . ."

According to a *Wall Street Journal* piece on Dow quoted in Richard J. Stillman's *Dow Jones Industrial Average:* "The men of the Street soon learned that this reticent, quiet-speaking man who took shorthand notes on his cuffs could be relied upon to quote them absolutely and without embellishment and moreover, that it was safe to tell him news in confidence . . ."

His talents led to a position with the Kiernan News Agency,

where he met Edward D. Jones and Charles M. Bergstresser. The three left together several months later to found Dow, Jones & Company. That was in November 1882.

DOW, JONES & COMPANY

Dow, Jones & Company ("Financial News Agents") distributed daily financial news bulletins to subscribers and published the Customer's Afternoon Letter, predecessor to *The Wall Street Journal.* Although Dow was the only partner without a college education, he was the analytical mind and writer. Jones, a Brown University graduate, had editorial and managerial rather than analytical skills and evidently had nothing to do with developing the average. Bergstresser, who had graduated from Lafayette College, had a lot of contacts and was mainly the marketing man. Why Bergstresser's name wasn't part of the company name is a mystery; perhaps it was just too much of a mouthful.

The three worked out of "a ramshackle building next door to the entrance of the Stock Exchange" that reminded an employee of a scene from Dickens' *Nicholas Nickleby:* "It was such a crowded scene that at first Nicholas saw nothing at all. By degrees, however, the place resolved itself into a bare hole with a few forms . . ."

THE DOW JONES INDUSTRIAL AVERAGE

Charles Dow first came up with a list of eleven of the most actively traded stocks, including nine railroads, Pacific Mail Steamship and (a bit of real high-tech) Western Union. These he simply listed with their closing prices added up and divided by 11.

The resultant simple arithmetic average was published in the

Customer's Afternoon Letter and then in *The Wall Street Journal* to become what is today the oldest continuously published index of stocks in the world.

During the next 12 years, much happened to change the business and economic landscape. These were the years leading up to the era of trust-busting that began with the Sherman Anti-trust Act of 1890. Small businesses were being consolidated into large corporations and trusts, which became the "action" for investors and speculators on Wall Street. Several changes in the average were made to reflect the new marketplace.

In 1896 the first purely industrial average was published in *The Wall Street Journal,* which was now seven years old. This average, published May 26, 1896, was composed of 12 stocks. They were:

American Cotton Oil	Laclede Gas
American Sugar	National Lead
American Tobacco	North American Company
Chicago Gas	Tennessee Coal & Iron
Distilling & Cattle Feeding	U.S. Leather Preferred
General Electric	U.S. Rubber

In 1902 Dow, Jones & Company was sold to Clarence W. Barron (founder of *Barron's National Business and Financial Weekly,* a Dow, Jones & Company publication), but Charles Dow, who appeared on *The Wall Street Journal*'s masthead following the sale, died that same year.

In 1916, the industrial average was increased to 20 stocks and on October 1, 1928, it was expanded to 30—the number of stocks comprising the average ever since. The original 30 companies were:

Allied Chemical	American Tobacco
American Can	Atlantic Refining
American Smelting	Bethlehem Steel
American Sugar	Bethlehem Steel

Chrysler
General Electric
General Motors
General Railway Signal
Goodrich
International Harvester
International Nickel
Mack Trucks
Nash Motors
North American
Paramount Publix
Postum, Inc.
Radio Corporation of America
  (RCA)

Sears, Roebuck &
  Company
Standard Oil of New
  Jersey
Texas Corporation
Texas Gulf Sulphur
Union Carbide
United States Steel
Victor Talking
  Machine
Westinghouse Electric
Woolworth
Wright Aeronautical

Counting a number of name changes, eight of that original list, or at least ancestors thereof, are still in the Dow in mid-1999. Allied Chemical became AlliedSignal, which became Honeywell International; American Can became Primerica Corp., which became Travelers Group, which is now Citigroup. Victor Talking Machine merged with RCA, which became part of General Electric, and Postum, Inc., changed its name to General Foods, which was acquired by Philip Morris. Standard Oil of New Jersey became Exxon, then became Exxon/Mobil. It is noteworthy how relatively few substitutions there have been between 1928 and now, especially considering that the Great Depression hadn't yet occurred. In fact, for two stretches of 17 consecutive years there were no changes whatsoever: between March 14, 1939, and July 3, 1956, and June 1, 1959, and August 8, 1976. In the last 60 years, there have been 24 substitutions.

CALCULATION OF THE DJIA

It's important to understand how the Dow is computed because the equation affects its value as a yardstick of the market. In 1928 the present method of calculating the average was adopted. Until then, the average was computed the original way, simply by totaling up prices and dividing by the number of stocks. For a while, the only problem with that was that it gave more weight to higher-priced stocks than lower-priced stocks.

To this day, the Dow is a price-weighted average, meaning that a $125 stock like IBM moving 10 percent influences the average five times more than a $25 stock like Disney with the same percentage change.

In 1928 a flexible divisor in place of the total number of stocks was introduced. This change became necessary when companies began splitting their stocks. As you probably know, a split occurs when a company increases its outstanding shares without increasing shareholders' equity. If a company whose stock was selling at $20 split it two for one (issued two shares for each existing share), the price per share would drop to $10. If the average were then to list the shares of that company at $10, it would reflect an artificial decline from $20. So instead of dividing by the number of shares, the publishers used a divisor that would make the average equal to what it was before the split.

The divisor in 1928 was 16.67. Today, after many adjustments made necessary not only by splits but by stock dividends, substitutions and mergers, the divisor is 0.197. The divisor is adjusted whenever an event would cause a distortion of 10 or more points in the average. Notice I say points. Another result of the flexible divisor was that changes became measured in terms of points rather than dollars, although dollar changes are, of course, what are being averaged.

Let me give you a simple illustration:

Assume the average consisted of only four stocks, selling for $10, $30, $60, and $80. Using the original formula, the total of the prices, $180, would be divided by the number of stocks, 4, to arrive at the average, $45.

$$10$$
$$30$$
$$60$$
$$\underline{80}$$
$$180 \div 4 = \$45$$

But now suppose the $80 stock was split 2 for 1. The unadjusted average following the split, assuming closing prices remained unchanged, would be:

$$10$$
$$30$$
$$60$$
$$\underline{40}$$
$$140 \div 4 = \$35$$

Since the market values of the companies didn't change but the average did, an adjustment must be made for the sake of continuity. One possibility would be to count twice the price of the stock that split, so it would look like this:

$$10$$
$$30$$
$$60$$
$$40$$
$$\underline{40}$$
$$180 \div 4 = \$45$$

But Dow, Jones & Company chose, instead, to get the same effect by changing the divisor, thus calculating as follows:

$$10$$
$$30$$
$$60$$
$$\underline{40}$$
$$140 \div 3.11 = 45 \text{ points}$$

The formula for arriving at the divisor is:

$$\frac{140}{x} = 45; \ 45x = 140; \ x = 3.11$$

Because the divisor gets smaller with each stock split or stock dividend, there is an increasing disproportion between the change in the actual prices of the 30 stocks making up the average and the change in the average. Thus when you say the Dow ended the week up 10 points, you are talking about a much smaller rise in the dollar value of the shares.

But the average nonetheless makes it possible to compare the magnitude and direction of price changes from day to day and year to year—in fact, with today's computers, from minute to minute.

THE DOW COMPARED WITH OTHER POPULAR INDEXES

The Dow Jones Industrial Average does have a few shortcomings, two of which we have already touched upon. The most serious, I think, is the fact of its being price-weighted. As we observed earlier, the same percentage change in an expensive stock like Merck moves the average more than in an inexpensive stock like Disney. In an extreme case, this could cause a misleading indication. A huge move in a few high-priced components could send the average one way even though a majority of the components went the other way and the other way was the way of the broader market.

But even under normal circumstances, price weighting creates distortions. It is simply a fact of market life that lower-priced shares tend to register greater gains and losses than higher-priced shares. If Disney is up or down $1.25 in a given day, which is 5 percent of $25, it's hardly big news. But when IBM is up or down $6.26 (the same percentage) in one day, you can bet it will be a news item. This is a factor (among several others) in a phenomenon Wall Street calls the small firm effect. Of course, "small firm" effect is a bit of a misnomer when you're talking about Dow stocks. Big stocks can have small prices, though, which is what the term refers to.

An interesting result of this is that if you in effect "unweight" the Dow—that is, if you bought an equal dollar amount of each of the 30 stocks (the same $125 would buy one share of IBM but five shares of $25 Disney)—the historical experience has been that in most years you would outperform the average (and, of course, most professionals). This happens because lower-priced stocks simply tend to move more percentage-wise than higher-priced shares. We'll take a closer look at this phenomenon when we discuss strategies later on.

When used in relation to the Dow, "weighted" and "unweighted" can be confusing. You'll see references to the unweighted Dow—the phenomenon just described. But you'll also see the Dow referred to as an unweighted average, which means it is a simple arithmetic mean in which no adjustments are made to make the various prices equal in their influence on the average. Unweighted thus means automatic price weighting. This distinguishes the Dow from other indexes that are deliberately adjusted to result in "market value" or "capitalization" weighting.

Let's look at some other major indexes.

By far the second most widely quoted stock index is the S&P 500 or just the S&P (although Standard & Poor's has less widely-used indexes of 400 stocks and 100 stocks). You'll usually see the performance of mutual funds and money managers compared to the S&P 500 because it is a broader measure of the overall market than the blue chip Dow. The S&P (as we'll call it throughout this book, unless otherwise specified) is made up of 379 industrial, 47 transportation and utility and 74 financial stocks. Most of its components are listed on the New York Stock Exchange (it accounts for something like 80 percent of the market value of all shares traded on the big board), but it includes some American Stock Exchange and NASDAQ (over-the-counter) stocks.

It is market value- (capitalization-) weighted, which means that each of its components is given a weight proportionate to its market capitalization (its share price times its shares outstanding). The effect of this is to give big companies with high market capitalizations more weight than smaller-cap companies.

To understand what this means compared with the Dow's price weighting, compare American Express, which has a market cap of $54 billion and a recent share price of $130, with AT&T, which has a market cap of $164 billion and a share price of $50. Given the same percentage change in price, American Express would affect the Dow more than AT&T because of its higher price. But in the S&P, AT&T would have more clout because of its higher total market value.

In comparing different indexes, however, weighting methods do not make that much of a difference under normal conditions. The blue chip Dow and the broader S&P have tended to parallel each other's movements. This happens because large-capitalization companies tend to have higher-priced shares.

YOU SHOULD also be familiar with several other indexes.

The Value Line Composite Index, like the S&P, is significant because it is widely used and the subject of abundant data. But whereas the Dow tracks the blue chips exclusively and the S&P tracks a broader group of blue chips and other mainly large ("secondary") stocks, the Value Line attempts to reflect the "typical" industrial stock. It is neither price- nor market value-weighted, but rather is an equally-weighted geometric average of approximately 1,700 NYSE, Amex and over-the-counter stocks followed by the Value-Line Investment Survey. Changes are expressed in index numbers related to a base value of 100 established in 1961.

Insofar as the trading of indexers and large institutions has a disproportionate influence on the Dow and the S&P 500, the equally weighted and broader-based Value Line is a more accurate measure of general investor sentiment. In 1998, for example, the Value Line had a negative return of −3.79% as the Dow and the S&P gained 16.10 percent and 26.78 percent respectively. This would indicate sagging public confidence in the market even as the institutions, buying selected blue chips, particularly those in the high-technology sector (more populous in the S&P), would give the opposite impression.

The NASDAQ (National Association of Securities Dealers Automated Quotations) Composite Index is made up of more than 5,400 companies listed on the NASDAQ Stock Market. The NASDAQ Stock Market combines the NASDAQ National Market, which lists the largest and most actively traded over-the-counter stocks, and the NASDAQ SmallCap Market, comprising emerging growth companies. Although the NASDAQ Composite Index includes such major names as Microsoft and Intel, it is heavily influenced by speculative smaller growth stocks, many of which are in the high-technology sectors. It is a market value-weighted index introduced with a base value of 100 in 1971.

The Wilshire 5000 Equity Index is a market value-weighted index that measures the performance of all U.S.-headquartered equity securities with readily available price data, now numbering some 7,000 securities. Its capitalization is approximately 81 percent New York Stock Exchange, 2 percent American Stock Exchange, and 17 percent NASDAQ Stock Market. It is thus the broadest of all indexes, running the gamut from large companies to small.

The above does not cover all the important stock indexes. Other major (nonspecialized) indexes include the aforementioned New York Stock Exchange Composite Index and the Amex Major Market Index (XMI) (the latter is made up of 20 NYSE-listed blue chips, 17 of which are Dow components, and is designed to be a proxy for the DJIA); the relatively new (and market value-weighted) Dow Jones Global-U.S. Index (formerly called the Dow Jones Equity Index); and the market value-weighted Amex Composite Index (XAX) of stocks listed on the American Stock Exchange. The XAX replaced the Amex Market Value Index (AXM) in 1997.

Also frequently quoted are three indexes published by Frank Russell & Company of Tacoma, Washington. The *Russell 3000*

Index consists of the largest U.S. stocks in terms of market capitalization. The highest ranking 1000 comprise the *Russell 1000 Index,* and the rest, the smaller components, make up the *Russell 2000 Index.*

AMONG THE stock averages published by Dow Jones, the Dow Jones Global-U.S. Index, a 700-stock index designed to measure broader market performance and essentially compete with the S&P 500, has its value, to be sure. But since it is relatively new and has not historically been important, we will focus instead, where comparisons with the Dow are appropriate, on the S&P 500. The S&P has been widely used to measure investment performance as a surrogate for the broader big-stock market.

Other Dow stock averages include the specialized Utility and Transportation stock averages and the Dow Jones Composite Average or, as it is also called, the 65 Stock Average, which combines the Industrial, Utility and Transportation averages.

The Dow Jones Utility Average comprises the common stocks of 15 geographically representative gas and electric utilities. Public utilities are heavily government-regulated and are permitted to raise their rates in order to meet certain cash-flow requirements. This tends to assure (but does not guarantee) their ability to pay common-stock dividends with the result that utility common stocks—and the Dow Jones Utility Average—tend to behave like bond substitutes. Utility common stocks usually have lower yields than utility bonds because the public puts more importance on the potential of common stocks to rise in price than it puts on the greater safety of bonds.

A significant drop in the Dow utilities average is like a drop in bond prices and has the same significance for the stock market. That is, it means interest rates are trending higher, which normally is negative news for ordinary common stocks.

The Dow Jones Transportation Average is made up of 20 air, truck and rail shippers and its principal significance is its use in the Dow Theory—a time-honored if controversial formulation arguing that when both the DJIA and the Dow Jones Transportation Average reach new highs or new lows a market trend is afoot. Conversely, when they don't, the theory goes, the market, whatever it's doing, will resume its existing trading range. The underlying logic of the Dow Theory is that transportation companies, which ship raw materials to factories and finished goods to distributors, provide a confirming indication of manufacturing and business activity and thus of the direction of the stock market.

I've never been much of a Dow Theory man myself. I'm really more interested in what stocks are going to do than what the market's going to do. Whatever you think of the Dow Theory, enough people believe in it for it to have some influence on market sentiment.

When it comes to sentiment, I reserve mine for Charlie Dow, the guy who gave us a Dow to beat.

SO TWO limitations of the Dow have to do with its being price-weighted (or, if you prefer, unweighted) and composed exclusively of blue chips, which are not always representative of the broader market.

A third limitation traditionally cited is that the 30 stocks don't adequately represent all the principal industrial sectors of the economy. Our discussions of the individual companies making up the Dow Industrials will show that the diversification of the component companies and recent substitutions have largely made that criticism anachronistic.

It's my conviction that the Dow Jones Industrial Average well represents the important segments of today's economy and that its blue chip composition reflects a securities marketplace dominated by large institutional investors.

The Dow's preeminence as a market indicator is therefore based as much on current realism as on long tradition. But by virtue of its being the world's most widely watched measure of the stock market, the Dow not only provides a reading of the investor psychology driving the market but also influences the psychology that is likely to underlie its movement in the future.

An investment strategy based on the Dow and using the Dow components is thus focused on both the nerve center and the brain of the investment marketplace. What better place is there for a contrarian with a yen for simplicity to find himself? And in such good company!

PART II

THE DOW INDUSTRIAL STOCKS

In THIS section we will gain an appreciation of the importance, the adaptability, and the resilience of the firms the Dow Jones Company has selected to comprise the average.

The Dow, as we know, is not without its critics, and one of their complaints is that by including so many "industrials" it inadequately reflects the American economy's service orientation and other recent developments and trends.

While it's true that the Dow Jones Company has put a higher priority over the years on continuity than on responding to short-term changes in the economic structure—that's how it has held on to its preeminence as a market barometer—this criticism ignores the dynamism of the companies themselves. Firms have themselves adapted to the changing economy even when the Dow has waited for opportunities created by mergers or other events to make substitutions reflective of the current business environment.

In response to shareholder expectations of profitability and growth, the Dow companies have modernized through internal diversification and through acquisitions and divestitures. They have recognized the need for globalization of their businesses and continue to expand their global vision. At the same time they are distinctly American enterprises, in most cases richly rooted in American tradition and yet often on the cutting edge of modern technology. To the extent that the Dow retains a "smokestack

America" bias, it is because manufacturing is the backbone of this country's economy. My strong belief, as I've said, is that we will see a revival of basic American industry. If we don't, I think we're in trouble.

THE DOW stocks can all be good investments, and the critical question of knowing when to buy and sell them for the greatest profit is the subject of later chapters.

You should read each of the following profiles as a way of becoming familiar with the Dow stocks, their history and especially their dynamism. Try to get a sense of the kinds of problems these stalwarts have encountered and solved, problems that, to contrarian investors, have been opportunities.

I've listed the companies' addresses and phone numbers at the end of this section, on pages 159–161, in case you wish to request annual reports or other company literature.

Consider each of them in the context of the megatrends I listed earlier—globalization of markets; cleaning up the environment; replacement and rejuvenation of the nation's crumbling highways, bridges, and other infrastructure systems; the growing need for sources of energy; revival of the manufacturing sector; increased literacy rate; the unification of Europe and expansion of the free world. I'm sure you'll think of some I haven't.

This may all sound kind of lofty for a book on how to make a buck. But it is the vital importance of the Dow companies in the larger economic and cultural framework that gives them their enormous viability. In practical terms, it turns any portfolio made up of them into a solid long-term investment. That they are run by humans, patronized by humans, and owned by humans guarantees that each and every one of them will have problems from time to time. And that's what every contrarian wakes up in the morning and thanks the good Lord for.

Here then, in capsule form, is the story of each of the 30 Dow stocks. Let's get to know them.

DJIA 30 COMPONENTS MARKET CAPITALIZATION AND YIELD AS OF AUGUST 31, 1999

Stock	Symbol	Share Price	Per-Share Div	Yield	Shares (in millions)	Market Cap
AlliedSignal	ALD	$61.25	$0.68	1.1	560.10	34,412,544,000
Alcoa	AA	64.56	.75	1.2	367.10	23,699,976,000
American Express	AXP	137.50	.92	.7	452.60	62,232,500,000
AT&T	T	45.00	.88	2.0	2,709.50	121,927,500,000
Boeing	BA	45.31	.56	1.2	1,010.70	45,794,817,000
Caterpillar	CAT	56.63	1.30	2.3	358.70	20,313,181,000
Citigroup	C	44.44	.56	1.3	3,387.00	150,518,280,000
Coca-Cola	KO	59.81	.64	1.1	2,465.50	147,461,555,000
Disney	DIS	27.75	.21	.8	2,048.70	56,851,425,000
Du Pont	DD	63.38	1.40	2.2	1,130.30	71,638,414,000
Eastman Kodak	EK	73.44	1.76	2.4	322.80	23,706,432,000
Exxon	XON	78.88	1.64	2.1	2,438.40	192,340,992,000
General Electric	GE	112.31	1.40	1.2	3,277.80	368,129,718,000
General Motors	GM	66.25	2.00	3.0	654.50	43,360,625,000
Hewlett-Packard	HWP	105.38	.64	.6	1,037.10	109,289,598,000
Home Depot	HD	62.50	.16	.3	1,563.12	97,694,750,000
IBM	IBM	124.56	.48	.4	1,845.70	229,900,392,000
Intel	INTC	82.19	.12	.1	3,318.00	272,698,125,000
International Paper	IP	47.06	1.00	2.1	307.30	14,461,538,000
Johnson & Johnson	JNJ	102.25	1.12	1.1	1,344.70	137,424,000,000

DJIA 30 Components Market Capitalization and Yield as of August 31, 1999 (Continued)

Stock	Symbol	Share Price	Per-Share Div	Yield	Shares (in millions)	Market Cap
J.P. Morgan	JPM	129.19	3.96	3.1	174.80	22,582,412,000
McDonald's	MCD	41.38	.20	.5	1,353.10	55,991,278,000
Merck	MRK	67.19	1.16	1.7	2,382.10	160,053,299,000
Microsoft	MSFT	92.56	–	–	5,046.92	467,715,535,000
3M	MMM	94.50	2.24	2.4	402.00	37,989,000,000
Philip Morris	MO	37.44	1.92	5.1	2,432.10	91,057,824,000
Procter & Gamble	PG	99.25	1.28	1.3	1,327.70	131,774,225,000
SBC Communications	SBC	48.06	.975	2.0	1,956.00	94,011,019,000
United Technologies	UTX	66.13	.80	1.2	225.80	14,932,154,000
Wal-Mart	WMT	44.31	.20	.5	4,446.90	197,042,139,000

Total Returns in Percentages*

Year	ALD	AA	AXP	T	C	BA
1973	73.41%	40.61	−31.24	.33		−48.96
1974	−38.97	−36.94	−39.72	−4.67		33.00
1975	22.26	33.77	44.27	21.62		61.19
1976	24.63	51.84	12.83	32.09		88.57
1977	15.86	−16.18	−8.74	1.73		29.54
1978	−32.01	6.49	−14.58	7.60		287.69
1979	80.07	20.37	8.62	−5.74		9.32
1980	13.83	14.49	41.29	1.44		−10.08
1981	−14.51	−7.96	14.60	33.79		−45.85
1982	−19.84	27.41	50.59	10.26		56.76
1983	79.61	48.63	5.42	13.43		33.27
1984	−2.39	−14.87	19.25	15.80		32.62
1985	40.72	7.30	44.32	34.36		41.15
1986	−3.48	−8.90	9.41	4.80		.14
1987	−25.11	41.55	−56.95	12.80		−30.37
1988	21.42	22.57	19.72	10.93		68.05
1989	12.86	38.79	33.67	62.43		49.79
1990	−17.42	−19.17	−38.00	−30.89		17.17
1991	68.4	14.8	4.5	34.2		7.4
1992	39.8	13.7	27.0	33.7		−13.9
1993	32.5	−0.9	28.1	5.3		9.9
1994	−12.3	27.0	8.3	−1.8		11.0
1995	42.0	24.2	43.3	31.5		68.9
1996	42.9	23.1	38.7	−7.7		37.3
1997	17.0	11.9	59.6	51.8	19.9	−7.0
1998	15.7	7.4	15.9	25.7	−6.7	32.2

TOTAL RETURNS IN PERCENTAGES* *(Continued)*

Year	CAT	KO	DIS	DD	EK
1973	3.01	-13.60	-60.03	-7.18	-20.74
1974	-25.15	-56.44	-54.51	-38.53	-44.15
1975	47.62	59.49	133.89	41.47	72.08
1976	27.87	-.74	-5.02	11.19	-17.01
1977	-2.66	-1.82	-15.01	-6.65	-38.12
1978	10.49	22.46	1.11	10.70	19.03
1979	-4.51	-16.92	13.03	2.65	-13.15
1980	11.72	3.00	15.81	10.84	51.29
1981	-.17	11.13	3.90	-4.76	7.00
1982	-23.38	56.89	23.35	2.75	25.85
1983	21.50	8.08	-14.90	51.64	-7.35
1984	-31.75	21.75	16.06	.77	-.91
1985	37.10	40.28	89.90	43.18	10.99
1986	-3.27	37.72	54.47	28.25	40.71
1987	55.76	3.96	38.13	7.95	-24.93
1988	3.83	20.20	11.61	5.25	-4.13
1989	-7.15	76.16	71.04	44.29	-4.42
1990	-17.37	22.46	-8.32	-6.46	6.08
1991	-5.3	74.6	13.5	31.5	20.7
1992	23.6	5.8	59.9	4.8	-11.9
1993	67.1	8.2	-0.3	6.1	43.8
1994	12.6	17.1	8.6	20.1	11.2
1995	8.7	45.8	28.8	28.1	43.7
1996	30.6	43.1	19.2	37.9	22.2
1997	31.3	27.8	42.7	30.2	-22.3
1998	-2.8	1.4	-8.5	-9.4	21.8

Total Returns in Percentages* *(Continued)*

Year	XON	GE	GM	HD	HWP	IBM	INTC	IP
1973	12.42	−11.57	36.67			−21.88		28.38
1974	−25.99	−44.48	25.96			−29.66		−27.87
1975	45.13	43.00	95.20			37.36		67.13
1976	26.93	24.15	45.82			28.04		22.73
1977	−4.66	−6.74	−11.24			1.57		−33.58
1978	8.98	−.69	−4.95			13.35		−12.00
1979	20.19	13.20	2.88			−9.13		7.40
1980	56.05	26.76	−4.10			10.78		20.00
1981	−15.06	−1.23	−9.11			−11.14		−1.13
1982	4.80	71.15	68.25			75.28		29.78
1983	36.05	27.39	23.73			30.61		26.93
1984	29.39	.00	17.47			4.28		−4.62
1985	30.19	32.36	.80			29.87		−1.35
1986	33.74	21.40	.89			−20.00		52.76
1987	−40.21	−45.69	.57			−.08		−40.49
1988	21.05	4.59	44.20			9.33		12.79
1989	18.86	47.93	8.38			−18.88		25.41
1990	8.30	−8.13	−11.54			25.20		−2.55
1991	22.1	37.0	−12.5			−20.4		35.4
1992	5.0	14.8	16.1			−38.0		−3.5
1993	8.0	26.4	73.3			16.6		4.6
1994	0.8	0.0	−21.8	16.6	29.5	31.9	3.6	13.7
1995	38.5	44.4	28.1	4.2	66.8	25.7	77.8	3.1
1996	24.6	40.0	8.5	5.7	21.1	67.2	131.2	9.6
1997	28.2	50.6	18.2	78.3	25.4	39.1	25.4	9.0
1998	22.2	40.7	21.1	108.3	10.3	77.0	69.1	6.2

TOTAL RETURNS IN PERCENTAGES* *(Continued)*

Year	JNJ	JPM	MCD	MRK	MMM	MO	MSFT	PG
1973		34.25	−25.25	−8.05	−7.67	−1.75		−16.09
1974		−22.68	−48.46	−16.09	−39.25	−14.95		−9.46
1975		6.86	98.72	6.41	23.27	12.42		11.53
1976		8.50	−8.39	.37	4.66	18.62		7.51
1977		−20.00	−3.13	−16.33	−11.35	2.53		−5.71
1978		10.64	−9.60	24.87	34.29	17.04		6.64
1979		7.48	−5.12	9.68	−16.59	5.53		−12.97
1980		17.68	14.26	19.94	22.99	24.36		−2.66
1981		10.16	36.18	3.50	−2.54	17.16		22.21
1982		31.91	40.39	1.85	43.49	27.84		52.22
1983		5.33	18.45	10.13	14.40	24.25		.01
1984		22.45	11.47	7.33	−.58	16.94		4.44
1985		68.98	58.40	49.13	18.60	14.38		26.93
1986		32.49	14.50	82.93	33.96	67.75		13.27
1987		−8.82	−26.51	29.94	−41.61	22.96		15.58
1988		.34	10.64	11.73	−.40	23.82		5.18
1989		30.92	45.69	37.04	32.63	68.55		65.29
1990		3.57	−15.23	18.72	11.36	27.87		25.87
1991		59.2	31.7	87.9	14.7	58.6		10.7
1992		−0.9	29.3	−20.2	9.0	53.3		16.5
1993		9.2	17.8	−18.4	11.4	−24.4		8.4
1994	24.5	−15.1	3.8	14.3	1.4	8.7	50.6	11.1
1995	58.5	48.3	55.2	75.5	27.9	63.3	44.3	36.3
1996	18.1	25.7	1.2	23.6	32.2	30.1	88.1	31.7
1997	34.1	19.2	5.9	35.3	1.4	24.4	56.2	49.7
1998	28.8	−3.5	61.6	41.0	−10.6	21.9	114.7	15.8

TOTAL RETURNS IN PERCENTAGES* *(Continued)*

Year	SBC	UTX	WMT	DJIA
1973		−43.71		−13.12
1974		48.75		−23.14
1975		48.28		44.40
1976		72.73		22.72
1977		−3.47		−12.71
1978		13.94		2.69
1979		16.27		10.52
1980		46.98		21.41
1981		−27.62		−3.40
1982		41.38		25.79
1983		32.56		25.65
1984		3.81		1.08
1985		24.55		32.78
1986		8.34		26.92
1987		−23.32		6.02
1988		25.98		15.95
1989		35.81		31.71
1990		−8.43		−.40
1991		17.1		23.9
1992		−7.9		7.4
1993		32.6		16.8
1994	1.0	4.5	−14.4	4.9
1995	45.9	54.2	5.6	36.4
1996	−6.4	42.0	3.2	28.9
1997	44.6	11.8	74.8	24.9
1998	49.0	51.3	107.1	17.9

*All stock returns throughout book exclude the effect of commissions and taxes.

ALLIEDSIGNAL INC. (ALD)
(HONEYWELL INTERNATIONAL)

By the time this book is printed, you may want to tear out these pages and insert them between Hewlett-Packard and IBM. That's because AlliedSignal agreed in June 1999 to acquire Honeywell, Inc. in a stock deal valued at $14.9 billion, and it has been decided that the name of the new company will be Honeywell International.

Shareholders of both companies overwhelmingly approved the merger at a special stockholders meeting September 1. The United States Department of Justice is continuing its investigation, and last month requested additional information about the merger. It is worried about overlap in avionics and other commercial cockpit equipment.

The European Commission, which concluded a one-month initial study and now has four months to decide whether to approve the transaction or request modifications, said the merger "may lead to the creation or strengthening of a dominant position on one or more markets for avionics products," according to a *Wall Street Journal* report August 31. Analysts, noting that the commission rarely blocks mergers or acquisitions, said the combined company may be forced to sell some overlapping avionics businesses to win European regulatory approval, but that they believe the merger remains on track to be completed in the fall.

When I wrote about AlliedSignal almost ten years ago, I noted that *Moody's Industrial Manual* used no fewer than 420 lines of fine print to record all its acquisitions and divestitures, most of them in the 1980s.

As I said then, if corporate genealogy doesn't do it for you, try a little romance. Remember Mary Cunningham, the blond and brainy Harvard MBA who helped young William Agee of Bendix Corporation attempt a hostile takeover of Martin Marietta, which then countertendered, adding the term "Pac-Man defense" to the colorful argot of high finance? Prior to their marriage in 1982, the pair had appeared as often in the gossip columns as in the financial pages.

Unlike Cunningham and Agee, Bendix and Martin Marietta never did merge. A white knight in the form of Allied came to the rescue, acquiring all of Bendix and 39 percent of Marietta, which was later spun off.

AlliedSignal was created in 1985 when Allied Corporation

(before that Allied Chemical, one of the original Dow 30) acquired The Signal Companies, a diversified group originally (but no longer) involved in oil and gas activities. In 1986 Allied spun off a collection of assorted businesses known now as The Henley Group (dubbed then "Dingman's Dogs," after the head of the management group that formed it). Even after that transaction, a *Wall Street Journal* headline read, "Allied Signal merger yields few benefits."

In 1991, however, Allied began a turnaround largely attributed to the management skills of CEO Lawrence Bossidy, who shed low-margin operations, expanded into more profitable businesses, and vastly improved operational efficiencies via the Six Sigma program. Six Sigma holds that almost any process, whether a production system or an order intake system, can be mathematically measured and refined so that errors or defects can be reduced to the statistically *de minimus* frequency of six sigma, or 3.4 defects per million opportunities. Achieving such levels results in huge cost savings from reduced scrappage, rework, and warranty costs, and stronger revenue growth from customers who appreciate higher-quality, lower-priced producers. ALD has risen at a 22 percent annual compound rate, versus 17 percent for the broader market.

Allied's 1998 sales of $15.1 billion came from four segments. Aerospace Systems (pollution control and power generation equipment, collision avoidance systems, wheels and brakes for commercial and military aircraft, and spare parts and maintenance/repair services) contributed 32 percent. Chemicals and Industrial Materials (specialty chemicals for the pharmaceutical, agricultural, refrigeration/air conditioning, and photography industries, and industrial materials for the food, pharmaceuticals, and electronic packaging industries) contributed 28 percent. The Turbine Technologies segment (jet engines for regional and business jet manufacturers, and auxiliary power generation equipment for the commercial air transport makers) contributed 24 percent; and the Transportation Products segment (a lower-margin

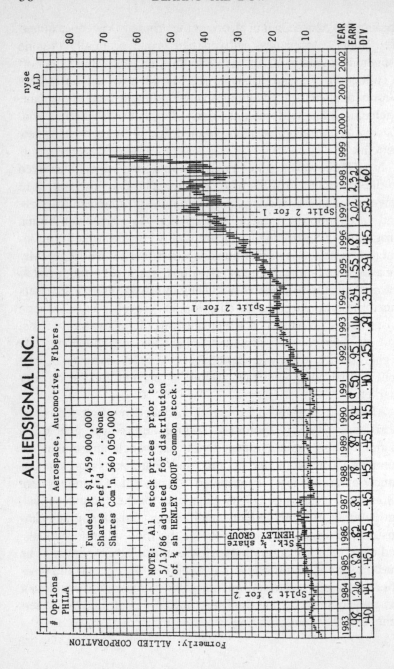

ALLIEDSIGNAL INC.

nyse
ALD

Aerospace, Automotive, Fibers.

Options
PHILA

Funded Dt $1,459,000,000
Shares Pref'd . . . None
Shares Com'n 560,050,000

NOTE: All stock prices prior to
5/13/86 adjusted for distribution
of ¼ sh HENLEY GROUP common stock.

Split 2 for 1

Split 2 for 1

Stk. ¼ share
HENLEY GROUP

Split 3 for 2

Formerly: ALLIED CORPORATION

YEAR	1983	1984	1985	1986	1987	1988	1989	1990	1991	1992	1993	1994	1995	1996	1997	1998
EARN	.98	1.20	.82	.82	.81	.78	.87	.84	d.50	.95	1.16	1.34	1.55	1.81	2.02	2.32
DIV	.40	.44	.45	.45	.45	.45	.45	.45	.40	.25	.28	.34	.39	.45	.52	.60

producer of brand name car care products such as Prestone antifreeze, Autolite spark plugs, and Simonize car waxes) contributed 16 percent.

Honeywell, Inc., with 1998 sales of $8.4 billion, makes thermostats and a wide range of products from humidifiers to airplane navigation systems. Allied expects the merger will reduce earnings cyclicality, yet boost sustainable earnings growth and profitability. Honeywell's general industrial earnings should climb when cyclical aerospace earnings fall, and vice versa. The merger will help Allied expand its highly profitable aircraft parts and services business. And ALD, whose international revenues are a relatively modest 20 percent of overall sales, is looking to the merger to increase its international exposure.

Finally, the merger will solve a succession problem. Mr. Bossidy wants to retire as chairman and CEO next April. Honeywell's CEO Michael R. Bonsignore wants to run the combined company. It works out just fine.

ALUMINUM COMPANY OF AMERICA/ALCOA (AA)

Chances are you're either wearing, riding in, sitting on or about to drink from something made using aluminum. Maybe you're even playing with it. According to the *World Book Encyclopedia,* aluminum had its first commercial application in the form of a toy rattle made for the baby son of Napoleon III in the 1850s. A century later, in 1959, Aluminum Company of America was added to the Dow.

Alcoa has mining, refining, processing, fabricating and selling locations throughout the world, and is the world's largest producer of primary and finished aluminum products. It is also the world's largest supplier of alumina, an intermediate raw material refined from bauxite and smelted into aluminum.

Processed aluminum is widely used in the packaging,

transportation, and construction markets. The packaging industry uses aluminum sheeting to make food and beverage cans and can ends, and for sheet and foil products. Aerospace and truck trailer makers are big users, and auto manufacturers increasingly use aluminum instead of steel in transmissions, wheels, doors, and roof racks. In construction, aluminum is used for siding, window frames, and numerous residential housing applications.

Throughout the 1990s the aluminum industry has been battered by low prices and global overcapacity. The Soviet Union was one of the world's biggest aluminum producers, and when it collapsed at the outset of the decade, Russia flooded the world market with aluminum in an effort to obtain hard currency. Economic turmoil in Russia, Asia, and Latin America in 1997 compounded the supply glut, while mergers in the automotive and aircraft industries created huge global buyers with the power to keep prices low. World prices fell some 30 percent from the 1980s, hitting a five-year low in March 1999.

In 1995, however, Alcoa, whose earnings since 1982 had moved in lockstep with the spot price of aluminum ingots on the London Metals Exchange, began taking action to increase profitability despite industry conditions. It has been amazingly successful with a program that combined new production efficiencies and acquisitions. It is ahead of schedule in its goal of shedding $1.5 billion in expenses by 2002, and expanded its world market share with the acquisition in 1998 of Alumax Inc., the third largest U.S. producer of aluminum, and two foreign state-owned aluminum companies, Alumix SpA of Italy and Inespal SA of Spain.

By early 1999, after two years of solid profit growth, AA had reached an all-time high of $70 7/8, adjusted for a two-for-one split in February. The company, which has paid continuous dividends since 1939, announced in January 1999 a 50 percent increase in its base quarterly dividend and a plan to repurchase 10 million (pre-split) shares. Alcoa also has a bonus dividend policy whereby the company pays out 30 percent of all earnings above a threshold that is adjusted periodically.

The biggest news, though, was breaking just as this was going

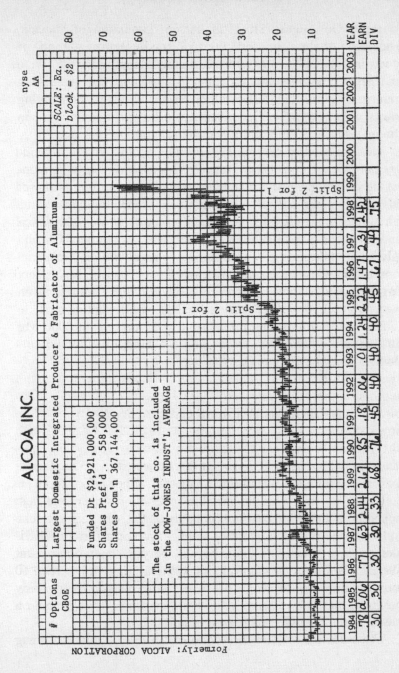

ALCOA INC.

nyse
AA

Largest Domestic Integrated Producer & Fabricator of Aluminum.

SCALE: Ea.
block = $2

Funded Dt $2,921,000,000
Shares Pref'd .. 558,000
Shares Com'n 367,144,000

The stock of this co. is included
in the DOW-JONES INDUST'L AVERAGE

Options
CBOE

Split 2 for 1

Split 2 for 1

Formerly: ALCOA CORPORATION

	YEAR	EARN	DIV
2003			
2002			
2001			
2000			
1999			
1998	2.42	.75
1997	2.3	
1996	1.47	.47
1995	2.22	.45
1994	1.24	.40
1993	.01	.40
1992	.06	.40
1991	.18	.45
1990	.85	.74
1989	2.67	.68
1988	2.44	.33
1987	.63	.30
1986	.77	.30
1985	2.06	.30
1984	.78	.30

to print. On August 11, 1999, Alcan Aluminum of Canada, Pechiney of France, and the Allusuisse Lonza Group of Switzerland (collectively referred to as APA) confirmed they were in merger talks that would create an aluminum and packaging giant with more than $21.6 billion in annual sales, supplanting Alcoa with its $15.5 billion in sales as the current number one in the industry.

Alcoa responded several days later by announcing a $4.4 billion merger agreement with Reynolds Metals Company, the number three producer, that would create a company with sales of $20.5 billion, virtually all from aluminum production. Since some $4 billion of APA's revenues would come from non-aluminum assets, Alcoa would remain number one. Both the APA and Alcoa/Reynolds mergers were subject to regulatory approval.

Whether the merger with Reynolds gets Justice Department approval or not, Alcoa's outlook is good. With the Asian and Latin American economies recovering, analysts are predicting a rise in industrywide shipments of 9 percent to 15 percent in 2000 and 2001. Having performed amazingly in a slump, AA should outperform decisively in an up cycle.

AMERICAN EXPRESS COMPANY (AXP)

The December 21, 1998, *Business Week* cover story, "The Rise of a Star," featured 47-year-old Kenneth I. Chenault, American Express Company's president, chief operating officer, and heir apparent. It noted that he serves not only on the American Express board, but also on the board of IBM. It quoted a former AmEx executive as saying, "I think he will be our generation's Jack Welch [CEO and wunderkind of General Electric]." Then it quoted Julius Erving, who's not in the Dow, but is a friend since boyhood and knows something about stardom: "He's a man of destiny, and a really good person besides."

When *Beating the Dow* first came out in 1990, AmEx's destiny was in the hands of then CEO James D. Robinson III ("Jimmy Three Sticks," as columnist Dan Dorfman used to call him, needling Robinson about his ubiquitous presence in the society pages in those days). AXP was selling below $20 and Robinson was having his troubles.

When we think American Express, most of us think traveler's checks and the credit card we can't leave home without. AmEx calls this group Travel Related Services (TRS). But Robinson had grand visions of AmEx that would carry it well beyond that and make it a vast global supermarket offering a diversity of financial services. In the early 1980s he prophesied, "By 1990 the typical consumer may have a stockbroker in California, a banker in New York, an insurance agent in Maryland, and a real estate agent jetting back and forth from Chicago to Boston. All on the American Express Card, of course."

So he embarked on a spree of acquisitions and by the end of 1990, Travel Related Services amounted to 40 percent of revenues and 60 percent of net income, the discrepancy due to "synergies" that didn't pan out. The Shearson Lehman Hutton unit, acquired in the 1980s and the second largest Wall Street firm after Merrill Lynch, lost over $800 million in 1990. the result of junk bond and bridge loan write-downs, bad loans, slow brokerage business, and massive layoffs.

AmEx's recovery began in 1993, when Robinson was replaced as CEO by Harvey Golub, a former management consultant with McKinsey & Co. Golub made his mark running AmEx's Minnneapolis-based money-management arm, now restructured as American Express Financial Advisors. With Ken Chenault at his right hand, Golub led AmEx back to basics, shedding many acquired assets like its insurance companies and Shearson Lehman, by then organized as separate companies (Shearson was sold to Primerica, Lehman was spun off to AXP shareholders), and by thoroughly restructuring others.

In 1998 Travel Related Services, comprising traveler's checks and 42.7 million credit cards, including the American Express Card (green, gold, and platinum), the Corporate Card, and the

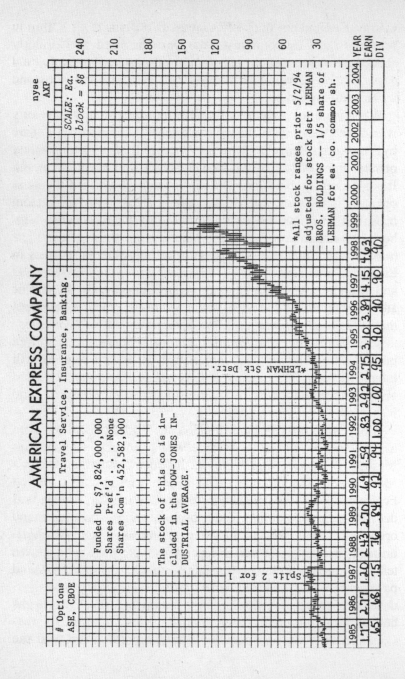

AMERICAN EXPRESS COMPANY

Travel Service, Insurance, Banking.

Funded Dt $7,824,000,000
Shares Pref'd . . . None
Shares Com'n 452,582,000

The stock of this co is included in the DOW-JONES IN-
DUSTRIAL AVERAGE.

Options
ASE, CBOE

nyse
AXP

SCALE: Ea.
block = $6

*All stock ranges prior 5/2/94
adjusted for stock dstr LEHMAN
BROS. HOLDINGS -- 1/5 share of
LEHMAN for ea. co. common sh.

*LEHMAN Stk Dstr.

Split 2 for 1

	1985	1986	1987	1988	1989	1990	1991	1992	1993	1994	1995	1996	1997	1998	1999	2000	2001	2002	2003	2004	YEAR
	1.77	1.77	1.20	2.43	2.70	.69	1.59	.83	2.92	2.75	3.10	3.89	4.15	4.63							EARN
	.65	.68	.75	.76	.84	.92	.94	1.00	1.00	.95	.90	.90	.90	.90							DIV

Optima Card, contributed 69 percent of AmEx's $19.1 billion in revenues and 61 percent of profits. Financial Advisors (formerly IDS) contributed 26 percent and 37 percent, respectively, and American Express Bank accounted for 5 percent of revenues and 2 percent of profits.

Today American Express considers itself a growth company with three overriding financial goals: to boost earnings per share by 12 percent to 15 percent annually, to maintain a return on equity of 20 percent, and to increase revenues by at least 8 percent a year. It is meeting the first two goals solidly and making good progress on the third. Growth in charge card volume is expected from higher spending per card member as well as increases in the number of cards outstanding.

American Express is also focusing on the Internet, seeking to expand its acceptance by on-line retailers and to broaden its travel and financial services. Web-based sites offering discounted airline and hotel rates, as well as complete travel packages, are a threat that AmEx aims to meet.

Incidentally, Warren Buffett's Berkshire Hathaway has been buying AXP over the years, and currently holds an 11 percent interest.

AMERICAN TELEPHONE & TELEGRAPH COMPANY/AT&T (T)

For many years AT&T, which has a record of consistent dividends dating from 1881, was considered the premier "widows and orphans" stock. Although much has changed since the court-ordered breakup of Ma Bell in 1984, to this day more people own telephone than any other American stock. But the staid dividend payer of old, even though it's still paying a relatively good dividend, is a cutting-edge telecommunications growth stock, a good bet, maybe, but no longer a sure thing.

The modern chronicle of AT&T began in 1956. By then Ma

Bell, or the Bell System as it was more formally known, had become an international telecommunications behemoth consisting of American Telephone & Telegraph Company (AT&T), the parent company of 22 operating subsidiaries; Bell Telephone Laboratories, engaged in research; and Western Electric, a manufacturer of equipment.

The fateful development that was to be the genesis of the new AT&T seemed relatively innocuous at the time. The Justice Department, which had been looming over Ma Bell like a tornado cloud for years, got the court in 1956 to issue a consent decree confining Western Electric's manufacturing to Bell System and government equipment and restricting AT&T from operating activities other than common carrier communications. Although this meant abandoning its promising cellular phone activities, it was preferable to the antitrust suit hanging over Western Electric.

But in the 1960s, two things happened.

The first was the introduction by non-Bell System makers of decorative telephones that replicated antiques, bananas, Snoopy— or were otherwise novel. The second development was the emergence of competitors in the long-distance business, such as Microwave Communications, Inc. (MCI), that offered cheaper rates if you used extra code numbers.

In response to the first development, the Federal Communications Commission (FCC) opened the way for an "interconnect industry" by abolishing all rules prohibiting AT&T customers from attaching their own phones to AT&T equipment. Score one against Ma Bell. In response to the second, the FCC authorized specialized carrier operations like MCI's. Score two. But Ma Bell didn't take it sitting down.

In 1974 the Justice Department charged Ma Bell with blocking both the interconnect and specialized carrier industries and filed an antitrust suit aimed at breaking up the Bell System.

Ma Bell now had the worst of all worlds: its core businesses, the sale of phones and phone service, were being threatened by antitrust action, and the consent decree made it impossible to enter

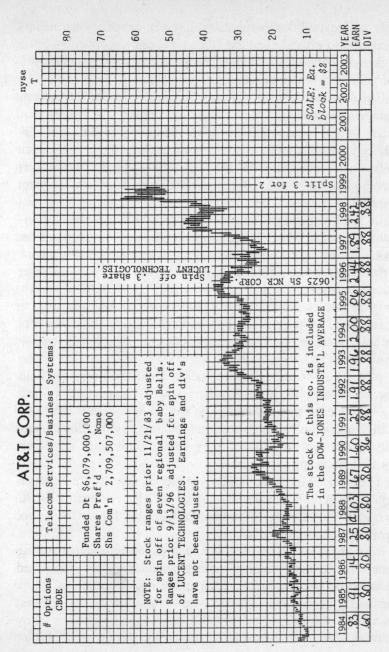

AT&T CORP.

Options CBOE

Telecom Services/Business Systems.

Funded Dt $6,079,000,000
Shares Pref'd . . . None
Shs Com'n 2,709,507,000

NOTE: Stock ranges prior 11/21/83 adjusted
for spin off of seven regional baby Bells.
Ranges prior 9/13/96 adjusted for spin off
of LUCENT TECHNOLOGIES. Earnings and div's
have not been adjusted.

The stock of this co. is included
in the DOW-JONES INDUSTR'L AVERAGE

nyse
T

SCALE: Ea.
block = $2

Spin off .3 share
LUCENT TECHNOLOGIES.

.0625 Sh NCR CORP.

Split 3 for 2

YEAR	1984	1985	1986	1987	1988	1989	1990	1991	1992	1993	1994	1995	1996	1997	1998	1999	2000	2001	2002	2003
EARN	83	91	14	1.25	d103	1.67	1.60	.27	1.91	1.96	2.00	06 2.44	06 2.41	1.89	2.42					
DIV	60	80	80	80	80	80	86	88	88	88	88	88	88	88	88					

new businesses. It was regulated like a monopoly—forced, for example, to provide service where it wasn't profitable—but it lacked a monopoly's immunity from antitrust actions and competition in areas where operations were profitable.

The next development put the FCC and the Justice Department at loggerheads and left AT&T squarely between a rock and a hard place. In 1980, responding to lobbying from Ma Bell, the FCC decided that starting in 1983 the company could enter into some unregulated businesses at arm's length—that is, through an unsubsidized subsidiary. But the Justice Department sued to block even this.

In 1982, realizing it couldn't live forever under the cloud of antitrust action, Ma Bell and Justice came to the agreement that would define the corporate basis of the AT&T we know today.

Under its terms, AT&T would divest itself of its 22 local operating companies. It would keep Western Electric, Bell Labs and its long-distance service. And it would be given the right to enter unregulated businesses through an unsubsidized subsidiary first called American Bell and later renamed AT&T Information Systems.

AT&T's 22 operating subsidiaries became seven regional holding companies (RHCs), familiar now as Nynex, Ameritech, Pacific Telesis, Bell Atlantic, US West, Southwestern Bell, and Bell South, which are regulated monopolies providing local phone service through subsidiaries (they are the Baby Bells, or BOCs, for Bell operating companies).

The ownership of the RHCs was passed directly to the shareholders of AT&T by a distribution of one share of each RHC for every 10 shares of AT&T common-held. All those widows and orphans made out very well.

Next, AT&T's dominance as a long-distance carrier was challenged with "equal access," which abandoned the extra digits required by MCI and other competitors and invited local phone customers to choose which of several long-distance carriers they wanted to use.

AT&T had total sales of $37.3 billion and profits of $2.7 billion in 1990, with 53 percent of revenues coming from long-distance operations and 45 percent from equipment sales and rentals.

For the next seven years, with the conservative hand of CEO Robert Allen at the helm, AT&T seemed to flounder. It knew it had to build on its basic long-distance services and equipment manufacturing to gain viability in an increasingly competitive marketplace, but it lacked a clear strategic vision.

In 1991 AT&T, in a major move, expanded its computer activities by acquiring NCR Corporation for about $7.40 billion. Global Information Systems, as it was renamed, lost money, and presumed synergies with the company's core communications services and manufacturing failed to materialize. The 1994 acquisition of McCaw Cellular for $12.6 billion and the 48 percent minority interest in LIN Broadcasting for $3.26 billion, although initially a drag on earnings, made AT&T a leader in wireless communication, which would become important later. Another innovation, the Universal Credit Card, was moderately profitable.

The next big milestone and the catalyst for all that's happened since was the Telecommunications Act of 1996, which deregulated the industry and put AT&T in direct competition with its one-time subsidiaries for local and long-distance business. Before, the Baby Bells needed AT&T (or MCI or Sprint et al.) for long-distance service, and AT&T needed the Baby Bells for local access. Now everybody would be going after the same business, meaning stiffer competition and lower margins. The need became clear for AT&T to succeed quickly in a host of new businesses in order to generate cash, lock in long-distance customers, and restore its direct link into people's houses.

AT&T's answer to the Telecommunications Act was to split the company into three new companies—NCR; Bell Labs, the equipment manufacturer, now renamed Lucent Technologies; and the new AT&T, which would include the telephone and wireless businesses, the credit card, and other new activities.

NCR, after losing billions, was spun off December 31, 1996, giving AT&T shareholders a value of around $2 per share of AT&T. Lucent Technologies was spun off September 30, 1996, with AT&T shareholders getting 32 percent of a Lucent share for each AT&T share, and has gained some 700 percent since the spin-off. On October 1, AT&T Capital Corp. was sold to a consortium of investors. The Universal Credit Card was sold in 1997 for around $2 billion.

So much for the "old" New AT&T. The real excitement—the "deal-a-minute" new New AT&T—began with the arrival in October 1997 of "intense and brilliant" 59-year-old C. Michael Armstrong, already dubbed "Pa Bell" by *Barron's*. The tennis-playing, Harley-riding Armstrong had transformed GM Hughes Electronics into a non-military telecommunications business in the early 1990s, and before that had been an IBM executive.

Promptly eliminating 20,000 jobs, Armstrong began in January by spending $12 billion to buy Teleport Communications Group, a provider of local phone service. Then he spent $53 million to buy TCI Group, the leading cable company. In July 1998 came a $10 billion joint venture with British Telecom, and in December a $5 billion deal to buy IBM's global network. In April 1999 he offered $62 billion for MediaOne Group, assuring that AT&T would own the cable TV lines that connect to nearly a quarter of America's 100 million homes. Then he got Microsoft to invest $5 billion in cash for agreeing to use that company's software in as many as 10 million set-top boxes that will allow cable TV subscribers to log on to the Internet through their TV sets.

Armstrong's vision, in short, is to offer customers a bundled service package consisting of telephony, digital TV, high-speed data and cellular, all for 25 percent less than the competition offers *a la carte*. Yet with all he's done, when asked recently by a *Barron's* reporter what inning the transformation of AT&T is in, he replied, "Maybe the second."

Having put most of the structure in place, Armstrong has made getting the stock up the immediate priority. He is the one plugging T as a "growth stock," and there is talk that he is reconsidering the idea of a tracking stock to highlight the worth of AT&T's cable subsidiary.

Ironically, the biggest problem facing this phenomenon of

deregulation right now is the risk of regulation. Under the 1992 Cable Act, no single company can reach more than 30 percent of the nation's homes, and AT&T is getting close to that limit. More important, there is the danger AT&T will be forced to open its network to competitors. This issue is currently being debated at the level of municipalities, but the Federal Communication Commission wants to have a national standard.

T hit an all-time high of 64 early in 1999 and in midyear has been hovering around 50. Some analysts say the company faces a series of hurdles that could hold its price down for a while. Another prominent research firm calls it "absurdly cheap." Take your pick.

THE BOEING COMPANY (BA)

Aerospace is one of the few industries in which the United States still leads the world, and Boeing is the leader of the industry, although Airbus Industrie, the European consortium and Boeing's arch rival, has a market share getting uncomfortably close to 50 percent.

In 1997 Boeing acquired the number three player, McDonnell Douglas, in a major industry consolidation. But Asian economic woes, curtailed defense spending, and ongoing production problems made for a disastrous 1998. As this is written in 1999, Boeing, which has always had a strong balance sheet and cash flow, is, operationally, a recovery story.

Boeing was founded just before World War I by a lumber executive named William Boeing. During World War II, it was the leading producer of bombers, including the B-29 Super Fortress that dropped the atomic bomb on Hiroshima.

Although jet engine technology had been developed during the 1940s, noise and high fuel requirements had to be weighed against jets' greater speed in the commercial market. Boeing pioneered commercial jet aircraft; its 707, which could travel nonstop across the Atlantic for the first time, was used for the first

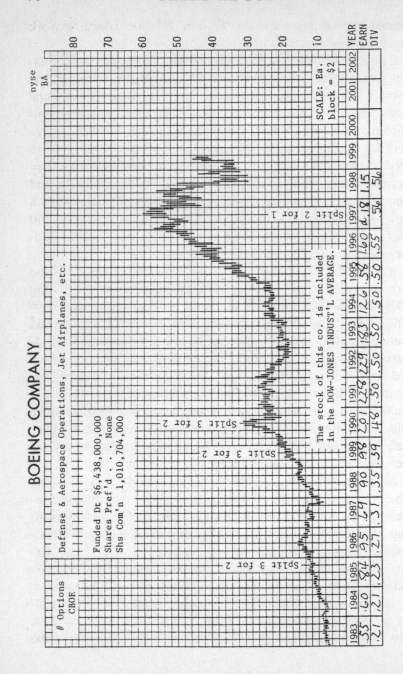

BOEING COMPANY

nyse
BA

Options
CBOE

Defense & Aerospace Operations, Jet Airplanes, etc.

Funded Dt $6,438,000,000
Shares Pref'd . . . None
Shs Com'n 1,010,704,000

Split 3 for 2

Split 3 for 2

Split 3 for 2

Split 2 for 1

SCALE: Ea.
block = $2

The stock of this co. is included
in the DOW-JONES INDUST'L AVERAGE.

YEAR	1983	1984	1985	1986	1987	1988	1989	1990	1991	1992	1993	1994	1995	1996	1997	1998	1999	2000	2001	2002
EARN	.35	.60	.84	.95	.69	.90	.98	2.01	2.26	2.29	1.83	1.26	.58	1.60	2.18	1.15				
DIV	.21	.21	.23	.27	.31	.35	.39	.48	.50	.50	.50	.50	.50	.55	5¢	56				

scheduled passenger jet service flight in 1958, between New York and London.

The development in the early 1960s of quieter, more fuel-efficient and far more powerful fan jet engines, inspired by the Pentagon's plans for the gargantuan C-5A cargo plane, led to the first Boeing 747 jumbo jet, built after Pan Am's Juan Trippe gambled his company on the idea of transporting 350 or more passengers at a time between continents.

The 1970s saw a shakeup and shakeout in the airframe industry as competitors like McDonnell Douglas, now part of Boeing, and Lockheed entered the widebody market with their somewhat smaller DC-10 and L-1011 airbuses capable of carrying up to 250 passengers 2,100 miles and later to be introduced in extended-range versions.

But by the mid-1970s, oil prices were on the rise again and the airlines began looking to replace their aging, narrow-body Boeing 707s, 727s, and Douglas DC-8s and DC-9s, and to add more fuel-efficient widebodies to their fleets. Boeing quickly established predominance with a $3 billion commitment to develop two mid-sized aircraft: a narrow-body 757 and a widebody 767, each accommodating about 200 passengers on trips of 2,000 miles. Both met FAA requirements for extended-range operations and the 767 exists in a model that can fly intercontinental routes. In the mid-1980s, oil prices plummeted, putting the carriers in a financial position to go ahead with long-delayed plans to modernize their fleets.

After several delays, 1989 saw delivery of the first 747-400, which features digital electronics and other technical improvements and can fly 400 passengers more than 8,000 miles, permitting nonstop service between destinations such as New York–Seoul, Los Angeles–Sydney and London–Tokyo. The 747-400 can also carry nearly 600 passengers on high-density domestic routes and is available in freighter and combination models.

The short-range 737, offered in three versions, is the bestselling jetliner in commercial aviation history. The 100-seat 717-200, launched in 1994 as the MD-95, is designed to serve the emerging short-haul, high-frequency regional market. The 300–500-seat 777, in service since 1995, is a two-engine plane larger than the 767 but smaller than the 747. It is adaptable to multiple sizes and all ranges, and was designed to replace aging DC-10 and 1-1011 fleets.

Of the 620 commercial deliveries scheduled for 1999, over 60 percent will be the new-type 717s, next-generation 737s, or 777s. For 2000, these types account for 75 percent of the 480 deliveries planned.

While the commercial aircraft segment contributed 64 percent of 1998 revenues of $56.2 billion, 35 percent came from Boeing's defense and space operations. With the 1996 acquisition of Rockwell International's defense and space units, the company is responsible for a substantial number of military-aircraft and defense-system products and programs, and is NASA's leading contractor. Congress reportedly is considering increasing the total defense budget by some $8 billion, good news for companies that serve the Pentagon.

The outlook for commercial aircraft is not considered bright at the moment. Commercial aircraft deliveries have peaked and are expected to decline 25 percent in 2000. Boeing's 747 deliveries are scheduled to fall from 57 in 1998 to 14 in 2000. The battle for market share between Boeing and Airbus Industrie has added price pressure to the reduced volume.

All this puts the focus on production efficiency, and Boeing has been working hard to reduce costs and improve margins. Recently announced second-quarter 1999 earnings reflected, in the words of *The Wall Street Journal,* "[a] recovery being driven by productivity gains that have begun to emerge in the company's commercial-jet division, along with steady improvement in military programs and an overhaul of the company's management and investment strategies. Lower research costs also contributed to the bottom line." Said a Wall Street analyst, "Emphasis is on execution and it's working."

BA is currently depressed and earnings momentum is unlikely to start building again until after 2000. Internally, however, cash flow is huge, and the company is reducing its debt, improving its productivity, and repurchasing its stock. We may have to wait a while, but BA is looking like a recovery story.

CATERPILLAR, INC. (CAT)

When they picked Caterpillar in May 1991 to replace Navistar in the Dow, I'll admit to being a bit wistful. Navistar, the truck maker evolved from farm equipment manufacturer, was a contrarian's dream. As they say out in farm country, it had been "rode hard and put to bed wet." At $3 and change, the cheapest stock in the Dow, it was a pure case of Murphy's Law. But it had a lot going for it and I felt it was a great comeback opportunity for the long run. In 1996 it began its revival, and today it's going strong.

Anyway, Caterpillar was substituted and we could have done lots worse. Caterpillar is America corpersonified (to coin a word). When Madison Avenue asks "Will it play in Peoria?" they refer to the all-American Illinois town where "Cat" is the dominant employer. The company's roots go back to the 1800s, when two inventors/entrepreneurs, co-founders Daniel Best and Benjamin Holt, helped revolutionize farming with the development of steam traction engines and combined harvesters. When, in 1904, Holt replaced wheels with tracks, creating the first track-type tractor, agriculture entered a new era.

Caterpillar is the world's largest manufacturer of earth-moving and construction machinery, and a leading producer of diesel and natural gas engines and turbines. Its products are used in the construction, mining, materials handling, forest products, and farming industries. It makes all types and sizes of earthmoving equipment, from small agricultural tractors to the largest mechanical drive mining truck in the world with a payload capacity of 240 tons.

Its diesel and natural gas engines range from 40 to 13,600 horsepower, and are used in earthmoving and construction machines, on-highway trucks, and marine, petroleum, agricultural, industrial, and other applications. CAT also makes turbines ranging from 1,340 to 15,000 horsepower primarily for use in electric power generation. The acquisition of Perkins Diesel for $1.325 billion in 1998 added sales of about $41.1 billion and expanded CAT's line of sub-200 horsepower reciprocating engines.

Caterpillar is vitally involved in worldwide infrastructure development and repair, but its earnings correlate with construction cycles domestically and with economic cycles abroad, especially in emerging markets About half the company's revenues are derived from sales outside the United States. Global 1998 revenue figures broke down this way: 57 percent North America; 25 percent Europe/Africa/Middle East; 10 percent Latin America; and 8 percent Asia/Pacific.

In 1998 CAT's earnings were severely affected by a combination of the economic turmoil in the Asia/Pacific region, sluggish economies in Europe and Latin America, and less directly, by low commodity prices and poor weather conditions hurting the farm economy in the United States. To the extent Caterpillar sells farm equipment, it had to deal with price cutting at farm machinery producers such as Deere and Case. By the same token, Deere and Case tried to offset slow farm sales by getting more competitive in the area of small construction machinery. So the domestic market for Caterpillar, which should have been strong because of federal spending on highway repair, was under price pressure.

CAT shares, which hit an all-time high in 1997 and revisited that high in 1998, experienced unusual volatility as reports on the Asian economies varied from optimistic to pessimistic and back again. In midsummer 1999 CAT was gaining on renewed market interest in the cyclical/value stocks, helped by a five-year share buyback program aimed at reducing outstanding shares by 11 percent.

The company also has been taking aggressive measures to cut costs and increase its minimum earnings in cyclical troughs.

CAT is a strong, well-managed company that should benefit in the longer term from worldwide economic improvement and a renaissance in American manufacturing.

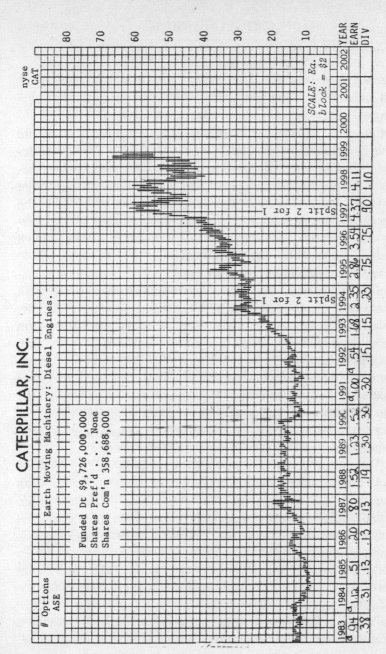

CATERPILLAR, INC.

Options
Options
ASE

Earth Moving Machinery: Diesel Engines.

Funded Dt $9,726,000,000
Shares Pref'd . . . None
Shares Com'n 358,688,000

nyse
CAT

SCALE: Ea.
block = $2

Split 2 for 1

Split 2 for 1

	1983	1984	1985	1986	1987	1988	1989	1990	1991	1992	1993	1994	1995	1996	1997	1998	1999	2000	2001	2002	YEAR
EARN	d.94	d1.12	.51	.20	.80	1.52	1.23	d1.00	d.54	1.68	2.35	2.86	3.54	4.37	4.11						
DIV	.38	.31	.13	.13	.13	.19	.30	.30	.15	.15	.23	.75	.75	.90	1.10						

CITIGROUP INC. (C)

There used to be a sign, I am reliably informed, that you'd see in gin mills: "They don't sell beer at the bank and we don't cash checks." Here's a story about a bank and a beer can that tie to a common ancestor whose bloodline still runs in the Dow family.

In her bestselling book about the junk bond era, *The Predator's Ball,* Connie Bruck describes a 1985 cocktail party encounter at the Beverly Hills Hotel between Gerald Tsai, then vice chairman of Dow component American Can Company, and Nelson Peltz of Triangle Industries, which had a subsidiary called National Can. Raising his voice over the music, Peltz, a guest of host Michael Milken of Drexel Burnham Lambert, told Tsai: "Someday I'd like to talk to you about buying your cans."

To make a long story short, Tsai, one-time wunderkind of the Manhattan Fund, a "go-go" fund of the sixties, had a run of bad luck and became involved with a tiny insurance company called Associated Madison, which he expanded into a direct-mail insurance operation later to be renamed Mutual Benefit Life. Tsai, no shrinking violet, approached the president of American Can, a leading maker of beer cans, Dixie cups, and large industrial cans, and persuaded him that American Can should buy Associated as a step toward diversifying into financial services. Tsai thus became American Can's resident financial services expert.

Tsai got American Can into a growing number of other financial services, increasing his importance in the process. When he was made president of American Can in 1986, he thought of Nelson Peltz—and talked to him, about cans. He sold the can business to Triangle Industries' National Can subsidiary for $580 million—raised, incidently, from Drexel Burnham Lambert, completing neatly the circle begun at the Beverly Hills cocktail party. American Can's remaining financial services business was renamed Primerica Corporation.

Primerica Corporation was then acquired by Baltimore-based Commercial Credit Corporation, an enterprise of one Sanford

Weill, formerly of American Express and the investment bank Shearson Loeb Rhodes. Weill took the helm at the merged company and had Commercial Credit's name legally changed to Primerica Corp. So American Can, one of the original 30 Dow stocks, became Primerica in two incarnations, all occupying the same slot in the Dow Jones Industrial Average. Until 1991.

In 1991, among other substitutions and deletions, Primerica was dropped from the Dow and replaced by J.P. Morgan, giving the Dow needed representation in the commercial banking sector.

In 1993 Primerica, which owned Smith Barney, later to be Salomon Smith Barney, acquired Travelers Inc., a huge life and casualty insurance company. This time Sandy Weill chose to retain the better-known Travelers name, and the company became Travelers Group. In 1997, when the Dow again changed several components, Travelers Group was added. Welcome back, American Can!

Nobody knows for sure who made the first move, but in 1998 two of the biggest forces in the world of financial services agreed to join in one of the largest mergers in corporate history. Citicorp, then vying with Chase Manhattan as the country's largest commercial bank, agreed to merge with Travelers Group to form a financial services behemoth with shareholders equity of $44 billion, assets of $697 billion, and a customer base of 100 million. The combined company would be called Citigroup, it would use the stock symbol C that once belonged to Chrysler, and it would occupy Travelers Group's place in the Dow. Two of the biggest egos in the business, John Reed of Citigroup and Sanford Weill of Travelers Group, would function as co-CEOs of the new company.

The deal, termed a "merger of equals," was completed in October 1998 with Travelers issuing 2.5 shares for each share of Citigroup in a tax-free exchange. The combined Citigroup would be owned equally by existing shareholders of both partners to the merger, although the new company's quarterly dividend of 18 cents a share was a raise for Travelers holders, who had last received 12½ cents, and a reduction for Citicorp holders, who last received 23 cents.

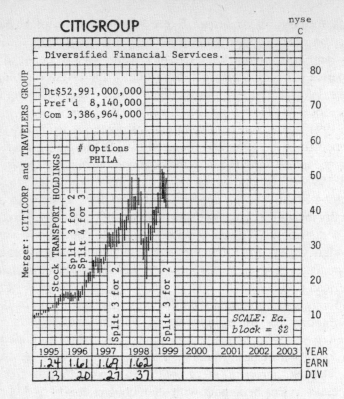

CITIGROUP   nyse C

Diversified Financial Services.

Merger: CITICORP and TRAVELERS GROUP

Dt$52,991,000,000
Pref'd 8,140,000
Com 3,386,964,000

Options PHILA

Stock TRANSPORT HOLDINGS

Split 3 for 2
Split 4 for 3

Split 3 for 2

Split 3 for 2

SCALE: Ea. block = $2

	1995	1996	1997	1998	1999	2000	2001	2002	2003	YEAR
EARN	1.24	1.61	1.69	1.62						
DIV	.13	.20	.27	.37						

At the time of the merger, Standard & Poor's observed that the combined company "would have a presence in virtually every financial services segment: banking, brokerage, asset management, and insurance. However, the success of the deal is predicated upon Citigroup's ability to leverage the potential for expense saving, economies of scale and cross selling opportunities."

Although there inevitably is speculation on how long it's going to be before Reed and Weill go for each other's throats, the combination so far seems to working reasonably well. A July 1999 *Business Week* article summarized the problem they both face: "The two men are attempting several revolutions at once. First, they are trying to offer consumers around the world everything from CDs and credit cards to mutual funds and insurance. At the same time they are trying to combine the Salomon Smith Barney investment bank with the Citibank corporate bank. And they are doing all this at a time when the Internet is rewriting the rules of financial services."

After three quarters, financial results seem encouraging. Says Argus Research in a July 1999 report, "Strong revenue and earnings momentum continued for BUY rated Citigroup. Citigroup has already completed $1.7 billion of the $2.0 billion expected cost savings this year and management expects to exceed their target. For the second quarter of 1999, diluted core EPS increased 25%. Core net income increased 21%. Overall business revenues advanced an impressive 12% in the quarter. For the first six months of 1999 core income per share increased to $1.40 from $1.17. . . . Citigroup is an excellent global recovery play."

According to *Business Week,* Reed says his internal measures show the deal has yet to prove itself. He has a "synthetic" Citigroup model that compares Citi's stock with an index of the bank's top competitors. Citi's stock has performed only slightly better than the index. Tough guy to please.

This will be fun to watch.

THE COCA-COLA COMPANY (KO)

It is just possible that there is nobody in the civilized world who hasn't heard of Coca-Cola, a brand name that has become synonymous with almost anything that is popular and ubiquitous. If you don't drink Coke, you may well drink one of the company's other products, like Tab, Sprite, Minute Maid juice, or Hi-C.

The formula for Coca-Cola was invented by an Atlanta pharmacist from coca leaves and kola nuts in 1886. The original formula contained just a touch of cocaine, but that was eliminated in 1903. Code-named Merchandise 7X, the formula for Coke remains one of the world's most closely guarded secrets. When an Indian court demanded the company turn it over to its local bottlers, Coca-Cola pulled out of India.

Marketed like nothing before or since, Coca-Cola was known all over the world by World War II. Ike liked it, making it a staple on military bases, which also meant setting up plants all over the globe to put it in the familiar green bottles.

Coke's nemesis, Pepsi-Cola, had been kicking around since the 1890s, but the famous "cola wars" really didn't begin until the 1950s. As Vice President Richard Nixon was shaking his finger at Nikita Khrushchev at the exhibition of American products in Moscow in 1959, Khrushchev was sipping a Pepsi for all the television world to see. That publicity coup was staged by Don Kendall, no mean marketer himself, who would later be Chairman of Pepsico, Inc. "Lifestyle" advertising by both companies in the 1960s, built on themes like "the Pepsi generation" and "Coke is the real thing," heightened the rivalry. By the 1980s Coke's predominant market share was being seriously threatened, despite its great successes with Diet Coke and caffeine-free varieties.

In 1985 Coca-Cola decided to meet the Pepsi challenge by making the first change ever in its century-old formula and introducing the "New Coke," with a smoother, sweeter, more Pepsi-like taste. The New Coke flopped in a colossal way, and Coca-Cola had egg all over its corporate face. Within three months, angry loyalists were forming opposition groups, such as "Old Coke Drinkers of America," major chains like McDonald's were dropping it, and the company was reintroducing the old formula (with corn syrup instead of sugar) under the name Coca-Cola Classic.

Today Coca-Cola, which operates in more than 200 countries, has 50 percent of the global market for soft drink sales, more than double the share of any competitor.

Some forays into diversification, such as its 1977 acquisition of Taylor Wines (sold to Seagram in 1983) and its 1982 purchase of 49 percent of Columbia Pictures (sold to Sony in 1989), were profitable investments and not serious distractions.

In 1986 the company created a new corporation, Coca-Cola Enterprises, Inc., to own its largest bottlers; CCE issued stock publicly. Coca-Cola Company owns 44 percent of CCE, which is separately listed on the New York Stock Exchange. Don't confuse it

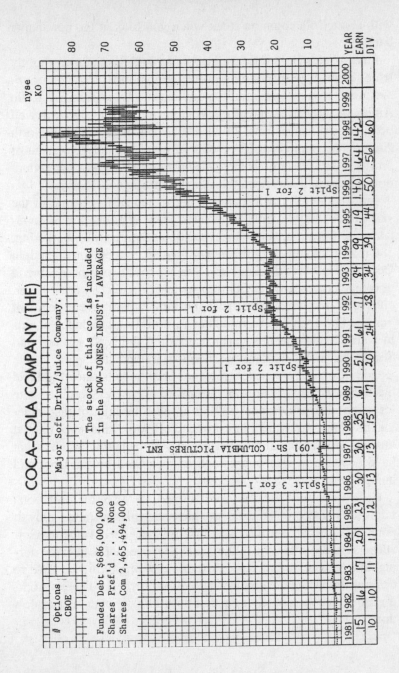

COCA-COLA COMPANY (THE)

nyse
KO

Major Soft Drink/Juice Company.

The stock of this co. is included
in the DOW-JONES INDUST'L AVERAGE

Options
CBOE

Funded Debt $686,000,000
Shares Pref'd . . . None
Shares Com 2,465,494,000

Split 2 for 1

Split 2 for 1

Split 2 for 1

Split 3 for 1

160 Sh. COLUMBIA PICTURES ENT.

YEAR	1981	1982	1983	1984	1985	1986	1987	1988	1989	1990	1991	1992	1993	1994	1995	1996	1997	1998	1999	2000
EARN	.15	.16	.17	.20	.23	.30	.30	.35	.61	.51	.61	.71	.84	.99	1.19	1.40	1.44	1.42		
DIV	.10	.10	.11	.11	.12	.13	.13	.15	.17	.20	.24	.28	.34	.39	.44	.50	.56	.60		

with Coca-Cola common stock when you look at the newspaper listings!

Coca-Cola's 1998 sales were about $18.8 billion, down slightly from the prior year. A strong dollar against most foreign currencies and weak economic conditions in Asia, Europe, Latin America, and Africa, have kept volume and earnings growth well below historical norms since 1995. Business outside North America accounted for 63 percent of net sales and 73 percent of profits in 1998. Earnings have also been affected by steep reductions in capital gains from the sale of bottling subsidiaries.

But historical growth patterns are expected to resume in the years 2002 to 2004. Soft drink sales grow as a function of population, civilization, economic vitality, and above all, marketing.

Growth should also be helped by an agreement signed in December 1998 with Cadbury Schweppes to purchase several beverage brands, such as Schweppes and Canada Dry tonic water, club soda, and ginger ale, Crush, Dr Pepper, and several regional brands. The acquisition, valued at $1.85 billion, includes brands in countries around the world (excluding the U.S., France, and South Africa) and concentrate plants in Ireland and Spain.

Coca-Cola has an unbroken record of dividends since 1893 and has increased its payout every year for the past ten years, despite less than ideal conditions. KO hit an all-time high of just under $90 in 1998, and while it has dropped off somewhat since then, it remains an example of the overpriced high-cap growth stocks that have kept the market overvalued as measured by the Dow and the S&P.

Coca-Cola once officially proclaimed, "We are the only bona fide global force in an industry blessed with unlimited growth potential." Doug Ivestor, who briefly succeeded Roberto Goizueta as CEO after the latter saw KO rise 3500 percent during his 16-year reign, has his own way of putting it: "We're dealing with human thirst," he told employees. "There's nothing about economic change that is going to change people's thirst."

How can I top that? It's a fabulous company and the market knows it. Maybe they'll do something dumb again like they did with New Coke, and give us a chance to buy it cheap.

WALT DISNEY COMPANY (DIS)

In an article titled "No Mickey Mouse Company," *Barron's* said: "Like Coca-Cola, Disney crosses cultural barriers and, for decades, has stood as an icon of American pop culture, making it one of the world's most powerful brand names—surpassing even McDonald's and IBM." I like that quote because it says a lot about Disney and gets four Dow names in one sentence.

Founded in a garage by creative genius Walt Disney back in the 1920s and built with the help of his business-minded brother, Roy, who is still active in the company, Disney was one of the three substitutions to the average made in May 1991, replacing USX. We needed some show biz; too much steel and oil can get tedious.

Disney breaks things down into three basic segments, which contributed to revenues of $23 billion and profits of $4 billion for the fiscal year ended September 30, 1998, as follows, according to Standard & Poor's:

The Creative Content segment had revenue of $10.3 billion and profits of $1.4 billion. This is the group that produces and distributes movies, TV shows, and home videos. It also includes merchandise licensing and a chain of more than 600 retail stores.

The Broadcasting Segment had revenue of $7.1 billion and profits of $1.3 billion. It owns and operates ten television stations, the ABC-TV network, and various radio stations. It owns and operates The Disney Channel, which is distributed through cable TV systems, and it owns 80 percent of various ESPN cable channels. Not included in the above figures are operations in which Disney owns 50 percent or less, such as the Lifetime, E, and Arts

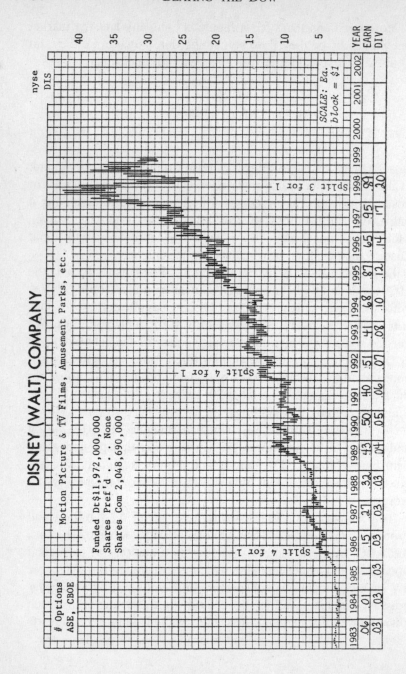

DISNEY (WALT) COMPANY

nyse DIS

Motion Picture & TV Films, Amusement Parks, etc.

Options
ASE, CBOE

Funded Dt$11,972,000,000
Shares Pref'd . . None
Shares Com 2,048,690,000

SCALE: Ea.
block = $1

Split 3 for 1
Split 4 for 1
Split 4 for 1

	1983	1984	1985	1986	1987	1988	1989	1990	1991	1992	1993	1994	1995	1996	1997	1998	1999	2000	2001	2002
YEAR																				
EARN	.06	.01	.11	.15	.21	.32	.43	.50	.40	.51	.41	.68	.87	.65	.95	.89				
DIV	.03	.03	.03	.03	.03	.03	.04	.05	.06	.07	.08	.10	.12	.14	.17	.20				

& Entertainment cable networks, in which it has interests of 50 percent, 39.6 percent, and 37.5 percent, respectively.

The Theme Parks & Resorts segment had revenue of and profit of $5.5 billion and $1.3 billion, respectively. This group includes the Walt Disney World Complex in Florida, which contains the Magic Kingdom, Epcot Center, the Disney-MGM Studio Theme Park, the Animal Kingdom, and at least 15 hotels owned by Disney. The company is also planning a $1.4 billion expansion of the Disneyland theme park resort in Anaheim, California. The expansion, expected to be completed in 2001, would include a new theme park, called Disney's California Adventure, and a 750-room hotel. In Japan, Tokyo Disneyland is licensed out to a local company, which plans to open a second theme park in 2001. This segment also owns interest in two California professional sports teams and Disney Cruise Line.

Disney also owns 39 percent of Euro Disney S.C.A., which operates the Disneyland Paris theme park business.

In July 1999 Disney announced a plan to combine various Internet-related assets with Internet company Infoseek, in which DIS already has a 43 percent equity interest. The resulting combination would be known as go.com, and DIS would own about 72 percent of a related tracking stock.

In late August 1999 DIS is trading at 29⅛, about where it started the year. That still gives it an outsized multiple of 40, but a lot of people aren't happy. According to a July 26, 1999, *Barron's* cover story picturing a dazed Mickey Mouse and titled "How to Revive Disney," investors are abandoning DIS in droves because earnings are stalled.

The problem, according to *Barron's,* is that the theme parks and cable properties are prospering, but its primary profit engine, the Creative Content segment, is under siege, having suffered a 33 percent drop in operating income to $74 million in the third quarter of the current fiscal year. In the preceding quarter, the unit's operating income had dropped 52 percent to $163 million.

Barron's says Creative Content's library of animated classics became a source of multiplying earnings when they were first being made available on videocassette. As the videocassettes were released, related Disney-character products would be sold, bringing in mounting billions. But by last year, sales growth flagged, leading management to conclude that many titles had been overexposed. So Disney decided to "rest" the library by moving to a ten-year release cycle from a seven-year cycle. That will save marketing costs and pay off in the long run, but the short-term effect is a reduction in income. Compounding the problem is the fact that ancillary product sales—the stuffed animals, backpacks, and posters—are licensed out and are almost pure profit. So CEO Michael Eisner is being unfairly criticized, say some people, for thinking long term rather than jumping at short-term opportunity.

Whatever the case, the sagging stock price has forced Mr. Eisner to become aggressively cost-conscious, and Wall Street always welcomes that.

In raising its rating from hold to accumulate, Standard & Poor's points to prospects for asset sales, cost cutting, and other efforts to improve profits. It also sees support coming from prospects for new animated films, two new Disney theme parks in 2001, and DIS's plan to create the new go.com tracking stock.

In 1990 we wrote, "Is Disney on the verge of getting too big to have growth potential? Can Disney make an elephant fly? Ask Dumbo."

Dumbo?

E. I. DU PONT DE NEMOURS
AND COMPANY (DD)

"Researchers are planning to use a gene from a spider to create a new artificial silk that, ounce for ounce, would be stronger than the strongest steel. A pencil-thin strand of this stuff could theoretically stop a 747 jet in full-powered flight, while a sheet not much thicker than a Kleenex could stop a high-powered bullet."

That news, quoted from a May 1998 *Barron's* article called

"New DuPont," dramatizes the kind of futuristic research DuPont is working on in its Life Sciences area, part of a major change of direction this traditionally cyclical chemicals company has taken in order "to supercharge its earnings growth and boost the earnings multiple investors are willing to pay."

A lot of people think of DuPont as the company that introduced women's nylon stockings. That was back in 1940 and was the beginning of this old gunpowder maker's preeminence in artificial fibers made from petrochemicals.

DuPont has a corporate legend that is rich in more ways than one. Pierre DuPont, a financial genius of sorts, bought the company in 1902 with $2,100 (when the assets of the company were valued at $24 million) and has been called the "architect of the modern corporation." He also got DuPont to buy, cheaply, 28 percent of a young company called General Motors, and he hired Alfred P. Sloan to build it into the world's largest industrial corporation. Following an antitrust suit, DuPont's GM shares were distributed to DuPont shareholders in 1962.

When we wrote about DuPont in the original *Beating the Dow,* the company was deriving about 40 percent of its sales from oil and energy-related businesses (mainly Conoco); another 43 percent from industrial and consumer chemical products, fibers, and polymers (Dacron, Teflon); and the balance from a group of diversified businesses ranging from agricultural products (herbicides, insecticides) to sporting goods (Remington firearms, fishing lines) and medical products and pharmaceuticals.

DuPont's 1998 annual report describes a company in the throes of a major restructuring. Revenues of $24.8 billion compare with the prior year's $45.1 billion, the difference largely reflecting discontinued operations, which account for 54 percent more of earnings than continuing operations. The discontinued operations are those of Conoco, 30.5 percent of which had been sold publicly in October 1998. Otherwise, 1998's sales were 47 percent foreign, and the total broke down as follows: agricultural and nutrition, 11 percent; pharmaceuticals, 4 percent; nylon intermediates, polymers, and fibers, 16 percent; polyester fibers (Dacron), films, and

PET resins, 10 percent; specialty fibers, 12 percent; coatings and polymers, 17 percent; pigments and chemicals, 13 percent; and specialty polymers, 15 percent.

As this is written in mid-1999, DuPont has just exchanged tax-free its remaining 69.5 percent interest in Conoco (COC) to DuPont shareholders for 108 million DD shares. The purpose of the so-called split-off was to eliminate a management distraction and gain flexibility to invest in life sciences such as biotechnology, crop pesticides, nutrition, and pharmaceuticals. The immediate financial rationale was that the lost revenue and earnings from Conoco would be offset by higher earnings-per-share resulting from what in effect was a share buyback.

As part of its strategy, DuPont plans to acquire the remaining 80 percent of Pioneer Hi-Bred International for $7.7 billion in DD stock and cash. DD acquired its 20 percent share of Pioneer, a producer of germ plasm and seed, in 1997 for $1.7 billion. In July 1998 DuPont purchased the other 50 percent interest in a pharmaceutical joint venture held by Merck for $2.5 billion (one of its products is the anti-HIV drug Sustiva), and plans to form other drug company alliances.

In February 1999 DD acquired the coatings unit of Hoechst for $1.9 billion, making it the world's largest supplier of auto coatings.

In an unusual wrinkle, the company is considering the issuance of a tracking stock for its life sciences businesses sometime in 2000. While not unprecedented—General Motors H (GMH) is a tracking stock for Hughes Electronics—tracking stock does not have voting rights and does not represent ownership. It would be designed to attract the higher multiple investors would give to a life sciences enterprise and would facilitate acquisitions on favorable terms. It would probably be dividended to existing DD holders. But the precise form it will take, if it is issued at all, and how it will affect the Beating the Dow portfolio strategies remains to be seen.

On July 30, 1999, DD was leading our Beating the Dow portfolios with a 32.7 percent total return for the year, but at 72⅛ it

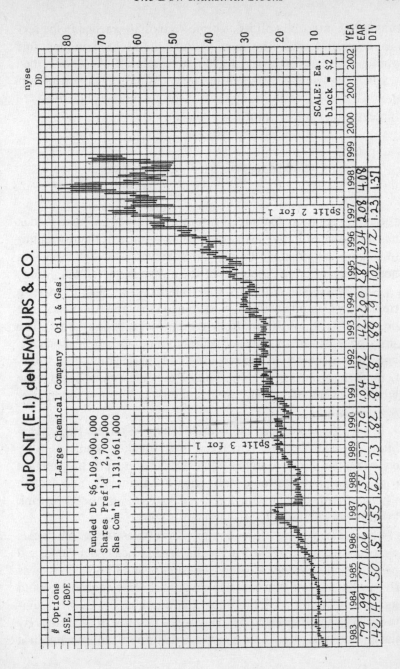

duPONT (E.I.) deNEMOURS & CO.

nyse
DD

Large Chemical Company – Oil & Gas.

Options
ASE, CBOE.

Funded Dt $6,109,000,000
Shares Pref'd 2,700,000
Shs Com'n 1,131,661,000

Split 3 for 1

Split 2 for 1

SCALE: Ea.
block = $2

YEAR	1983	1984	1985	1986	1987	1988	1989	1990	1991	1992	1993	1994	1995	1996	1997	1998	1999	2000	2001	2002
EAR	.79	.99	.77	1.06	1.23	1.52	1.77	1.70	1.04	.72	.42	2.90	2.81	3.24	2.08	4.08				
DIV	.42	.49	.50	.51	.55	.62	.73	.82	.84	.87	.88	.91	1.02	1.12	1.23	1.37				

was still significantly off its all-time high of 80 reached in the second quarter of 1998. The "new DuPont" had soared on favorable publicity and the prospect of a lucrative spin-off of Conoco, then taken a dive when its second-quarterly earnings declined 16 percent. CEO Charles Holliday says, "Our governing objective is to increase shareholder value."

EASTMAN KODAK COMPANY (EK)

I'm not going to try to count the number of times Eastman Kodak has restructured in the last twenty years—some of the restructurings were called streamlinings or whatever—but the result has been a very different corporation, and a very skeptical Wall Street.

This famous old company was founded in the late nineteenth century by George Eastman, who coined the name Kodak because he liked the letter K (his mother's maiden name began with it). The story goes that he once described the company's product development as a brainstorming process that kept on going until somebody in the group said, "How simple." When Eastman heard those words, he knew they were on to something. He was a man after my own heart.

If only his successors had been listening. By 1991 EK's $18.9 billion in sales derived 37 percent from Imaging (cameras, film, etc.) and the rest in roughly equal proportion from Information (office copiers, electronic equipment), Chemicals, and Health (Sterling Drugs, which made Bayer Aspirin, and Lehn & Fink Products, best known for Lysol disinfectant).

Operationally, the office copier market was weak, chemicals were in a down cycle, the drug business had a heavy debt load, and overall results were lackluster. The camera and film business was strong, but the company had made a questionable decision to build its future on traditional, high-quality film photography when digital technology seemed to be the wave of the industry's future. By the end of 1992, after four major restructurings failed to produce significant results, a Dean Witter analyst summed things up: "This is a hate stock, with a high level of bearish opinion."

Kodak's new direction really started in late 1993 with the appointment as CEO of 52-year-old outsider George M.C. Fisher, a PhD in applied mathematics credited with leading Motorola through a period of explosive growth and record profitability.

That December, with shareholder pressure having become intense, the company spun off its chemicals division to EK shareholders, creating Eastman Chemical. The spin-off reduced EK's debt by $2 billion, and EK shareholders, who now got two dividend checks equaling the old one, got a 43.8 percent total return for the year.

Fisher's next major move was an organizational restructuring that created a separate unit to specialize in the development of digital electronic imaging technology. Aggressive competition from Fuji Film had shrunk profit margins on traditional film from 23 percent to 18 percent in three years.

To raise cash and reduce debt, Fisher put Sterling Drug and Lehn & Fink on the block. By October 1994 both divisions had been sold for a total of just under $8 billion, with the proceeds used to reduce debt, to develop and introduce a new line of Advanced Photo System (APS) products, and to launch Digital Imaging as the fastest-growing part of the company.

Eastman Kodak's 1995 annual report had one word printed on the familiar yellow background: "Smile." Fisher was about to celebrate his second full year as CEO by announcing stronger-than-expected first-quarter earnings and the second stock buyback program in six months. EK had produced a 40-month total return of 113.5%.

But there was much work to be done. Kodak's Digital Imaging activities required huge amounts of cash and were not projected to be profitable until 1997. Also, digital technology required an about-face in EK's corporate culture. Fisher was successfully challenging EK's obsession with privacy and replacing it with the open exchange of ideas that characterized Silicon Valley, but it was taking time and exacting a cost. The company's one

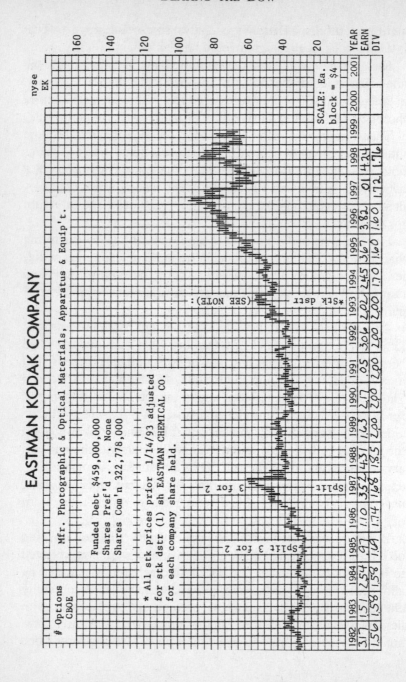

EASTMAN KODAK COMPANY

Mfr. Photographic & Optical Materials, Apparatus & Equip't.

Options
CBOE

Funded Debt $459,000,000
Shares Pref'd . . . None
Shares Com'n 322,778,000

* All stk prices prior 1/14/93 adjusted
for stk dstr (1) sh EASTMAN CHEMICAL CO.
for each company share held.

nyse
EK

SCALE: Ea.
block = $4

*Stk dstr   (SEE NOTE):

Split 3 for 2

Split

3 for 2

YEAR	1982	1983	1984	1985	1986	1987	1988	1989	1990	1991	1992	1993	1994	1995	1996	1997	1998	1999	2000	2001
EARN	3.17	1.51	2.54	.97	1.10	3.52	4.31	1.63	2.17	.05	3.06	2.02	2.45	3.67	3.82	.01	4.24			
DIV	1.56	1.58	1.58	1.09	1.74	1.68	1.85	2.00	2.00	2.00	2.00	2.00	1.70	1.60	1.60	1.72	1.76			

remaining non-core activity, Commercial Imaging (office copiers), was a drag on earnings and a buyer was still being sought. And Fuji Film, already predominant in Japan, loomed as aggressive competition in the U.S. film market.

In mid-1999, Commercial Imaging has finally been sold, eliminating a distraction and a cost drain; but it was not sold at a profit. Fuji has become a major U.S. competitor, eroding market share with its aggressive price-cutting in economy film lines and forcing Kodak to spend more to develop and market high-end film products. Digital Imaging continues to grow, but also to run losses, although progress is being made.

The company has just completed two encouraging quarters, but has also announced yet another round of massive cost-cutting that will cause a $300 million charge in the third quarter. It seems to be positioned now for real progress as a photography company, and it is selling at a bargain-basement price. But Wall Street is yelling "show me," with its heels dug in cement.

EXXON/MOBIL CORPORATION (XOM)

Before it was renamed Exxon, and even longer before Mobil was added, this company was called Esso, the initials for Standard Oil. Esso was Standard Oil of New Jersey, called Jersey Standard, the original company of the Rockefeller family oil empire and the one the U.S. Supreme Court busted up in 1911 to create 34 separate companies (including what is now Chevron).

But Standard Oil of New Jersey remained a big, national company—so big, in fact, that the Supreme Court delivered another jolt in 1969 by ruling that the company couldn't use the trade name Esso in states where other Standard Oil companies operated.

Standard Oil of New Jersey spent an estimated $100 million in 1969 dollars on advertising and managed almost overnight to burn the name Exxon into the national consciousness. Remember the "tiger in your tank" ads?

If there was anybody 20 years later who didn't know the name, that changed overnight when the tanker *Exxon Valdez* ran aground in Alaska's Prince William Sound in January 1989.

Horrible as that disaster was, it is a remarkable comment on the resilience of Exxon that although its stock dropped 7 percent on the news, it quickly rebounded.

With $106.4 billion in 1998 sales, Exxon ranked as the nation's largest oil company. It is a totally integrated producer of oil and natural gas, with activities ranging from exploration to transportation and marketing. It is a major producer of coal and manufacturer and marketer of petrochemicals.

Since 1882 Exxon has paid generous portions of its immense profits in dividends, with annual increases year in and year out.

On December 1, 1998, in keeping with an oil-industry consolidation trend, Exxon announced it would acquire Mobil in a deal by which 1.32 shares of XON would be newly issued and traded for each share of Mobil. Subject to regulatory approval, the merger should be completed during the second half of 1999. Mobil's 1998 sales were $52.1 billion, and the combined company will be the largest publicly owned oil company in the world. In all probability, some properties may have to be shed to obtain regulatory approval.

Like Exxon, Mobil is involved in all major segments of the oil industry, including natural gas and chemicals. Mobil was also part of the Standard Oil Trust, then became Standard Oil.

According to Value Line's analysis, possibilities for cost reductions from the merger are substantial. Exxon has determined that nearly $3 billion of redundant expenses can be eliminated by the merger. Value Line estimates that will add about $0.50 a share to the earnings of the combined company in two to three years. The merger provides a good way to boost profits in this mature, and often cyclical, business.

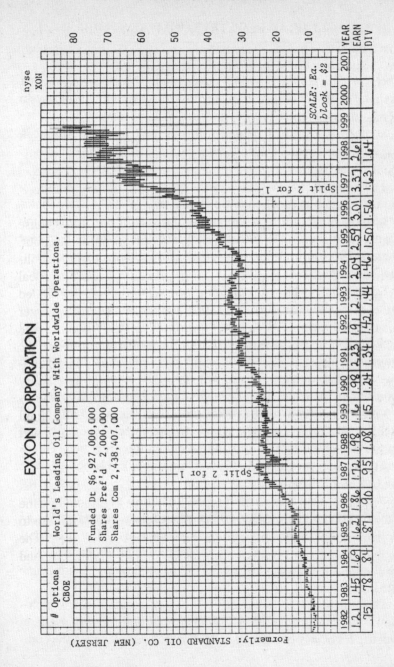

EXXON CORPORATION

World's Leading Oil Company With Worldwide Operations.

Funded Dt $6,927,000,000
Shares Pref'd 2,000,000
Shares Com 2,438,407,000

Options
CBOE

nyse
XON

SCALE: Ea.
block = $2

Split 2 for 1

Split 2 for 1

Formerly: STANDARD OIL CO. (NEW JERSEY)

YEAR	1982	1983	1984	1985	1986	1987	1988	1989	1990	1991	1992	1993	1994	1995	1996	1997	1998	1999	2000	2001
EARN	1.21	1.45	1.69	1.62	1.86	1.72	1.98	1.16	1.98	2.23	1.91	2.11	2.04	2.59	3.01	3.37	2.61			
DIV	.75	.78	.84	.87	.90	.95	1.08	1.15	1.24	1.34	1.42	1.44	1.46	1.50	1.56	1.63	1.64			

GENERAL ELECTRIC COMPANY (GE)

The April 12, 1999, *Barron's* cover read, "Meet the Next Jack Welch." (The rest of the cover copy asked why Dennis Kozlowski of a company named Tyco is such a well-kept secret.)

Some pages back, I quoted a former colleague of American Express' heir apparent, Ken Chenault. She called him "our generation's Jack Welch."

The February 15, 1999, *Barron's* cover read, "Jack's Magic." It pictured a smiling face beneath a classic case of male-pattern baldness and a hand pulling a rabbit out of a hat. In this instance the cover copy read, "For nearly 20 years, Jack Welch has kept General Electric's profits rising apace. How can his successor follow this act?"

I guess that's what you call a high-class problem, how a corporation goes about topping 20 years of rising profits.

In 1990 I wrote, "This year—this decade—according to CEO Jack Welch, the focus will be on people: using new concepts of management, such as employee involvement, to bring out the ingenuity and energies of working people. GE employs almost 300 thousand of them and the challenge of the 1990s, as Welch sees it, is a 'need for speed' in responding to today's pace of change. Said one Harvard professor, who is among two dozen academics and consultants hired by GE to help implement the program: 'This is one of the biggest planned efforts to alter people's behavior since the Cultural Revolution.'

"Coming from any other corporation, this might sound like annual report rhetoric. But GE is no ordinary company. In the 1980s, its philosophy was strength through diversity. It accomplished that by a program of divestiture and acquisition that resulted in the thirteen businesses GE has today. By design, each one is at, or very close to, the top in its global market."

The June 21, 1999, *Wall Street Journal* updated Jack Welch's views on managing people: "As chairman and CEO of General Electric for nearly two decades, Jack Welch has reshaped the com-

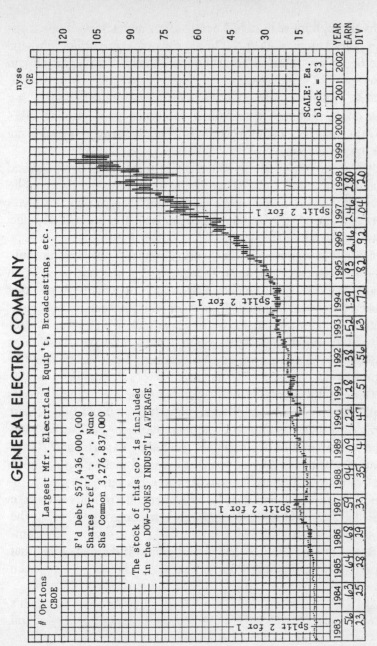

GENERAL ELECTRIC COMPANY

nyse
GE

Largest Mfr. Electrical Equip't, Broadcasting, etc.

Options
CBOE

F'd Debt $57,436,000,C00
Shares Pref'd . . . None
Shs Common 3,276,837,000

The stock of this co. is included
in the DOW-JONES INDUST'L AVERAGE.

SCALE: Ea.
block = $3

Split 2 for 1

	1983	1984	1985	1986	1987	1988	1989	1990	1991	1992	1993	1994	1995	1996	1997	1998	1999	2000	2001	2002	YEAR
	.56	.63	.64	.68	.59	.94	1.09	1.22	1.28	1.38	1.52	1.39	1.93	2.16	2.46	2.80					EARN
	.23	.25	.28	.29	.33	.35	.41	.47	.51	.56	.63	.72	.82	.92	1.04	1.20					DIV

pany through more than 600 acquisitions and achieved one earnings record after another. Yet he says his most important job—the one he devotes more time to than any other—is motivating and assessing GE's employees.

"Mr. Welch recently sat down in his New York office for a long talk about motivation, including his practice of grading GE's 85,000 managers and professionals annually on a curve and firing the lowest scorers.

" 'You have to go along with a can of fertilizer in one hand and water in the other and constantly throw both on the flowers,' he says. 'If they grow you have a beautiful garden. If they don't you cut them out. That's what management is all about.'" Clearly, he's not running a welfare agency.

GE is a conglomerate that works, which is probably an oxymoron. What it really says, though, is that the businesses that make it up are of secondary importance to whatever it is that makes them work together. That's why GE, more than most companies, is its prime mover, in this case Jack Welch. The story is never GE. It's always Jack Welch. That's why the question of GE's future is a question of who succeeds Jack Welch when he retires in two years.

General Electric vies with Microsoft for the highest market capitalization of any public company. It is engaged in a diverse array of service, technology, and manufacturing industries. More than 30 percent of GE's revenues (including exports) and 20 percent of profits are derived overseas, and globalization is one of the company's guiding themes. Key to GE's business plan is the requirement that businesses be first or second in market share in their industries. Businesses that aren't are divested.

Segment contributions and operating profit margins in 1998, as reported by Standard & Poor's, were:

	Revenues	Profit Margins
GE Capital	48%	7.8%
Industrial products and systems	11%	17%
Aircraft engines	10%	17%
Power systems	8.3%	15%
Plastics	6.5%	24%
Appliances	5.5%	13%
NBC	5.2%	26%
Technical products/services	5.2%	21%

Operations are divided into two groups: Product, Service and Media comprises 11 businesses, and GE Capital Services operates 28 financial businesses.

The company has been raising its dividend year after year, although its yield of 1.2 would classify it as a growth stock. It has been one of the stocks leading the bull market (it's had 40 percent–plus returns for the past three years), and at a current price (August 1999) of 116⁹⁄₁₆ and a PE of 39 it is overvalued, even for a company expected to see 14 percent earnings growth.

Welch's vision for GE's future, he told *Barron's,* is that of "an increasingly postindustrial company in which intellectual capital and information will continue to replace brawn and hard assets. Products and services must be continuously revamped, and costs must be relentlessly driven further downward."

Welch is coy on the subject of his successor, saying only that he or she must be strong in the "four Es"—energy, ability to excite, edge, and execution.

Says *Barron's,* "Under Welch, the company has been known for nurturing talented executives in a rigorous meritocracy where performance is lavishly rewarded and failure mercilessly punished. Still, Welch's size 10 shoes will be difficult to fill, no matter how adept his successor."

GENERAL MOTORS CORPORATION (GM)

In September 1998 General Motors, trading at an incredible eight times earnings, looked poised for take-off. It sort of did take off, rising 40 percent to around $90 and a PE of 20 by January 1999. It had recently ended the latest in a series of crippling strikes with significant productivity gains and improved relations with the United Auto Workers. And investors were anticipating the spin-off of GM's remaining interest in Delphi Automotive Systems, Inc., its parts-making subsidiary, confident it would call attention to the fact that Wall Street was giving no value at all to GM's vehicle manufacturing operations.

Delphi became a fait accompli in late May 1999. GM's second-quarter results broke records. Its midyear balance sheet looked like Fort Knox. Blue chip value stocks were back in vogue. The Dow skyrocketed. GM, as this is written, sells at eight times earnings.

Wall Street calls this kind of thing a "hope stock." The value's there but the market won't recognize it. How did this happen? What's it going to take?

General Motors is the world's largest manufacturer of cars and trucks. Its 1998 sales of $155.9 were approximately 2 percent of the United States gross domestic product. But size hasn't always equaled smarts.

For most of the 1980s, GM was run by Roger Smith, who presided over an unprecedented 10 percent plunge in North American market share to under 30 percent last year. Smith's seeming obliviousness to public sensibilities was even the subject of a satirical movie called *Roger and Me*.

Not everybody blames Roger Smith for GM's lackluster performance in the 1980s, however. GM's preeminence 15 years earlier was achieved via a weak Ford, an unhealthy Chrysler, and an absence of serious competition from Japanese producers.

Before that, it was taken for granted. Remember "Engine Charlie" Wilson, who went on to be President Eisenhower's secretary of defense after he retired from GM in 1953? It was Wilson who made the famous remark, "What's good for General Motors is good for the country."

But a strong Ford, a strong Chrysler (now Daimler-Chrysler), and vigorous competition from Europe and the Far East were there to greet current CEO John F. (Jack) Smith when he took over the reins of a struggling GM in 1992, and *Time* magazine's cover ominously read, "Can GM Survive?"

GM was selling at around 30 back then, and its once dominant North American operations were bleeding red ink. But Smith hit the ground running. He meat-axed payrolls, passed health care costs on to staff, closed excess plants, modernized facilities, began outsourcing parts and supplies, and cut unprofitable sales to fleet owners. These savings went straight to the bottom line, generating profit improvements of about $1 billion a quarter for eight straight quarters. GM's dramatic turnaround sent its stock price soaring to a peak of just over $65 in 1994.

But the celebration was premature. Although 1994 would be the first year since 1988 when North American operations showed a full-year profit, the year, which was not a strong one for interest rate–sensitive auto stocks, saw GM plunge to 21 percent. GM had overcome old quality and styling bugaboos, but had trouble meeting demand because of production delays affecting new models. Investors, who had inflated expectations, became disillusioned. When GM announced that North American Operations showed a $328 million loss in the third quarter, the stock skidded to below $40. Rumors began circulating that the turnaround was stalling out.

But it wasn't. By the end of 1995, with GM around 50 and paying an increased $1.10 annual dividend, some investors began seeing progress. J.P. Morgan gave GM a strong buy, saying, "It's a restructuring story: management continues to cut costs and improve margins, even in a weak vehicle market; a de-leveraging story: over the past three years, it has added more than $22 billion to its pension fund and by next year it will have eliminated most of its preferred stock, cutting preferred dividends by 70 percent;

finally, it's a cash-flow story: we expect the company's free cash flow to total almost $28 billion, suggesting significant dividend increases and share repurchases."

The next year began and ended with costly countrywide strikes, but GM got a three-year UAW pact that goes a long way toward permitting efficiencies that should give it cost-per-car equality with Ford, Daimler-Chrysler, and Japanese competition by the early 2000s.

Earnings and cash flows, adjusted for the strikes, continued to make progress. GM split off EDS Corp. for $500 million and signaled it would do something with GM-Hughes in 1997. GM ended the year in the mid-50 range after reporting, as expected, lower fourth-quarter earnings. But cash flow rose to an astounding $17 billion from $10 billion the year before, permitting the third 10 cent quarterly dividend increase since May 1995 (to $2 annually) and the first-ever plan to increase earnings per share by buying back $2.6 billion of stock.

In January 1997 GM announced a series of actions intended to unlock shareholder value in the Hughes business segments. In December Hughes's defense operations were spun off to shareholders and merged into Raytheon Co. in a $9.8 billion transaction. GM Class H common stock was recapitalized into a new class of GM common stock that will track Hughes's telecommunications and space business (Hughes Telecom). GM also transferred Hughes's automotive electronics subsidiary, Delco Electronics, to the Delphi Automotive Systems unit.

A work stoppage in mid-1998 at two Flint, Michigan plants effectively shut down North American plants dependent on their parts, and cost the company $2 billion in lost profits. The UAW national contract is up for renewal in 1999, and a strike is not expected.

In February 1999 GM completed the initial public offering of 17.7 percent of Delphi Automotive systems. The remaining shares were distributed to GM shareholders in May.

GM announced second-quarter 1999 earnings July 20. Excluding Delphi, the profit of $2.66 compared with 40 cents in the strike-impacted prior year quarter, beating analysts' expectations of $2.56. GM fell 1.8125 on the news to $66.50.

Profits were stronger in North America and Europe but turned to losses in Latin America and worse losses in Asia. "Consolidated results show the strength of our globally integrated company," said CEO Smith. U.S. market share was off 2.1 percent to 29.5 percent, but is expected to continue improving. Company cash reserves stood at $16.7 billion, up from $11 billion at midyear 1998. GM has spent some $7.3 billion repurchasing 15.2 percent of its stock since January 1997 and bought back $520 million in the quarter. Costs were trimmed to the tune of $1.8 billion.

Profit margins worldwide were 4.2 percent, short of the company's own goal of 5 percent. Margins hit 5.1 percent in North America, exceeding the goal for the third consecutive quarter. (Ford's North American margins were 7.7 percent.)

On balance, then, GM's news is of solid progress. Why won't Wall Street recognize it?

Analysts think the Street needs a little more "show me." Analyst Rod Lache of Deutsche Bank said, "The Street's not giving GM any credit for 2000 earnings. As it becomes increasingly clear that North American demand is going to remain strong, you're going to start to see the Street give GM credit for that." Mr. Lache has a target price of $93 a share over the next six to nine months.

Other GM watchers focus on the company's breakup value. Oscar Schafer told the *Barron's* Midyear Roundtable '99, "GM's current management, unlike prior generations, is focused on shareholder value and return on invested capital. If you take GM's share of the market value of publicly-owned companies in which it owns stakes, give a multiple to GMAC that's comparable to other asset-backed lenders, and net out the cash on GM's balance sheet, you get the car company for absolutely zero. If you then assign a multiple of 9 times to the $5.50 a share of auto earnings, you get $49.50. Add that to other saleable assets and cash, and you

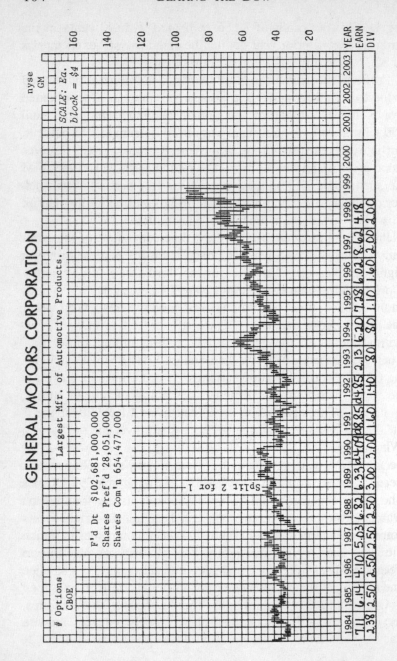

GENERAL MOTORS CORPORATION

Largest Mfr. of Automotive Products.

nyse
GM

SCALE: Ea.
block = $4

F'd Dt $102,681,000,000
Shares Pref'd 28,051,000
Shares Com'n 654,477,000

Options
CBOE

Split 2 for 1

YEAR	1984	1985	1986	1987	1988	1989	1990	1991	1992	1993	1994	1995	1996	1997	1998	1999	2000	2001	2002	2003
EARN	7.11	6.14	4.10	5.03	6.82	6.33	d4.09	d8.85	d4.85	2.13	6.20	7.28	6.02	8.62	4.18					
DIV	2.38	2.50	2.50	2.50	2.50	3.00	3.00	1.60	1.40	.80	.80	1.10	1.60	2.00	2.00					

get $1155 when GM is trading at 64. I'm really talking about spinning off some assets and realizing the value that's locked up in the company."

A Merrill Lynch Research Bulletin dated July 12, 1999, states, "We are maintaining our accumulate rating on GM because, although the company's fundamentals remain under pressure, it is increasingly a break-up play. Hughes (GMH) now accounts for 40 percent of the value of GM common and we think it will be separated from GM next year." GM is on record as opposing any divestiture of Hughes, believing vehicles that use its technology for directional aids, in-car faxes, and the like will have an edge.

A *Barron's* article, "How to Fix GM," quotes Kevin Risen of Neuberger & Berman as saying, "There's clearly an incredible amount of value that GM management can create if they pull the right levers."

My opinion is that if the market hasn't recognized GM's value in the six to twelve months it needs to prove its recovery is real, the pressures on GM's management to pull some of those levers will be irresistible.

HEWLETT-PACKARD CO. (HWP)

When AT&T spun off Lucent Technologies in 1996, one of the people integral to its spectacular success was the executive who headed Lucent's global-services division, Carla "Carly" Fiorina. She sensed that investing in a telephone equipment manufacturer was inherently about as exciting as watching paint dry, but that something evoking cutting-edge twenty-first century telecommunications might be received differently. The name Lucent Technologies, if not her brainchild, was inspired by her insight; and the rest, as they say, is history.

On July 19, 1999, Carly Fiorina became the first outsider in history to be named president and CEO of the venerable Hewlett-Packard, and the first woman ever to head one of the nation's 20 largest publicly held companies. HWP makes a good and reliable computer printer, but the name is hardly synonymous with state-of-the-art Silicon Valley innovation. So there's an image problem to be addressed.

There were also a number of H-P executives, all of them valuable, who had their hearts set on Ms. Fiorina's job. She is known to have a gift for making harmony out of dissonance, asserting herself in a warm way, and one of her challenges will be making peace with Hewlett's top executives. She will succeed Lewis Platt when he retires December 31 and Hewlett-Packard splits into two separately traded companies. Back to that in a minute.

Not that Hewlett-Packard is doing badly. Next to Alcoa, HWP has the highest year-to-date total return in the Dow, 54.7 percent, and soon after Fiorina's appointment was announced, it hit an all-time high of 118⅞₆. But back in March, things looked different. As *The Wall Street Journal* put it in announcing Fiorina's appointment, "Back then, H-P seemed to be stuck in a rut, outmarketed by fleet-footed rivals such as Sun Microsystems and IBM. Although it continued to increase earnings, H-P's revenue growth sagged thanks to the Asian economic crisis, sluggish server sales, and a new competitive challenge from low-cost inkjet printers."

Already, though, H-P appears to be bouncing back. Again to quote the *Journal,* "Its new 'e-services' campaign, designed to highlight the way H-P technology supports the growth of electronic services over the Internet, has given H-P a focused message that appears to be winning over some customers. A new line of midrange servers is selling well, its PC division is profitable, and the company is expected to report a big jump in revenue for the fiscal third quarter, which ends July 31."

In March, H-P announced plans to spin off its test and measurement, chemical analysis, components, and medical operations into a separate company. These units had 1998 sales of $7.6 billion, 16 percent of the total. The remaining operations, which contributed 84 percent of revenues, will comprise the computer and printing units. The move is already bringing a better focus to the

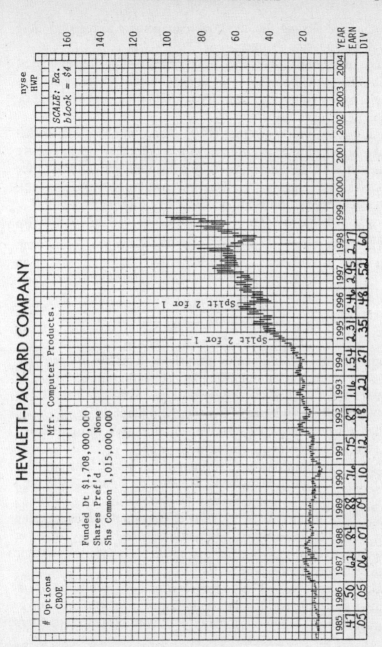

HEWLETT-PACKARD COMPANY

Mfr. Computer Products.

Funded Dt $1,708,000,000
Shares Pref'd . . . None
Shs Common 1,015,000,000

Options
CBOE

nyse
HWP

SCALE: Ea.
block = $4

Split 2 for 1

Split 2 for 1

YEAR	1985	1986	1987	1988	1989	1990	1991	1992	1993	1994	1995	1996	1997	1998	1999	2000	2001	2002	2003	2004
EARN	41	50	62	84	88	76	75	87	1.16	1.54	2.31	2.46	2.95	2.77						
DIV	05	05	06	07	09	10	12	18	23	27	35	48	52	60						

two businesses, and should allow management to respond more rapidly to industry changes.

The measurement business, to be called Agilent Technologies, will make a public offering of approximately 15 percent of its shares by the end of this year. By mid-2000 the rest of it will be spun off to Hewlett shareholders.

Argus Research notes that HWP "trades at about the market multiple, which may seem cheap for a computer stock. But we note that H-P's Internet business is not significant yet, giving the stock less of a valuation than its peers." Argus believes H-P's computer networking arm combined with Ms. Fiorina's communications knowledge will bring an excellent fit to H-P's e-services strategies.

HOME DEPOT, INC

Home Depot's 1998 Annual Report shows a person in a red flannel shirt pondering an unfinished kitchen and asking, "Where do I start? What do I need? Where do I go? Who can help?" The answer to all four questions, it's clearly implicit, is Home Depot, which *Fortune* magazine has named America's Most Admired Specialty Retailer for six consecutive years.

Inside, Bernard Marcus, chairman of the board, tells how this $30 billion corporation opened 137 new stores during 1998 for a total of 761, and how it improved the performance of its existing stores: "We did this by listening to our customers' needs, offering new products and services, and utilizing technology or other resources to allow our associates to spend more face-to-face time with customers in the store aisles."

Home Depot was added to the Dow in 1999, replacing Sears. Sears was having an identity crisis ("Am I a department store or a general merchandiser?") while HD was clearly a discount

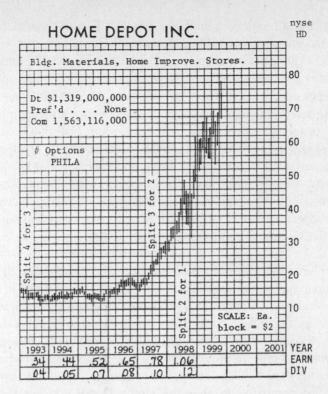

HOME DEPOT INC.

nyse
HD

Bldg. Materials, Home Improve. Stores.

Dt $1,319,000,000
Pref'd . . . None
Com 1,563,116,000

Options
PHILA

Split 4 for 3

Split 3 for 2

Split 2 for 1

SCALE: Ea.
block = $2

	1993	1994	1995	1996	1997	1998	1999	2000	2001	YEAR
	34	44	.52	.65	.78	1.06				EARN
	04	.05	.07	08	.10	.12				DIV

retailer—one with ties to the economically vital home construction sector.

Standard & Poor's Stock Report, not usually given to editorial embellishment, describes Home Depot as "a do-it-yourselfer's paradise." That the stock quadrupled in the three years prior to fiscal year end January 31, 1999, is pretty good evidence that Bernie Marcus' explanation of his company's success is more than empty words. Home Depot actually trains its employees (called "associates") to be knowledgeable about the products in the stores and many of them also have trade skills or direct experience in using the products.

Home Depot was founded in 1978, went public in 1981, and is the world's largest home improvement retailer, ranking among the

10 largest retailers in the United States. The 761 stores operating at the end of fiscal 1998 included 707 Home Depot stores and 8 EXPO Design Center stores in the United States; 43 Home Depot stores in Canada; 2 Home Depot stores in Chile; and one Home Depot store in Puerto Rico. Subsidiaries include Maintenance Warehouse, a direct mail distributor of maintenance and repair products to property maintenance managers, and National Blinds and Wallpaper, Inc., a telephone mail order service for wallpaper and custom window treatments. The company has 157,000 associates.

In virtually every financial respect, Home Depot has shown consistently dramatic progress. Revenues have been increasing at an annual rate of 25 percent for the past five years and net income at a 29% rate. Earnings per share are expected to grow 23 percent to 25 percent annually in the foreseeable future.

Home Depot's store base has been increasing at a 20 percent annual rate and is projected to grow at a 22 percent rate in the next several years. Sixteen hundred stores are expected to be in operation by the end of 2002. The company currently has a dominant 14 percent share of a highly fragmented $140 billion do-it-yourself home improvement market. The competitive environment is expected to ease as small regional players thin out.

The company believes the Home Depot concept is ripe for global expansion and it also has comprehensive plans to exploit the Internet's marketing possibilities. With its outstanding record of growth, HD deserves to trade at a premium to the market and it does. But if you've ever had to beg a plumber or other repairman to come to your house—and who hasn't—you have some feeling for the potential size of the do-it-yourself market. It's hard to think of a better DIY play than Home Depot.

INTEL CORPORATION

Before the first microprocessor was introduced by Intel Corporation in 1971, the word wasn't even in Webster's Dictionary.

Microprocessors, or "chips" as they are popularly called, and other products that enhance the capabilities of personal computers, are now a $25 billion industry and Intel, based in Santa Clara, California, has 80 percent of the market.

Intel was one of the "new economy" stocks added to the Dow on November 1, 1999. Intel and Microsoft, which are traded on the NASDAQ, were the first non–New York Stock Exchange-listed companies to be admitted to the Dow.

A microprocessor is the central processing unit (CPU) of a computer, analogous to the brain in an organism. Computer power depends on the number of transistors that can be fit on a microprocessor. Intel has dominated the personal computer market for nearly thirty years by following a tenet known as Moore's Law, named for Gordon Moore, a young engineer who later became Intel's CEO. Moore's law postulated that technological advances would allow the number of transistors on a chip to double every 18 to 24 months. Intel catalyzed the explosive computer revolution by introducing a steady stream of microprocessors—8086, 286, 386, 486 and the Pentiums I, II and III—each faster than the one before, each setting a new standard of performance and selling at a premium price.

In the process, Intel grew from a small startup company building semiconductor memory products to a technology giant with 1998 sales of over $26 billion, net profits of over $6 billion, and nearly 65,000 employees. Forty-five percent of Intel's sales are to customers in North and South America, 28 percent are in Europe, 20 percent in the Asia-Pacific region and 7 percent in Japan.

Today, Intel supplies the computing industry with the chips, boards, systems and software that are the "ingredients" of computer architecture. These products are used by industry members to create advanced computing systems. Intel's mission, according to company literature, is to be the preeminent building block supplier to the connected computing industry worldwide.

Intel's business, however, faces dramatic changes on the eve of the year 2000. What has happened is that personal computers are already sophisticated enough to provide the functions important to

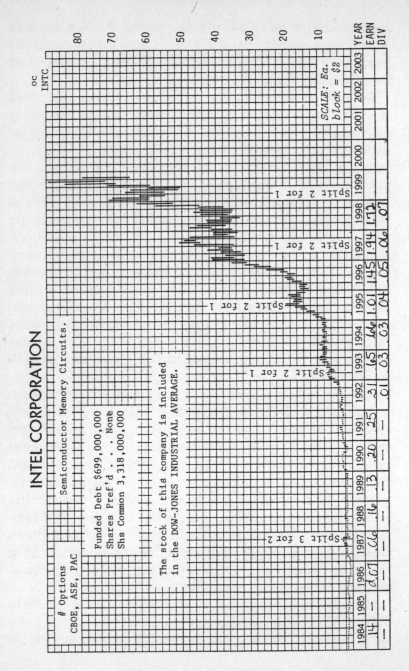

INTEL CORPORATION

OC
INTC

Options
CBOE, ASE, PAC

Semiconductor Memory Circuits.

Funded Debt $699,000,000
Shares Pref'd . . . None
Shs Common 3,318,000,000

The stock of this company is included
in the DOW-JONES INDUSTRIAL AVERAGE.

SCALE: Ea.
block = $2

Split 2 for 1
Split 2 for 1
Split 2 for 1
Split 2 for 1
Split 3 for 2

YEAR	1984	1985	1986	1987	1988	1989	1990	1991	1992	1993	1994	1995	1996	1997	1998	1999	2000	2001	2002	2003
EARN	.14	—	.07	.66	.16	.13	.20	.25	.31	.65	.66	1.01	1.45	1.94	1.72					
DIV	—	—	—	—	—	—	—	—	.01	.03	.03	.04	.05	.06	.07					

most consumers. Home and business applications such as word processing, e-mail and financial management already run as fast as people can think and write, and so consumers are looking not for more power but for lower computer prices.

According to a recent *Barron's* article, the sudden popularity of PCs selling for less than $1000 is cannibalizing the longstanding sales growth of high-end PCs using the state-of-the-art microprocessors made by Intel. From less than 30 percent in 1997, sub-$1000 PCs account for more than 60 percent of units sold in 1999. This threatens Intel's ability to maintain its historic annual earnings growth rate of nearly 30 percent. Thus Intel's 2000 earnings are expected to rise by less than 20 percent.

Intel, which is rated one of America's best-managed companies, recognizes the problem, but sees the solution in the Internet. Intel wants to become a supplier of chips to servers and networking devices, the high-end computers that power the Internet. The server market alone is growing at around 35 percent a year, compared to just 15 percent for PCs.

But as the *Barron's* article points out, "Powerhouses in the server business, like IBM and Sun Microsystems, are not likely to willingly cede market share to Intel. And heavyweight networking chipmakers like Motorola and Texas Instruments aren't likely to roll over and play dead either."

Another problem is that continued explosive Internet growth depends on the timely rollout of broadband access to American homes. If companies like AT&T and SBC Communications, which aim to provide the broadband access, are slow to deliver, demand for Intel-powered servers and networking devices may not prove strong enough to make up for the slowdown in the company's revenue growth from the PC market.

Intel's stock, adjusted for five splits, has risen from under $2 in 1985 to over $80 as this is written. That's a 6300 percent gain, versus an 800 percent gain for the Standard & Poor's 500 Stock Index. Investors are expecting INTC to gain another 25 percent to $100 by the end of 2000.

INTERNATIONAL BUSINESS MACHINES
CORPORATION (IBM)

If you're long enough in the tooth, you'll no doubt remember IBM's original (early 1920s) corporate slogan, THINK, which became ubiquitous almost overnight and was used for several decades. Today you see THINK signs everywhere, either hanging upside down or with the last two letters squished together in a horrendous failure of forethought. And just about everybody's forgotten where it all began.

"Big Blue," as stock traders call IBM (after the color of its corporate logo), led America into the computer age and for many years *was* the computer industry.

But, as somebody said, when other computer companies started being called "the next IBM," it was a clear sign Big Blue was in for a bumpy ride. And bumpy it has been.

It's interesting, the kind of problems a company has when an industry comes of age in a relatively few years. For instance, one of the biggest problems IBM's top management was having in the late 1980s was mediating internal squabbling among managers—those whose careers were made on traditional proprietary products and those who see the future in "open systems."

The latter refers to a free-for-all competitive environment characterized by inexpensive open-system workstations that run on industry-standard software, and that is where IBM is putting its money in the 1990s.

Because computers are now such a part of everybody's life, it's hard to believe that before the mid-fifties they were virtually nonexistent. But that all changed when Thomas Watson founded IBM and IBM developed the first computer, right?

Wrong.

The company that became IBM started when Charles Randall Flint combined a group of small businesses making grocery scales, slicers, time clocks and tabulating machines into a company called Computing-Tabulating-Recording Company. He

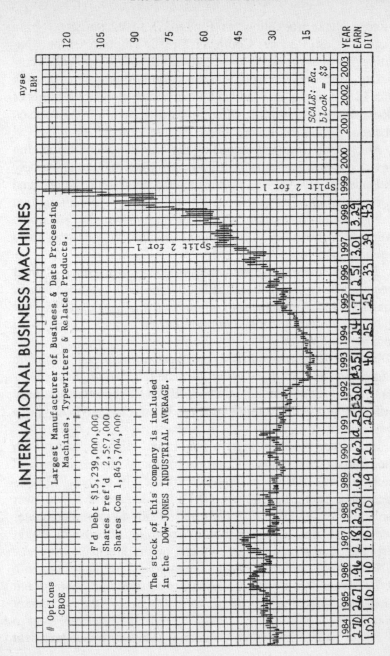

INTERNATIONAL BUSINESS MACHINES

nyse
IBM

Largest Manufacturer of Business & Data Processing
Machines, Typewriters & Related Products.

F'd Debt $15,239,000,000
Shares Pref'd 2,5?7,000
Shares Com 1,845,704,000

The stock of this company is included
in the DOW-JONES INDUSTRIAL AVERAGE.

Options
CBOE

SCALE: Ea.
block = $3

Split 2 for 1

Split 2 for 1

	1984	1985	1986	1987	1988	1989	1990	1991	1992	1993	1994	1995	1996	1997	1998	1999	2000	2001	2002	2003	YEAR
	2.70	2.67	1.96	2.18	2.32	1.62	2.63	2.25	2.30	d3.51	1.24	1.77	2.51	3.01	3.29						EARN
	1.03	1.10	1.10	1.10	1.10	1.19	1.21	1.21	1.21	.40	.25	.25	.33	.39	.43						DIV

hired a young marketing whiz named Tom Watson away from National Cash Register Company. Watson emphasized the tabulating part of the business and, by stressing what is now called corporate culture, which included the slogan THINK, built a superbly managed business that fed off the insatiable accounting needs of Social Security and other New Deal programs. In 1924, Watson changed the name to International Business Machines.

Meanwhile, research was being done on electronic computing devices at such places as Bell Labs, Harvard, and the University of Pennsylvania. At Penn, two eggheads named John Mauchly and J. Presper Eckert assembled a Rube Goldberg-type contraption using electronic vacuum tubes that they called the Electronic Numerical Integrator and Computer, which was demonstrated publicly in 1946.

The two men recognized the commercial potential of their invention and, to keep the patent, quit Penn and started a company to market their computers, which they now named UNIVAC. But they weren't businessmen and they lacked capital, so they went looking for a buyer.

They first approached IBM, but Watson turned thumbs down. Computing devices using electronics, he felt, had no future. They had better luck at Remington-Rand, IBM's chief competitor in the office supply field. Remington-Rand bought the UNIVAC business in 1950.

Remington-Rand could have used UNIVAC to walk away with the computer revolution. Almost immediately they struck a deal with CBS to use UNIVAC to predict the results of the 1952 presidential election. By 9:00 P.M. UNIVAC forecast the Eisenhower landslide. Although CBS wasn't quite ready to trust a computer and waited for confirming ballot counts, millions heard Walter Cronkite tout this electronic miracle, helping to make the name UNIVAC as synonymous with computers as Frigidaire was with refrigerators. But Remington-Rand, which became Sperry-Rand in 1955, hesitated to expend the capital to exploit the full market potential of UNIVAC.

In the meantime, Thomas Watson was succeeded as president

of IBM by his son, Thomas Watson, Jr. Young Tom Watson clearly saw that the future belonged to computers, and in 1952 introduced the 701, the first of several generations of IBM computers that would dominate the marketplace for two decades.

In the 1960s, IBM undertook the most massive privately financed corporate project in history with its $5 billion development of the IBM 360 series of computers. Designed for any kind of commercial data processing need, these huge "mainframes," which cost $1 million or more, were aimed at large organizations such as corporations and government agencies.

Soon after its April 1964 debut in 62 U.S. cities and 14 foreign countries, the 360 had so established IBM's market dominance that analysts referred to the industry as "IBM and the Seven Dwarfs," the dwarfs being Sperry-Rand, Control Data, Honeywell, RCA, NCR, General Electric and Burroughs.

Unfortunately for IBM, its dominance and power to set industry standards and compete for new business (there was a saying that IBM may not be the best, but nobody ever got fired for buying it) was not lost on the Department of Justice. An antitrust suit, filed in 1968, haunted IBM until it was dropped in January 1982.

The 1970s were a rocky period for IBM. Independent firms began undermining IBM's mainframe leasing business by offering lower rental rates, while others started selling IBM-compatible peripheral equipment ("clones") at prices cheaper than IBM's.

IBM's efforts to counter this competition resulted in a series of small but nettlesome lawsuits. The Seven Dwarfs, now down to five and renamed the BUNCH (Burroughs, Univac, NCR, Control Data and Honeywell), continued to nibble away at IBM's market share.

But the biggest development was the blossoming of the minicomputer industry, featuring smaller, more flexible systems that companies could adapt more easily to their particular needs. Digital Equipment had been first with an inexpensive $120,000 system. They grew like crazy, and were joined by Data General, Hewlett-Packard and others.

IBM had missed the boat on minicomputers and saw its overall market share drop from 60 percent to 40 percent by the end of 1979.

The 1980s were the era of the home microcomputer for data processing and entertainment. Steve Jobs started in the early 1970s "phonephreaking" (making little electronic boxes that beat the phone company out of the cost of calls) with his pal Steve Wozniak. He worked for Atari, then he rejoined Wozniak in a now-famous garage. Jobs had already built Apple Computer into an organization with sales of $117 million when IBM introduced the PC (for personal computer) in 1981.

Determined not to miss out in microcomputers as it had in minicomputers in the 1970s, IBM took advantage of Apple's early growing pains and by 1983 was the dominant producer of microcomputers in a crowded field that included Commodore, Texas Instruments, Tandy, Osborne, Atari, Coleco and others, most of which have since fallen by the wayside.

By the middle 1980s, Apple had successfully launched its Macintosh, and many IBM "clones" were on the market, but despite heightened competition and price wars, IBM continued to dominate, albeit with reduced market share.

On the commercial mainframe front, IBM introduced a medium-scale entry called the 4300 at the outset of the decade that met heavy demand early on but got bogged down in production delays and other problems. These affected earnings, sent the stock price south, and opened the way for increased competition from makers of compatible equipment. The company also brought out new generations of high-end mainframes with mixed success.

The mid-1980s was a time of slackened growth in the computer industry generally. IBM, having the most to lose in terms of market share, was the biggest loser.

Referring to the company's stubborn adherence to a strategy emphasizing proprietary products, especially its giant mainframe computers, one IBM insider was quoted as saying, "We took our eye off the ball."

In early 1990 CEO John Akers announced a line of open-system workstations known as AIX and a policy of encouraging links between these smaller computers and IBM's big models.

In the fall of 1991, as it neared the end of its first year of declining sales since 1946, IBM, which in February traded at $144, was selling at under $100 and yielding over 5 percent. It seemed strange to view IBM, a name synonymous with technology and growth, as a yield stock.

But with technology investment writedowns behind it and a historical shakeup under way in its organizational structure, IBM was ready to focus again on growth. In a rare display of executive ventilation, CEO Akers addressed IBM employees with the widely quoted words: "The fact we are losing market share makes me goddam mad. . . . everyone is too comfortable at a time when the business is in crisis."

IBM ended 1990 with sales of $69 billion. Said a *Business Week* article marking the start of a difficult decade: "Big Blue is so big that if at first it doesn't succeed, it can try, try again."

Those were prophetic words. IBM began a downward spiral that by the fall of 1993 would see Big Blue selling at 10, adjusted for two subsequent splits. The market's consensus: IBM was a dinosaur doomed for extinction. (I said buy it big! Forgive me, but I just had to get that in.)

To take a subtotal, IBM was in deep trouble because 1) it was overdependent on mainframes, a high-margin area for IBM, but the smart money was on desktop computing; 2) it was committed to proprietary hardware in a market that wanted open systems compatible with other manufacturers' products; 3) it was emphasizing hardware in an industry where software and services had become the name of the game; and 4) it couldn't get new product to market as quickly as smaller competitors.

Lou Gerstner, the comeback veteran of American Express and RJR Nabisco, came on board in 1993, bringing with him Lawrence Riccardi, his close aide and corporate counsel, and the guy who in November 1998 negotiated the $14 billion deal with AT&T involving the sale for $4 billion of the IBM Global Network data-communications pipeline.

Gerstner, who would succeed CEO John Akers when he retired in 1994, saw 40,000 people slashed from the payroll in 1992, part of a program aimed at reducing SG&A costs by $1.5 billion that year. He would help implement a restructuring begun by Akers that had a goal no less ambitious than turning inside out the buttoned-down corporate culture for which IBM has become famous.

In an effort to push centralized power downward, IBM restructured as 13 autonomous divisions consisting of nine "LOBs" (manufacturing and development Lines of Business) and four geographically organized "M&S" companies, Marketing and Services units that would sell LOB's products directly. A highly publicized alliance with competitor Apple Computer providing for collaboration on the next generation of chips for workstations became symbolic of efforts to share risks, gain expertise, and increase sales through partnerships with competitors here and abroad.

In June 1999 *Business Week* noted that "the one-two punch of Gerstner and Riccardi is paying off handsomely for IBM. The $82 billion computer giant's revenue growth, stuck in the low single-digit range for most of Gerstner's six-year tenure, has begun to edge up, hitting 15% for the first quarter. IBM stock, meanwhile, is up 23% from 91 since the beginning of the year (having split May 27 for the second time in two years)."

What can I tell you about dinosaurs? Look at the accompanying stock chart.

INTERNATIONAL PAPER COMPANY (IP)

There's a very good chance International Paper made the page you're reading, and that the tree was cut from one of 7.5 million acres of southern real estate the company owns. That's about half the area of the state of West Virginia. International Paper has the distinction of being America's largest private landowner.

International Paper Company, which celebrated its centennial in 1998, is one of the world's largest producers of packaging, printing and writing papers, as well as corrugated boxes, photographic papers and films, lumber and wood products. Through more than 290 outlets, it distributes paper and building materials mainly manufactured by others. Through subsidiaries, it makes products like turpentine and resin as well as other chemicals used in flavoring, fragrance, and aroma applications. It is also involved in oil and gas exploration and drilling through royalty arrangements with oil companies, and is engaged in real estate activities.

In April 1999, following a consolidation trend in an industry plagued by overcapacity, IP acquired for $7.9 billion the Union Camp Corporation, significantly enhancing its standing in the containerboard and uncoated printing paper markets and expanding its timberland holdings by 25 percent. Both companies had been aggressive costcutters and IP expects cost reductions and operations improvements from the merger to amount to another $300 million by the end of the year 2000. IP's 1998 sales were approximately $20 billion and Union Camp's approximately $5 billion. Sales to customers in some 130 nations outside the U.S. contributed 30 percent of 1998 revenues.

Paper is a cyclical business, waxing and waning with the economy generally and the construction sector specifically. But it is also a growth business, tied to growing worldwide literacy and also to economic activity. Environmental concerns currently favor paper packaging over nonbiodegradable plastics.

An industry up cycle was in progress until a strong U.S. dollar and Asian financial problems came into the spotlight in 1997. Prospects have improved since late 1998, thanks to a vigorous U.S. economy, some weakening of the dollar, industry efforts to reduce capacity, and indications that the Asia/Pacific economies are recovering.

Prior to the Union Camp acquisition in 1999, IP had completed a plan to sell $1 billion in nonstrategic assets under a July 1997 reorganization program, and another $500 million of asset sales were planned for 1999. That restructuring included a 10 percent workforce reduction in printing papers. A further restructuring

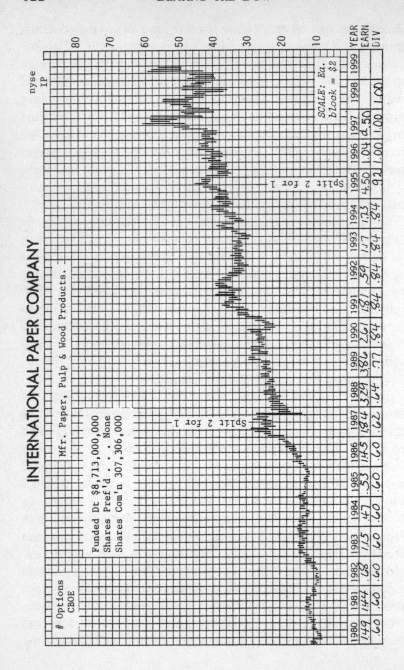

INTERNATIONAL PAPER COMPANY

Mfr. Paper, Pulp & Wood Products.

nyse
IP

Funded Dt $8,713,000,000
Shares Pref'd . . . None
Shares Com'n 307,306,000

Options
CBOE

Split 2 for 1

Split 2 for 1

SCALE: Ea.
block = $2

YEAR	1980	1981	1982	1983	1984	1985	1986	1987	1988	1989	1990	1991	1992	1993	1994	1995	1996	1997	1998	1999
EARN	1.49	1.44	.68	1.15	.47	.53	1.45	1.84	3.29	3.86	2.61	1.81	.59	1.17	1.73	4.50	1.04	d.50		
DIV	.60	.60	.60	.60	.60	.60	.60	.62	.64	.77	.84	.84	.84	.84	.84	.92	1.00	1.00	1.00	

announced in October 1998, also involving printing papers and a shutdown of certain facilities, was expected to save another $85 million annually.

IP in mid-1999 was on the verge of revisiting highs registered before Asia's troubles began in 1997, helped by all the above factors plus a market rotation into cyclical value stocks. With overhead reductions and purchasing and logistical savings from the recent merger, IP seems well positioned for the next peak cycle in paper prices expected in 2001.

JOHNSON & JOHNSON (JNJ)

Band-Aid is actually listed in Webster's Dictionary, defined as "metaphorically, emergency temporary patch applied to a basic problem." Dow watchers have seen many Band-Aids applied to corporate problems over the years, but there's probably not a soul in the Western world who hasn't reached for one to cover a razor nick and doesn't associate the name with Johnson & Johnson.

Johnson & Johnson was founded over 110 years ago by two brothers, James and Edward Mead Johnson. Most people think of it as a medical products and hospital supplies firm, but JNJ is also a major producer of pharmaceutical drugs. About 75 percent of sales in 1998 represented product lines in which the company has the number one or number two market share on a global basis.

Revenues in 1998 were $23.7 billion. Pharmaceuticals, which include over 90 different prescription drugs, contraceptives, and veterinary products, represented 36 percent of sales and 69 percent of operating profits. Professional products, which include sutures, wound closure products, surgical accessories, and orthopedic products, as well as coronary stents, angioplasty catheters, and disposable contact lenses, accounted for 36 percent and 22 percent respectively. Consumer products, which include the well-known Tylenol and Neutrogena as well as bandages and toiletries and Johnson's Baby Products, contributed 28 percent of sales and 9 percent of profits. Of all the health care companies, JNJ is among the most geographically diversified. Forty-seven percent of 1998 sales were in 150 countries internationally.

In 1998 Johnson & Johnson acquired DePuy, a prime mover in the $9 billion orthopedic business. DePuy is a leading maker of spinal implants, and also produces things like knee and hip replacements.

The company recently announced plans to acquire Centocor in a stock deal valued at about $4.9 billion. Centocor has some promising drugs to treat rheumatoid arthritis, Crohn's disease, and cardiovascular disease. Centocor makes Remicade, which is approved for Crohn's, but is awaiting government approval for rheumatoid arthritis drugs, a potentially enormous market where there are few competing drugs. According to a *Wall Street Journal* article, J&J would get access to Centocor's hot-selling ReoPro anticlotting medicine, as well as another type of anticlotting medicine, Retavase. ReoPro had sales last year of $365 million, and sales are expected to soar to about $700 million in a couple of years.

J&J received FDA approval to market Benecol, which contains the dietary ingredient stanol ester and has been patented for use in reducing cholesterol as much as 14 percent. According to a Value Line report, JNJ began a national product launch late in May of 1999 and will begin selling the product as both a margarine and a cream cheese spread. It is expected to generate sales upwards of $500 million.

Another promising pharmaceutical product is Remiyl, which increases the amount of acetylcholine in the synaptic space, thus facilitating nerve impulse conduction. Memory and cognitive loss in Alzheimer's disease has been shown to be associated with the depletion of acetylcholine in the brain.

JNJ has held up quite well in 1999, with a 22.5 percent total return through August despite weakness in the top-tier pharmaceutical sector generally. At 102¼ and with a PE of 42, though,

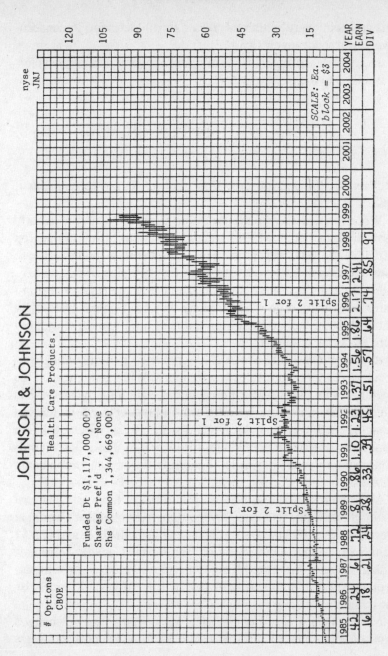

JOHNSON & JOHNSON

nyse
JNJ

Health Care Products.

Funded Dt $1,117,000,000
Shares Pref'd . . None
Shs Common 1,344,669,000

Options
CBOE

SCALE: Ea.
block = $3

Split 2 for 1

Split 2 for 1

Split 2 for 1

	1985	1986	1987	1988	1989	1990	1991	1992	1993	1994	1995	1996	1997	1998	1999	2000	2001	2002	2003	2004	YEAR
EARN	.42	.24	.61	.72	.81	.86	1.10	1.23	1.37	1.56	1.86	2.17	2.41								
DIV	.16	.18	.21	.24	.28	.33	.39	.45	.51	.57	.64	.74	.85	.91							

this great company, which has raised its dividend for 36 consecutive years, seems overpriced.

JNJ, which has increased its dividends for 36 consecutive years, was added to the Dow in 1997.

McDONALD'S CORPORATION (MCD)

McDonald's has been described as "the world's largest small business."

When it opened a restaurant on Red Square in Moscow in early 1990, nothing better symbolized the imminent lifting of the Iron Curtain—the hamburger, an American tradition named after a West German city, served with an order of French fries.

McDonald's is a great source of impressive statistics. I don't know how many billion hamburgers they have sold to date (they know, though; look at their sign the next time you drive by), but here are a few others:

At the end of 1998, McDonald's reported its thirty-third consecutive year of record sales and earnings. When it announced the opening of its twenty-five thousandth restaurant August 1999 in Chicago, 20 miles from Des Plaines, Illinois, where founder Ray Kroc opened the first McDonald's in 1955, CEO Jack M. Greenberg noted that McDonald's now serves more than 40 million customers every day in 117 countries, the latest addition being Gibraltar.

McDonald's operates, licenses, and services the world's largest chain of fast food restaurants. According to Standard & Poor's, at December 31, 1998 there were 12,472 units in the U.S. and 12,752 units in foreign countries, mostly in Japan, Canada, Germany, Brazil, Taiwan, the United Kingdom and Australia. Sixty-one percent of their restaurants were owned by franchisees, 23 percent by the company, and the rest by affiliates.

McDonald's is also a real estate company, owning or leasing a substantial amount of the real estate used by franchisees. Rents

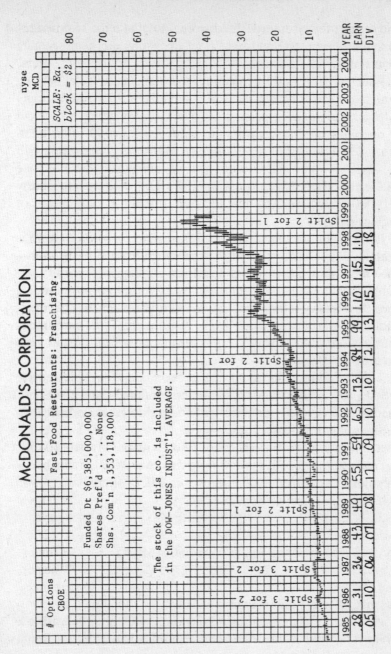

McDONALD'S CORPORATION

Fast Food Restaurants: Franchising.

nyse
MCD

SCALE: Ea.
block = $2

Funded Dt $6,385,000,000
Shares Pref'd . . . None
Shs. Com'n 1,353,118,000

The stock of this co. is included
in the DOW-JONES INDUST'L AVERAGE.

Options
CBOE

	1985	1986	1987	1988	1989	1990	1991	1992	1993	1994	1995	1996	1997	1998
EARN	.28	.31	.36	.43	.40	.55	.59	.65	.73	.84	.99	1.10	1.15	1.10
DIV	.05	.10	.06	.07	.08	.17	.09	.10	.10	.12	.13	.15	.16	.18

Split 3 for 2 (1986), Split 3 for 2 (1987), Split 2 for 1 (1989), Split 2 for 1 (1994), Split 2 for 1 (1999) and service fees from franchisees often total at least 11.4 percent of sales. Real estate and restaurant decisions are kept separate financially.

With the free world expanding, there seems to be almost no limit to the growth potential of McDonald's. In 1998 international sales accounted for 51 percent of systemwide sales and 56 percent of operating profits. According to Value Line, in 1999 a net addition of 150 domestic units is likely, while the global chain will expand by some 1700 units net of closings. There is one McDonald's per 22,000 people in the U.S. and one for every 605,000 elsewhere. And new locations are not its only means of increasing sales.

Even where they have saturated their markets—where there is seemingly not an empty belly left in which to stuff a Big Mac—they have shown themselves to be remarkably resourceful marketers, coming up with innovations like drive-in windows, a breakfast menu, salad bars, and chicken sandwiches. The latest: McBagel. Under pressure from health-conscious consumers, they've found a new way to cook fries without beef fat and whip up lower-fat shakes.

They're doing their bit for the environment, too. "McRecycle USA" uses recycled paper napkins and containers, and gives preference to recycled materials when building, remodeling, or reequipping their restaurants.

Sad to say, all of this has not gone on with the investing public in the dark. McDonald's is currently way overpriced at a PE of 36. In a normally valued market, however, MCD offers both growth and defensive characteristics.

MERCK & CO., INC. (MRK)

If I had to name one company to illustrate the ability of a Dow component to adapt to radically, and quite suddenly, changed conditions, I couldn't think of a better example than Merck.

No company inside or outside the Dow has worn the blue chip mantle with more elegance and genuine merit than Merck. Named "America's Most Admired Corporation" by a Fortune poll year in and year out, Merck has exemplified good science, financial strength, and managerial vision as the world's largest manufacturer of prescription medicines.

With massive investment in basic research, the company has been a steady source of new products, which traditionally were marketed through doctors at prices that, although kept within the inflation rate by company policy, virtually guaranteed annual increases in sales, profits, and dividends. From the mid-eighties until 1993, MRK spiraled upward like a kite in a stiff wind.

Then, overnight, arrived the managed care revolution and a marketplace dominated by cost-conscious HMOs. The new Clinton administration's aggressive health care reform agenda brought the issue of drug company pricing and profits front and center. Although accounting for a surprisingly small portion (less than 7 percent) of the health care dollar, the drug manufacturers, with their visibly high profit margins, were a natural to become the bad guys. It was open season on drug stocks. MRK peaked in early 1992 at 39 (adjusted for subsequent splits), then sunk to a 30-month low of 15 in August 1993.

But Merck took the bull by the horns. Forward looking as always, Merck, the world's largest drug company, acquired Medco, the nation's largest mail-order marketer of prescription drugs. If they couldn't make it on margins, they'd make it on volume. They paid $6 billion, or 47 times Medco's 1993 earnings, for the acquisition in July 1993; it looked high at the time, but Merck's competitors were soon to follow suit, paying 58 times and 100 times earnings for similar acquisitions.

The acquisition, however, meant assimilating different corporate cultures and management teams, and raised questions about Merck's ability to sustain its historical growth rate as a volume company. Moreover, Merck issued stock to acquire Medco, diluting earnings per share. The stock continued depressed well into 1994 under a cloud of pending health care reform and because of a delay in naming a successor to Merck's highly esteemed CEO, Doctor P. Roy Vagelos. He was scheduled to retire in November 1994, and one likely successor, Medco's CEO Martin Wygood, had resigned in May.

By mid-1994, though, things had started looking up. Although first-quarterly earnings were flat on a per-share basis because of dilution, sales were up 48 percent and earnings up 10 percent. That reassured analysts that lower margins would be offset by higher volume in the new Merck. A dividend increase was paid in the second quarter. In June the succession problem was solved with the appointment of Raymond V. Gilmartin, who had gained needed managed care experience as head of Becton Dickinson. In October, with the stock beginning to take notice, Gilmartin announced significant reorganization plans aimed at Merck's success in the price-competitive managed care environment. To counter the dilutive effects of Medco-related stock, a $2 billion stock buyback plan was announced along with plans to sell noncore Kelco and Calgon to finance their repurchase.

With competitors reporting flat earnings, Merck announced a 15 percent increase in fourth-quarter profits on the same increase in sales. That met analysts' ambitious expectations and gave evidence that the Merck-Medco assimilation had been successfully accomplished. Even more encouraging was the revelation that proprietary products were not as vulnerable to substitution as analysts had feared. First-quarter-1995 income was up 13 percent, about in line with the industry, on the strength of newer products and continued growth in Merck-Medco managed care business. One analyst called that "reasonable growth" and spoke optimistically about "a new product story that's unfolding."

Merck's shares have gained steadily since the beginning of 1995 and peaked at 87⅜ early in 1999. At 68⅛ as this is written in late summer, the drop-off is explained by general weakness in the drug sector as investors have rotated into cyclicals, some concern about impending patent expirations, and worry that proposed Medicare drug benefit changes might result in price controls.

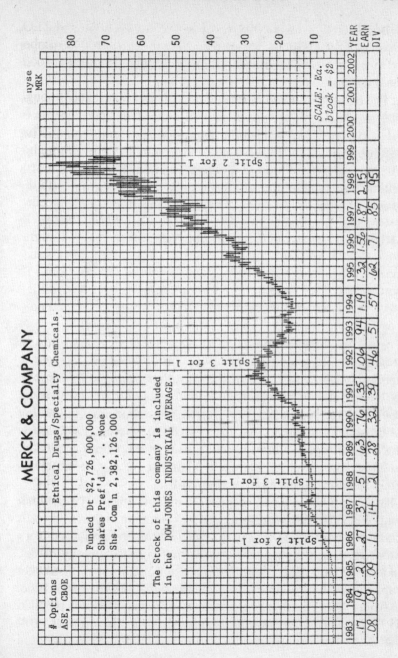

MERCK & COMPANY

Ethical Drugs/Specialty Chemicals.

nyse MRK

Options
ASE, CBOE

Funded Dt $2,726,000,000
Shares Pref'd . . . None
Shs. Com'n 2,382,126,000

The Stock of this company is included in the DOW-JONES INDUSTRIAL AVERAGE.

Split 2 for 1

Split 3 for 1

Split 3 for 1

Split 2 for 1

Split 2 for 1

SCALE: Ea.
block = $2

	1983	1984	1985	1986	1987	1988	1989	1990	1991	1992	1993	1994	1995	1996	1997	1998	1999	2000	2001	2002
YEAR																				
EARN	.17	.19	.21	.27	.37	.51	.63	.76	1.35	1.06	.94	1.19	1.32	1.50	1.87	2.15				
DIV	.08	.09	.09	.11	.14	.21	.28	.32	.39	.46	.51	.57	.62	.71	.85	.95				

But Merck, whose 1998 revenues of $26.9 billion and net income of $5.2 billion both set records, and whose 1999 sales are expected to grow 20 percent, retains its status as the class act in the drug industry.

The current Standard & Poor's stock report notes that "Merck-Medco Managed Care provides mail order drug and related services to over 51 million people. Merck-Medco represented about 43% of Merck's total 1998 sales, but less than 5% of profits . . . The huge success of Merck's drugs has enabled it to support a $1.8 billion R&D program, which promises to spawn an ongoing stream of blockbuster drugs in the years ahead."

Oh, and a footnote to the S&P report on Merck: value of $10,000 invested five years ago, $44,264.

MICROSOFT CORP.

The mid-November 1999 issue of *Time* has a cover depicting an about-to-be-punctured party balloon with the bulging eyes, rosy cheeks and hubristic grin of the world's richest enfant terrible, William Gates III. "Busting Bill" is the caption and it refers, of course, to the November 1999 Justice Department action finding Microsoft a monopoly. As this is written, Microsoft's future is unclear, with possibilities ranging from an innocuous settlement to a breakup of the company à la AT&T in 1982, with the analogous creation, in this case, of Baby Bills.

Microsoft became part of the Dow in November 1, 1999, along with Intel, Home Depot and SBC Communications. Microsoft and Intel, both NASDAQ-listed, became the first non–New York Stock Exchange companies, and the first high-technology stocks, to join the Dow. Some said it was about time. Microsoft's market capitalization at the time was bigger than that of General Electric.

Micro-Soft (the hyphen was later eliminated) was started in 1975 by a twenty-year-old, soon-to-be-Harvard dropout, Bill Gates, and a twenty-three-year-old University of Washington dropout, Paul Allen, in Albuquerque, New Mexico. Gates, on the long end of a 60/40 split, later moved the company to Washington so he could be closer to his parents.

William Henry Gates III was born in 1955 to a well-to-do family in Seattle, Washington. When he was eleven, being "overly energetic and prone to getting into trouble," according to one report, he was sent to the Lakeside School, an all-boys prep school. Lakeside had a primitive computer, a teletype machine connected by telephone to a time-share computer. "A nerd before the term was invented," according to a teacher, he quickly mastered BASIC (Beginner's All-purpose Symbolic Instruction Code), one of the early operating languages written for mainframe computers, and with his fellow classmate Paul Allen spent countless hours writing programs, playing games, and generally learning about computers.

Gates went on to Harvard, where in December 1974 he received a phone call from an excited Paul Allen, already a college dropout working in computers with Honeywell in Cambridge. *Forbes Greatest Business Stories of All Time*, by Daniel Gross and the editors of *Forbes* magazine (Wiley, 1996), tells the story of how Allen had picked up on an article in *Popular Electronics* describing a breakthrough new minicomputer using the Intel microprocessor. Called the Altair 8800, it was made by a New Mexico company called MITS. No computer language existed for microcomputers, the forerunners of personal computers, and Allen and Gates saw an opportunity to supply one.

Allen wrote the inventor of the Altair saying he and his partner had developed BASIC for the machine, which, at that point, they hadn't. The inventor told them to bring it to New Mexico, which gave Allen and Gates eight weeks of all-nighters to come up with something. But they did it. Their language program worked, and in the summer of 1975 they started Microsoft and the software industry. The new firm signed a contract with MITS, under which MITS would pay royalties in exchange for licensing rights, an arrangement that paid royalties of $16,000 the first year.

In the scattered computer community of the sixties, much,

including computer languages like BASIC, was in the public domain and Gates was determined to prevent hackers from copying software and capitalizing on his innovations. Selling software already installed in computers was one way of protecting himself and in one of its first important deals, Microsoft licensed Tandy Corporation to install its BASIC computer language in its TRS–80, the 1970s' most popular forerunner of today's PCs.

In mid-1980 IBM, then a $30 billion company, decided to produce its first desktop computer. Needing an operating system, it sought out fledgling Microsoft, by then a $4 million company, and signed an agreement in 1980 that paid Microsoft a royalty for each unit sold while Microsoft retained ownership rights. The only problem was that, again, Gates had made a commitment before he had developed the product.

This time, a nearby company called Seattle Computer Products had developed an operating system that ran on an Intel 8086 chip. Seattle Computer considered its system an experiment, but Gates saw its adaptability to IBM's new machine and Paul Allen paid the company $25,000 to license the system to undisclosed (a condition imposed by IBM) end users. The following year Microsoft bought all intellectual and physical rights to the system, called 86-DOS before it was renamed MS-DOS, for $50,000.

Microsoft's retention of ownership rights was to prove a bonanza as other computer companies, led by Compaq, began producing lower-priced IBM clones using MS-DOS.

Clone makers around the world called Microsoft to negotiate the right to install MS-DOS in their machines. Gates responded by setting up a worldwide sales force to make MS-DOS the international standard, pricing the system cheaply for installation as original equipment, and immediately began working on a new version. With 80 percent of the market for PC operating systems, Microsoft's sales rose from $16 million in 1981 to $97 million in 1984. In 1986, Microsoft celebrated its tenth birthday with sales of $200 million and 1500 employees.

In 1988, the company introduced the Excel 2.0, the improved, IBM-compatible, version of Excel 1.0, a spreadsheet package de-

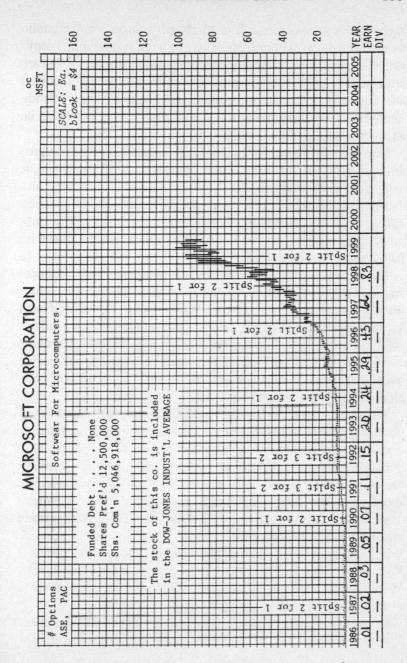

MICROSOFT CORPORATION

Softwear For Microcomputers.

OC
MSFT

SCALE: Ea.
block = $4

Funded Debt. . . . None
Shares Pref'd 12,500,000
Shs. Com'n 5,046,918,000

The stock of this co. is included
in the DOW-JONES INDUST'L AVERAGE

Options
ASE, PAC

Split 2 for 1
Split 2 for 1
Split 2 for 1
Split 2 for 1
Split 3 for 2
Split 3 for 2
Split 2 for 1
Split 2 for 1

YEAR	EARN	DIV
2005		
2004		
2003		
2002		
2001		
2000		
1999		
1998	.83	—
1997	.77	—
1996	.43	—
1995	.29	—
1994	.24	—
1993	.20	—
1992	.15	—
1991	.11	—
1990	.07	—
1989	.05	—
1988	.03	—
1987	.02	—
1986	.01	—

signed earlier for Macintosh as Microsoft's answer to the block-buster Lotus 1–2–3. Microsoft Word was next, and eventually MS-DOS was replaced by a new concept called "Windows," which became the industry standard and put Microsoft ahead of IBM as the dominant force in information technology. Mainly on the strength of Windows, Microsoft's sales rose from $590.8 million in 1988 to $1.183 billion in 1990.

Windows 95 marked Microsoft's entry into the business of Internet access and in early 1996, it joined with NBC to form the television network MS-NBC.

Microsoft today is a company with revenues of just under $20 billion. Standard & Poor's stock report dated October 25, 1999, says, "The company's revenues will be driven over the near term by new product cycles for Office 2000 and Windows 2000. In addition, SQL Server, the company's database software, is show-ing strong growth. MSFT's many Internet properties are experi-encing rapid revenue growth, both from advertising and e-commerce. The company boasts cash and equity investments totaling nearly $34 billion, leading to high levels of interest income and investment gains. The shares continue to merit their premium valuation, in light of MSFT's strong competitive posi-tion and its future growth prospects."

Of course, that summary preceded the finding of facts in *U.S. v. Microsoft*. Since the November 5, 1999 finding, both sides have retired to their corners to consider how antitrust law should apply. Public statements by Microsoft haven't shed much light. "We've welcomed any opportunity to settle," Gates told shareholders November 10. "[But] we aren't going to compromise on the prin-ciple of freedom to innovate," President Steven A. Ballmer told *BusinessWeek* a few days later.

MINNESOTA MINING AND MANUFACTURING COMPANY (MMM)

When the relics of capitalist society are studied a million years from now, one artifact that might cause archeologists some head-scratching will be the ubiquitous "suggestion box." It sends a double message. On one hand, it acknowledges that fresh ideas are needed and welcomed. Yet by promising anonymity, it implies that the employee who ventures a new idea might otherwise do so at some risk of job security.

Of course we all know that is exactly what does happen, however subtly, in corporations. The people who get promoted are usually those who play the game and don't challenge the accepted way of doing things. The down side, unfortunately, is that the really creative people all too frequently pack up and leave.

At 3M, which for my money is the world's most interesting corporation, there's no suggestion box because none is needed.

This remarkable organization has been built on a steady stream of new products, some 60,000 in all, that are largely the inventions of 73,600 employees who work in 60 countries. Scotch tape and Post-it notes are among the most familiar examples.

How 3M managed to create this entrepreneurial environment is a fascinating tale.

To begin with, the word "mining" in the corporate name is a misnomer stemming from a mistake. In 1902 a bunch of Minnesota boys, thinking they had found a corundum mine, established a quarrying plant and formed a company called Minnesota Mining and Manufacturing. What they really had, they were to discover, was nothing but a sand bank, so they got some financing and started making sandpaper. That's how it all started.

The first major success occurred in the 1920s with a product called Wetordry, a sandpaper that could be used with water and represented a breakthrough in sanding automobiles.

Today 3M coats adhesives to film (Scotch brand tapes), abrasive granules to paper (sandpaper), low-tack adhesives to paper

(Post-it brand notes), iron oxide to plastic backing (magnetic recording tape), glass beads to plastic backing (reflective sign materials), light-sensitive materials to metal (printing plates), nutrients to film (bacteria culture dishes), ceramics to granules (roofing granules), and dozens of others.

But coatings are just one product category. Others include non-woven fibers, fluorochemistry, industrial abrasives and hardware ranging from hand-held tape dispensers to sophisticated equipment for open-heart surgery and a range of other medical, dental, and pharmaceutical products.

The 3M system that so uniquely rewards creativity and, just as important, rewards sharing ideas with other people is really rather formalized.

According to Blamer and Shulman, 3M's tradition of innovation and problem solving began with a bookkeeper-turned-salesman named William McKnight, who joined the company in 1907 and later headed it for several decades.

Lacking formal sales training, McKnight tried an unusual tack. Instead of presenting his card at a potential customer's front office, he went directly to the production areas, where he would ask the workers what they liked or didn't like about the products they worked with. To this day, 3M gets 50 percent of its new product ideas from soliciting customers' suggestions.

Internally, entrepreneurship is encouraged with a "15 percent rule" that permits employees to spend 15 percent of their time pursuing their own ideas. Once an idea is born and determined to have high profit potential, programs such as Pacing Plus kick in to ensure that sales potential is maximized.

If employees with ideas can't persuade their own divisions to fund them, they are encouraged to shop the idea around the company's other 40 or so divisions or certain special sources. Division managers, though, aren't quick to reject ideas, since they are expected to meet a requirement that 30 percent of divisional sales come from new products developed in the last four years and 10 percent of sales from products introduced within the last year.

Once funding has been lined up, the employee has to recruit and organize a project team. This helps separate the ideas with market potential from those that are simply ingenious. And once the project team is put together it stays together as long as the project meets the company's financial and marketing criteria.

Post-it brand notes were invented by a 3M scientist who sang in his church choir and got frustrated every time the page marker fell out of his hymnal. Remembering a colleague's discovery of a barely sticky adhesive, he brushed some on a piece of paper and it worked perfectly. He was able to sing without interruption thereafter, and the success of Post-it is now legendary.

In 1996, 3M spun off its printing and publishing, data storage, and imaging systems as an independent, publicly owned company, now known as Imation Corp. (IMN), in which 3M holders received one share for ten MMM. Imation gained, and 3M holders realized a total return of 32.2 percent that year.

In 1998, 3M had sales of $15 billion, roughly level with its sales before the Imation spin-off. Fifty-two percent of revenues and 54 percent of operating profits derived from international sales. Overall, sales come from three groups: the Industrial and Consumer segment—which makes most of the traditional products, and to a lesser extent, specialty chemicals, electronics, and telecommunications equipment—contributed 52 percent of revenues; the Transporta-tion, Safety, and Specialty Material Markets segment—which includes reflectors (used for highway signs, construction equipment, and personal safety applications) and products used for electronic surveillance and counterfeiting protection—contributed 21 percent; and the growing Health Care segment—which makes products for the medical, dental, and personal hygiene markets—contributed 21 percent.

Because it sells to a diverse range of other producers, 3M traditionally has been viewed as a barometer of general business conditions and as a bellwether stock. Its unusually high exposure to foreign economic risk and unfavorable currency conversions has, however, dampened results in the late 1990s.

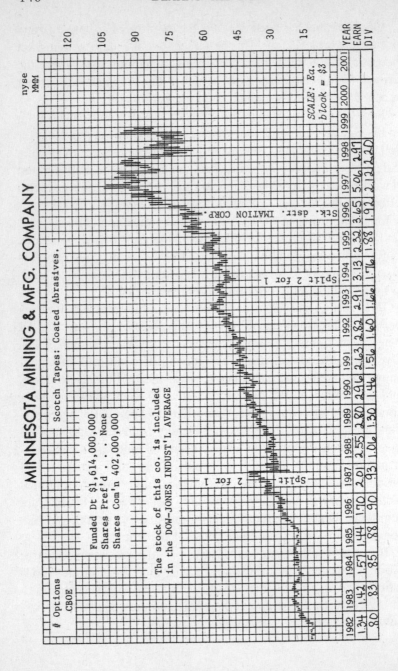

MINNESOTA MINING & MFG. COMPANY

nyse MMM

Scotch Tapes: Coated Abrasives.

Options
CBOE

Funded Dt $1,614,000,000
Shares Pref'd . . None
Shares Com'n 402,000,000

The stock of this co. is included
in the DOW-JONES INDUST'L AVERAGE

SCALE: Ea.
block = $3

YEAR	1982	1983	1984	1985	1986	1987	1988	1989	1990	1991	1992	1993	1994	1995	1996	1997	1998	1999	2000	2001
EARN	1.34	1.42	1.57	1.44	1.70	2.01	2.55	2.80	2.96	2.63	2.82	2.91	3.13	2.32	3.65	5.06	2.91			
DIV	.80	.83	.85	.88	.90	.93	1.06	1.30	1.46	1.51	1.60	1.66	1.76	1.88	1.92	2.12	2.20			

In midsummer 1999, MMM is outperforming the market as its results reflect economic recovery in Asia and Latin America, aggressive cost-cutting and productivity gains, large share repurchases, the strong U.S. economy, and a revival of market interest in the traditional industrial sector.

3M has raised its dividend for 41 consecutive years.

J.P. MORGAN & CO. INCORPORATED (JPM)

"Never be a bear on the United States," said J.P. Morgan, who is among the most quoted of America's business pioneers. The fact that he put his money where his mouth was had a lot to do with America's growth to industrial preeminence.

The substitution in May 1991 of Morgan for Primerica Corporation, a non-bank financial services conglomerate, ended criticism that the Dow was incomplete without a major commercial bank.

Interestingly, although Morgan remains at its core a commercial bank, it has shifted its emphasis to asset management and servicing, finance and advisory services, asset and liability management, and market making. This includes debt and equity securities underwriting to an increasing degree. Morgan has thus become more of an investment bank than a traditional commercial bank.

While J.P. Morgan was making itself over, Primerica, the non-bank it replaced in the Dow, merged with Travelers Inc., the insurance company, to become Travelers Group, which was added to the Dow in early 1997. In October 1998 Travelers Group merged with Citicorp, a commercial bank in the conventional sense, to form Citigroup, which remained in the Dow and was discussed earlier.

So the Dow, by both design and serendipity, has its representation in the commercial banking sector. But what about this hybrid enterprise known as J.P. Morgan?

Technically, J.P. Morgan & Co. Incorporated is a bank holding company that owns Morgan Guaranty Trust Company, located in New York City. Morgan ranks among the top money-center banks, but it has always been a wholesale bank rather than a retail bank, meaning that even where traditional commercial banking is concerned, Morgan deals with a corporate clientele and with wealthy individuals. It has always had the largest trust department in the United States. It isn't out hustling installment loans, credit cards, and special checking accounts.

But Morgan has a distinct competitive position among the big banks. As its CEO, Douglas A. Warner III, said in his 1998 Letter to Shareholders, "We are the only wholesale financial firm that combines investment banking, commercial banking, and asset management capabilities globally on a meaningful scale."

In 1998, 65 percent of revenues derived from global finance, which includes advisory, capital raising, and market making activities, such as investment banking, foreign exchange trading, interest rate risk management and making loans. Twenty-one percent of revenues came from management of portfolios totaling $216 billion in asset value, including portfolios of pension plans, governments, endowments and foundations, financial services for individuals, 401K and similar plans, and mutual fund distributions. The remaining 14 percent came from proprietary investments, including private equity investments, and taking market and credit risk for its own account.

Because more than half of JPM's revenues derive from trading operations, it has been subject to earnings volatility, and Wall Street has been inclined to give its shares the multiple it gives investment banks, which is lower than that of commercial banks whose earnings are more predictable. Part of the problem has been Morgan's slow progress in bringing costs and expenses under tighter control.

After falling sharply in the third quarter of 1998 because of emerging markets turmoil, the shares in mid-1999, thanks to growing investor confidence based on successful cost control, are approaching record levels. Rumors of a takeover by Deutsche

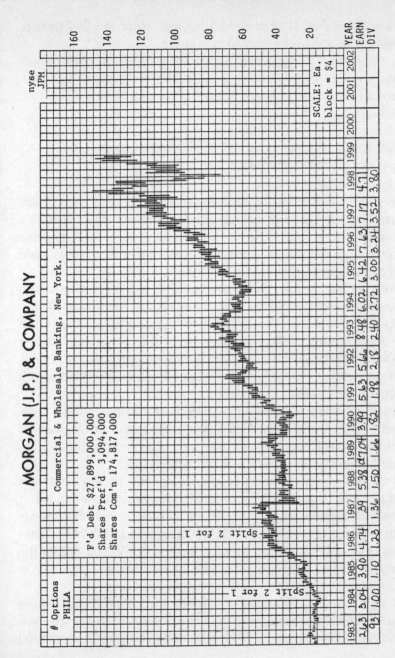

MORGAN (J.P.) & COMPANY

nyse
JPM

Options
PHILA

Commercial & Wholesale Banking, New York.

F'd Debt $27,899,000,000
Shares Pref'd 3,094,000
Shares Com'n 174,817,000

Split 2 for 1

Split 2 for 1

SCALE: Ea.
block = $4

YEAR	1983	1984	1985	1986	1987	1988	1989	1990	1991	1992	1993	1994	1995	1996	1997	1998	1999	2000	2001	2002
EARN	2.63	3.04	3.90	4.74	.39	5.38	d7.04	3.99	5.63	5.46	8.48	6.02	6.42	7.63	7.17	4.71				
DIV	.93	1.00	1.10	1.23	1.36	1.50	1.66	1.82	1.98	2.18	2.40	2.72	3.00	3.24	3.52	3.80				

Bank had driven JPM to an all-time high close to 150 earlier in 1998. JPM was trading at 140 at midyear.

The company repurchased $750 million of its stock in 1998 and approved a plan to repurchase a similar amount in 1999. Dividends have been raised in each of the last 24 years.

PHILIP MORRIS COMPANIES (MO)

The April 1990 *Forbes* cover showed Philip Morris' then Chairman Hamish Maxwell tucking a napkin under his chin beside a caption asking, "Who's Next?" It was a reference to PM's appetite for acquisitions, which, together with internal growth, made it one of the hot growth stocks of the 1980s.

Citing the rises in this stock even after lackluster results with the acquisitions of Miller Brewing, General Foods, and Seven-Up, Peter Lynch observed back then that at Philip Morris even diworseification couldn't hurt the stockholders. In fact, had he been able to see what was coming for Philip Morris, Mr. Lynch might even have agreed that the diworseification was an idea with considerable merit.

Philip Morris, as everyone knows, is an old-line tobacco company, famous originally for its own brand name ("Call Fooooor Phil-ip Maaaaar-ace"), then later for Parliament, Virginia Slim, and Marlboro, the world's bestselling cigarette.

Of course, when you are an oligopsony of sorts and have folks addicted to your product, profitability comes easy. At the end of 1990, 41 percent of PM's revenues and 68 percent of earnings came from cigarette sales. The company was marketing aggressively overseas to offset steadily declining tobacco use in the United States, although its market share here was and still is growing.

With the acquisition of Kraft, Inc., in 1988 Philip Morris became the largest and most diversified food and beverage company in the United States. With sales of $44 billion, of which food

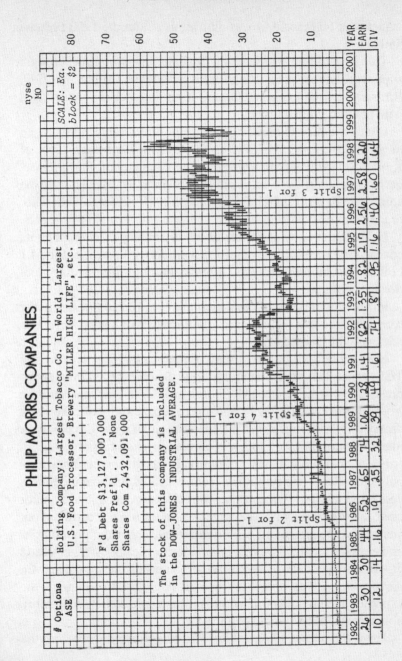

PHILIP MORRIS COMPANIES

nyse
MO

SCALE: Ea.
block = $2

Holding Company: Largest Tobacco Co. In World, Largest
U.S. Food Processor, Brewery "MILLER HIGH LIFE", etc.

F'd Debt $13,127,000,000
Shares Pref'd . . . None
Shares Com 2,432,091,000

The stock of this company is included
in the DOW-JONES INDUSTRIAL AVERAGE.

Options
ASE

Split 3 for 1
Split 4 for 1
Split 2 for 1

	1982	1983	1984	1985	1986	1987	1988	1989	1990	1991	1992	1993	1994	1995	1996	1997	1998	1999	2000	2001
YEAR																				
EARN	.26	.30	.30	.44	.52	.65	.74	1.06	1.28	1.41	1.82	1.35	1.82	2.17	2.56	2.58	2.20			
DIV	.10	.12	.14	.16	.19	.25	.32	.39	.49	.61	.74	.87	.95	1.16	1.40	1.60	1.64			

is just over 50 percent, it was number seven on the 1990 Fortune 500 list.

The $5.7 billion purchase of General Foods in 1986 brought such well-known products as Maxwell House Coffee, JELL-O, Birds Eye frozen foods and Oscar Meyer, but lacked product lines with real growth potential.

Hence the record-breaking—until the RJR Nabisco leveraged buyout (LBO)—$13 billion acquisition in December 1988 of Kraft, Inc., with Kraft cheeses, Breyers ice cream, Parkay margarine, Light n' Lively and a range of popular brands that gave the combined Kraft General Foods Division 10 percent of the U.S. brand-food market.

In 1990, the company took an important step to strengthen its competitiveness in European food markets by acquiring, for $4.1 billion, Jacobs Suchard AG, a Swiss-based coffee and confectionary company.

Philip Morris is one of the richest and best-run companies in the world. But the specter of tobacco liability awards hangs over it like the sword of Damocles.

Until 1993 MO gained steadily on increased sales and profits. Then came "Marlboro Monday," a decision by the company to drastically cut the price of Marlboros in order to grab market share from competitors. In 1993 profits were substantially off, the stock dropped to 1990 levels, but the Marlboro man was riding high on market share. By 1994 MO was climbing steadily again.

For the next couple of years, tobacco was the target of negative publicity, there were rumblings from Washington about the FDA's desire to classify tobacco as a controlled substance, and a major class action suit was seeking (but didn't get) certification. Generally, though, the legal environment, if not the public relations environment, was still favorable for the industry, cigarette profits were good, and analysts were expressing the view that even if the industry was forced to trade off its ability to advertise, the expense saved would be a boon to profits while the effect on sales, if significant at all, would be gradual.

Then, in August 1996, a Florida jury surprised everybody by

reaching the stunning conclusion that Brown & Williamson Tobacco Corp. was liable for Grady Carter's lung cancer and should pay him and his wife $750,000 because cigarettes made by the company were "unreasonably dangerous and defective." MO dropped 14 percent on the news, the significance being that nicotine addiction, for the first time, played a major role in a plaintiff's case. "Litigation jitters" entered the financial news journalist's vocabulary.

In March 1997 *The Wall Street Journal's* "Heard on the Street" was headlined, "Cigarette Stocks Are Smokin'," and observed that tobacco stocks were rising on "mounting speculation that a magic bullet legislative solution will wipe away the regulatory and legal attacks that have dogged cigarette makers." It referred to efforts begun by industry lawyers to negotiate with states' attorneys general some sort of monetary settlement in exchange for immunity from punitive damages. State Medicaid suits were considered the industry's only really significant liability threat, class actions being impractical and individual suits almost never succeeding.

Then began an off-again, on-again succession of multi-billion-dollar settlement proposals, complete with political grandstanding and a growing recalcitrance on the part of anti-tobacco forces. When it looked good for a settlement favorable to tobacco, MO spurted. When it looked like a deal was dead, MO declined.

Finally, in November 1998, 46 states and five U.S. territories agreed to accept a $206 billion settlement, payable over 25 years. Said one prominent analyst, "This removes the threat of bankruptcy from the stocks and reduces the litigation discount that had plagued them since 1994. We are back to business as usual." MO hit a new high of 60, split adjusted, and ended 1998 with a 21.9 percent total return.

End of story? Not quite. Earnings from tobacco operations are being adversely affected by higher prices being charged to pass on the costs of the landmark settlement. And individual and class action liability suits, which had not been considered a serious problem for the industry, have suddenly loomed in 1999 as a threat of potentially colossal proportions. Two personal liability cases in two states resulted in substantial damages, and a class action suit has received certification for the first time ever.

All this has sent tobacco stocks in general and Philip Morris in particular back into the doldrums. MO currently trades under 40. Despite its attorneys' optimism that recent rulings lack legal merit and will be reversed on appeal, investors worry that younger, more anti-tobacco juries, influenced by incriminating corporate documentation now on record, have begun an unstoppable legal assault on tobacco that will result in ever more numerous and higher monetary awards, ultimately threatening Philip Morris financially. There is also the fact that 62 percent of MO is institutionally held, and vulnerable to a sell-off if public attitudes demand it.

Of course, that's only one view, a worst-case scenario that ignores the values in MO and gives no value at all to the food and beverage business, which is both expanding and improving in profitability.

Argus Research made the positive case as follows in its February 1999 report: "Despite the legal problems, we believe MO's food and beer assets, as well as its international tobacco business, offer compelling value to shareholders. . . . We believe strong underlying profit growth should make investors willing to tolerate the litigation risk."

Argus crunched the company's numbers assuming a spin-off of the domestic tobacco operations, which would free the remaining assets from litigation risk. They came up with asset values of $60 to $65 billion for food and beer and $135 billion for international tobacco, for a total of $200 billion, sans domestic tobacco (which is still a profitable business). That yields $82 a share, 75 percent higher than the current level (39⅛).

PROCTER & GAMBLE COMPANY (PG)

Try to guess what happened the year one company said the following in its Letter to Shareholders: "We are reasonably pleased with the results of the past year. And yet, as we have stated in previous letters, the long-term development of the business is more important than the results of a single year."

In most annual reports words like "reasonably" and "long-term" mean things weren't so hot. But don't underestimate the modest self-confidence of Procter & Gamble. The annual report from which that quote was taken highlighted an 18 percent increase in earnings and a dividend increase for the thirty-third consecutive year. Now it's forty-one years. That's pretty good going.

Procter & Gamble began in 1837 making soap and candles out of pig fat in Cincinnati, then jokingly called "Porkopolis." The company's identification with such household staples as Ivory soap, Mr. Clean, Head & Shoulders, Crest, Pampers, Charmin, Bounty and Tide makes it one of the most visible consumer products companies in the world. Not to mention the "soaps" sponsored by P&G, like *Search for Tomorrow* and *As the World Turns,* that have fulfilled more than a few fantasies over many years. Although personal care and household products amount to some 80 percent of sales, the company's food products are equally familiar: Folgers coffee, Crisco, Jif, and Pringles potato chips. The company estimates that 98 percent of American households contain at least one P&G product.

In the fiscal year ended June 30, 1998, laundry and cleaning products contributed 30 percent of the company's $37.1 billion of sales; paper, 29 percent; beauty care, 19 percent; food and beverage, 12 percent; health care, 8 percent; and corporate and other, 2 percent. North America accounted for 50 percent of total sales and 65 percent of operating profits; Europe, the Middle East, and Africa, for 32 percent of sales and 29 percent of profits; Asia, for 9 percent of sales and 5 percent of profits; Latin America, for 7 percent of sales and 7 percent of profits; and corporate, 2 percent of sales and minus 6 percent of profits.

PG's success obviously depends on a stream of new products and applications. Olean, for example, a recently approved cooking oil developed in the Food & Beverage segment, is made from soybeans and allows frying without adding fat or calories. The

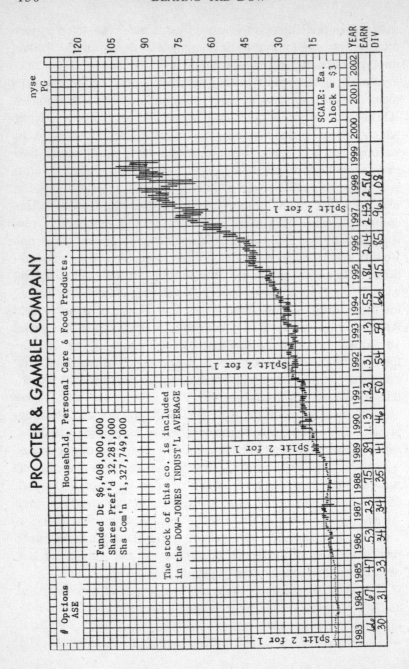

PROCTER & GAMBLE COMPANY

Household, Personal Care & Food Products.

nyse
PG

Funded Dt $6,408,000,000
Shares Pref'd 32,281,000
Shs Com'n 1,327,749,000

The stock of this co. is included
in the DOW-JONES INDUST'L AVERAGE

Options
ASE

SCALE: Ea.
block = $3

	1983	1984	1985	1986	1987	1988	1989	1990	1991	1992	1993	1994	1995	1996	1997	1998	1999	2000	2001	2002
YEAR																				
EARN	.66	.67	.47	.53	.23	.75	.89	1.13	1.23	1.31	1.12	1.55	1.86	2.14	2.43	2.56				
DIV	.30	.31	.33	.34	.34	.35	.41	.46	.50	.54	.59	.60	.75	.85	.96	1.08				

Split 2 for 1

Laundry and Cleaning Products segment has developed Dryel, a fabric care product that enables consumers to clean and freshen clothing labeled "dry clean only" in home dryers. A recently launched face-cleaning cloth combined technological advances from the company's food, paper, and beauty units.

In a recent development, the company announced June 9, 1999, a major restructuring involving the elimination of 15,000 jobs, the closing of ten factories, and the cutting of $1.9 million in costs over the next six years. The reorganization, which will streamline manufacturing and create seven brand-centered business units, is designed to accelerate revenue growth to 6 percent to 8 percent annually over the long term and increase per-share earnings from operations 13 percent to 15 percent a year during the next five years.

In 1995 the company said it would double sales to $70 billion by 2005, a goal it obviously no longer believes it can attain.

CEO Durk Jager said, "These are the most far-reaching changes in the history of P&G. The result will be bigger innovations, faster speed to market and greater growth."

The Wall Street Journal noted that the goal of this restructuring differs from the last one, when 13,000 jobs and 30 plants were eliminated in 1993. Then the goal was to cut prices to compete with cheaper, private-label rivals. Now the goal is technological advances that will allow higher prices and drive sales growth.

The reorganization will have the aim of standardizing manufacturing operations. New acquisitions would likely be in the areas of baby care, feminine protection, and hair care, Jager said.

The company expects savings from the restructuring to reach $900 million a year by 2004.

P&G is another one of the consumer growth stocks that have led the current bull market. At a price of 98 and a PE of 38, it is overvalued even if its earnings goals materialize.

SBC COMMUNICATIONS, INC.

This not-so-little combination of Baby Bells joined the Dow in 1999.

In 1997, when it was a combination of formerly independent Southwestern Bell and PacTel (Pacific Bell), it was in merger discussions with Dow component AT&T. That would have been a homecoming of sorts, AT&T having once been Ma Bell, but the talks fell through, reportedly because SBC's CEO Ed Whiteacre didn't want to play second fiddle to AT&T's Mike Armstrong.

After that, AT&T went into cable TV in a big way and SBC went on to acquire, in November 1999, still another Baby Bell, Ameritech (midwestern U.S.). That makes SBC Communications the largest local telephone company in the country, ranking just ahead of Bell Atlantic GTE. All three, AT&T, SBC, and Bell Atlantic GTE, are competing for preeminence in the telecommunications industry where deregulation and converging technologies have made bundled phone and data services via "broadband" the name of the game. AT&T with cable, and SBC and Bell Atlantic GTE with local phone lines, each has access to about one-third of American homes.

SBC Communications, Inc. is a global communications leader and a formidable contender.

Through some of the strongest brands in the industry— Southwestern Bell, Pacific Bell, Ameritech, SBC Telecom, Nevada Bell, SNET, and Cellular One—SBC provides local and long-distance phone service, wireless and data communications, paging, high-speed Internet access and messaging, cable and satellite television, security services and telecommunications equipment, as well as directory advertising and publishing.

In the United States, the company presently has 87.3 million voice grade equivalent lines and 10.3 million wireless customers and is undertaking a national expansion program that will bring SBC service to an additional 30 markets.

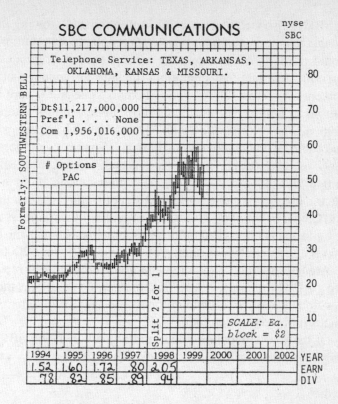

SBC COMMUNICATIONS

nyse
SBC

Formerly: SOUTHWESTERN BELL

Telephone Service: TEXAS, ARKANSAS, OKLAHOMA, KANSAS & MISSOURI.

Dt$11,217,000,000
Pref'd . . . None
Com 1,956,016,000

Options
PAC

Split 2 for 1

SCALE: Ea.
block = $2

	1994	1995	1996	1997	1998	1999	2000	2001	2002	YEAR
EARN	1.52	1.60	1.72	.80	2.05					
DIV	78	.82	85	.89	94					

Internationally, SBC has telecommunications investments in 22 countries. With more than 200,000 employees, SBC is the fourteenth-largest employer in the United States. Its 1998 revenues of $27.8 billion put it among the largest Fortune 500 companies.

According to an August 24, 1999, Standard & Poor's valuation report, revenues should advance about 8 percent in 1999, with wireless and data services being key catalysts. Shares are expected to continue to outperform the market as the company looks to evolve from a regional local provider of telephone services to a national end-to-end provider of communications services.

The company should get the FCC go-ahead to offer long-distance services in its own markets in early 2000.

SBC is also well positioned to exploit the fast-growing international telecommunications market. Over 50 percent of all international traffic to Mexico and 20 percent to Asia originates in its territory. International operations include an approximately 10 percent interest in Telefonos de Mexico, cable and telecommunications operations in the U.K. and Chile, wireless interests in France, South Korea, and South Africa, and long-distance alliance and cable television operations in Israel. Ventures were formed in 1997 in Switzerland, South Korea, and Taiwan, and SBC has joined with 13 other international companies to build a trans-Pacific fiber-optic cable for long-distance traffic between the U.S. and China. In late 1998, the company and 11 other partners agreed to build an undersea communications pipeline between the United States and Japan, which should be completed by mid-2000.

Argus Research Corporation, in a November 1999 report rating SBC "buy," said, "We think the carrier is among the best-positioned players to become one of a handful of international giants in the coming decade."

Of the four companies added to the Dow in 1999, SBC is the only one with an above-average dividend yield.

UNITED TECHNOLOGIES CORPORATION (UTX)

This is one of those companies better known for its parts than its whole. The "United" comes originally from United Aircraft and Transport, a company formed in the twenties and split up in 1934, creating United Airlines, Boeing, and United Aircraft. The latter was the predecessor of United Technologies.

United Aircraft and its subsidiaries, Hamilton Standard and Pratt & Whitney, were synonymous with aircraft propellers and engines during World War II. Today Pratt & Whitney vies with General Electric and Rolls Royce for dominance of the world market for jet engines.

Another subsidiary, Sikorski, was the main supplier of helicopters during the Vietnam War and continues as a major producer of rotary-wing aircraft for government and commercial use.

Like other major aerospace and defense contractors in the early 1970s, United Aircraft began a diversification program aimed at reducing its dependence on those sectors.

Under the leadership of Harry Gray, who was recruited from the conglomerate Litton Industries, United made some major commercial acquisitions, including Otis Elevator, Carrier Corporation (heating, ventilating and air conditioning equipment) and several other businesses that were later sold.

Today United Technologies, which was renamed in 1975, has sales of $25.7 billion from four categories of activities. Pratt & Whitney, which represents about 30 percent of revenues, is one of the world's three leading jet engine makers and also supplies spare parts and provides overhaul service to the aircraft aftermarket, a growing business as airlines increasingly modify and repair older aircraft. The Carrier division, which represents another 30 percent of revenues, is the world's largest maker of heating, ventilating, and air conditioning (HVAC) systems and equipment. It also makes commercial refrigeration equipment and generates 52 percent of its revenues from international sales. The Flight Systems division, 20 percent of revenues, makes Sikorsky helicopters and Hamilton Standard propellers, fuel systems, and aircraft controls equipment. Sikorsky, Standard & Poor's notes, is compensating for flat military orders by offering civilian versions of its helicopters. The Otis division, also 20 percent of revenues, is the world's largest maker of elevators and escalators. It generates over 80 percent of its sales overseas, and has been restructuring to improve its profit margins.

The company recently agreed to sell its low-margin, slow-growing auto components unit. It also agreed to buy Sunstrand, a highly profitable maker of aircraft power systems, such as generators. That business will become part of the Flight Systems division.

Thanks to superb management, a five-year annual earnings per share growth of 23 percent, a return on investment of more than

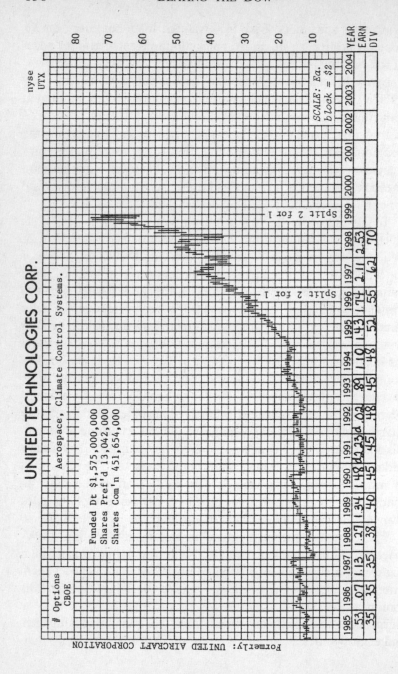

UNITED TECHNOLOGIES CORP.

Aerospace, Climate Control Systems.

Options
CBOE

Funded Dt $1,575,000,000
Shares Pref'd 13,042,000
Shares Com'n 451,654,000

nyse
UTX

SCALE: Ea.
block = $2

Split 2 for 1

Split 2 for 1

Formerly: UNITED AIRCRAFT CORPORATION

YEAR	1985	1986	1987	1988	1989	1990	1991	1992	1993	1994	1995	1996	1997	1998	1999	2000	2001	2002	2003	2004
EARN	.53	.07	1.13	1.27	1.34	1.48	d2.23	d.02	.89	1.10	1.43	1.74	2.11	2.53						
DIV	.35	.35	.35	.38	.40	.45	.45	.48	.45	.48	.52	.55	.62	.70						

20 percent, and generous stock buybacks, UTX has risen like an Otis elevator run amok. For seven years straight, the shares have increased at an annual rate of 22 percent, outperforming the Dow and the S&P handily.

UTX currently trades at around 68, and as PE's go these days, UTX sells at a relatively low 17 times. But while the earnings outlook is good, it is not expected to continue at an annual growth rate of 23 percent. Standard & Poor's projects 15 percent, and while that is nothing to sneeze at, it suggests the stock is appropriately priced where it is.

WAL-MART STORES INC (WMT)

In an interview conducted for Wal-Mart's 1998 Annual Report, CEO David D. Glass was asked if the 106 percent increase in Wal-Mart stock last year was something that could be expected to continue. He answered by saying, "Unfortunately, we don't directly control the stock market."

Unfortunate, indeed. Wouldn't it be nice if every time we went into the stock market, we were met by a folksy official greeter, were assured of everyday low prices and good value, and could look forward to the phenomenal growth and success this business has enjoyed? We'd all be in the Forbes 400 with young Bill Gates and old Sam Walton.

Wal-Mart replaced Woolworth (now Venator) in the Dow in 1997, and with an average total return of 91 percent for the past two years, we don't hear many complaints.

Wal-Mart is the world's largest retailer, operating about 1,850 discount stores, 565 supercenters (a one-stop concept including sizable food and grocery departments), and 450 Sam's Clubs (membership discount warehouses) in the United States, plus 870 foreign stores, mainly in Latin America and Canada, but also in Germany, Korea, and before this ink is dry, in the United Kingdom and elsewhere.

This gang just seems to have it all together. Its two main growth areas, the U.S. supercenter segment (now about 35 percent of domestic selling space) and its foreign operations (expected to expand 15 percent this year and next and to represent 25 percent to 30 percent of overall top- and bottom-line gains over the next three to five years), reflect intelligent management and planning, and not just the good luck of a booming economy.

The supercenters, for example, focus on economies of scale, increased private-label merchandising, and expense-leveraging same-store sales growth, and are already approaching the profit margins of the discount stores. The foreign stores, expanded internally by applying working formulae developed domestically, have also increased in number because the company sees soft economies as opportunities—opportunities to acquire real estate and businesses at favorable prices before the recovery inevitably begins.

In general, Wal-Mart has made a major strategy point of substituting information for inventory. Company literature quotes Sam Walton as saying, "People think we got big by putting big stores in small towns. Really we got big by replacing inventory with information." This is more than talk. The company has been a leader in developing and implementing retail information technology in managing its inventory. As a result of efficient inventory management, WMT has reduced prices on a broad assortment of items by 10 percent, leading to strong market share gains.

The company recently completed its best year ever (its fiscal year ended January 31, 1999) with sales of over $137 billion, up 17 percent, which is more than $20 billion (International Paper's total sales were less than that) more than last year. Impressive as that is, earnings per share, reflecting higher margins, increased by 27 percent; return on assets improved to 9.6 percent; and the company paid dividends of almost $700 million to shareholders.

Commenting on the second quarter of 1999 ended July 31, Argus research noted, "During the quarter, Wal-Mart showed gains across the board with strong categories including women's apparel, consumables, and hot weather-related merchandise. . . .

In light of a stronger than expected second quarter, we are raising our EPS estimates and reiterating our buy recommendation on the shares of this top-tier retailer. In recent weeks, the shares have dropped more than 18 percent from their recent highs and more than 25 percent from the 52-week high. We view the recent sell-off as a good buying opportunity for investors seeking high quality retail exposure. Keep in mind though, that at current prices, the shares are not cheap and are still susceptible to interest rate fallout."

Wal-Mart is exercising knowledgeable caution in its approach to Internet merchandising. "Very few, if any, Internet retailers have made a profit, and issues like the cost of delivery, merchandise returns and data security all have to be resolved before this business model is validated," says Walton. "When and if the business proves viable, we will be there with the technology, distribution, assortment and the lowest price." A relaunch of its Internet site is planned for the fall, prior to the important holiday season.

THE DOW COMPANIES' OFFICES

AlliedSignal Inc.
(Honeywell International)
Columbia Road & Park Avenue
Morristown, NJ 07962
(201) 455-2000

Aluminum Company of America
1501 Alcoa Building, 425 6th Avenue
Pittsburgh, PA 15219
(412) 553-4545

American Express Company
American Express Tower
World Financial Center
New York, NY 10285
(212) 640-2000

AT&T Corp.
32 Avenue of the Americas
New York, NY 10013-2412
(212) 387-5400

The Boeing Company
7755 East Marginal Way South
Seattle, WA 98108
(206) 655-2121

Caterpillar, Inc.
100 North East Adams Street
Peoria, IL 61629
(309) 675-1000

Citigroup
399 Park Avenue
New York, NY 10043
(212) 559-1000

The Coca-Cola Company
1 Coca Cola Plaza NW
Atlanta, GA 30313
(404) 676-2121

Walt Disney Company
500 South Buena Vista Street
Burbank, CA 91521
(818) 560-1000

**E.I. du Pont de Nemours and
   Company**
1007 Market Street
Wilmington, DE 19898
(302) 774-1000

Eastman Kodak Company
343 State Street
Rochester, NY 14650
(716) 724-4000

Exxon Mobil
5959 Las Colinas Boulevard
Irving, TX 75039-2298
(800) 252-1800

General Electric Company
3135 Easton Turnpike
Fairfield, CT 06431
(203) 373-2211

General Motors Corporation
3044 West Grand Boulevard
Detroit, MI 48202
(313) 556-5000

Hewlett-Packard Co.
3000 Hanover Street
Palo Alto, CA 94304
(415) 857-2030

Home Depot, Inc.
2455 Paces Ferry Road
Atlanta, GA 30339
(770) 433-8211

Intel Corporation
2200 Mission College Boulevard
P.O. Box 58119
Santa Clara, CA 95052-8119
(408) 765-8080

**International Business
   Machines Corporation**
Old Orchard Road
Armonk, NY 10504
(914) 765-1900

International Paper Company
2 Manhattanville Road
Purchase, NY 10577
(914) 397-1500

Johnson & Johnson
One Johnson & Johnson Plaza
New Brunswick, NJ 08933
(908) 524-0400

McDonald's Corporation
McDonald's Plaza
Oak Brook, IL 60521
(312) 575-3000

Merck & Co. Inc.
One Merck Drive
P.O. Box 100
Whitehouse Station, NJ 08889-
   0100

J.P. Morgan & Company Incorporated
60 Wall Street
New York, NY 10005
212-483-2323

Microsoft Corporation
One Microsoft Way
Redmond, WA 98052-6399
(425) 882-8080

Minnesota Mining and Manufacturing Company
3M Center Building
St. Paul, MN 55144
(612) 733-1110

Philip Morris Companies
120 Park Avenue
New York, NY 10017
(212) 880-5000

Procter & Gamble Company
1 Procter & Gamble Plaza
Cincinnati, OH 45202
(513) 983-1100

SBC Communications, Inc.
175 E. Houston
P.O. Box 2933
San Antonio, TX 78299
(210) 821-4105

United Technologies Corporation
United Technologies Building
Hartford, CT 06101
(203) 728-7000

Wal-Mart Stores, Inc.
702 S.W. 8th Street
Bentonville, AR 72716
(501) 273-4000

PART III

MARKETS AND CYCLES

BEFORE WE get to the strategy section, I think it's important that we talk a bit about the inevitable ups and downs of the market that occur over time.

Market cycles may be as inevitable as the tides, but that doesn't mean their timing can be predicted with the same exactitude. Not that people will ever stop trying. Part of the fun of being a contrarian has been to keep a file on just how wrong experts can be. I'll share some of my favorite examples in a minute.

When it comes to soothsaying, I'm no better than anybody else, which is to say that I don't know now, never have known, and never will know in advance what the market is going to do. Nobody does.

Beating the Dow is about buying good stocks when they are cheap, and how that can make you money regardless of what the market does.

But to look at the way stocks, big and small, have behaved in relation to each other, to fixed-income investments and to inflation over the years will help us understand why money management will never be an exact science and why no market strategy—even mine—works perfectly each and every year.

Which we should be glad for. Markets being what they are, a strategy that worked without exception would put itself out of business. It's the occasional off-year that allows anomalies, like the strategies we'll be discussing, to exist.

It's popularly observed that historical market comparisons going back prior to 1970 aren't really relevant today. Institutional domination, deregulation of brokerage commissions, globalization, computerized markets, derivative instruments like index futures and index options that make possible index investing and give rise to program trading, floating foreign exchange rates—these, and a host of other developments affecting the financial markets in important ways, all happened after 1970.

In general, prior to 1970 the stock market was supported by wealthy personal investors who bought stock primarily for income and switched to bonds when interest rates exceeded the dividends and expected growth of stocks.

Today the market is supported by mutual funds, retirement plans, and other institutional investors who invest for total returns, looking for capital gains plus dividends (in the case of stocks) or capital gains plus interest (in the case of bonds). As observed earlier, competitive pressures force a short-term focus.

It's probably true that enough has changed to make most such comparisons dubious. But I also know that the human forces of fear and greed, the basic determinants of market psychology, have been with us since day one, causing the extremes of euphoria and pessimism that have defined market tops and bottoms over the years. The best line to use when the cocktail party talk turns to the stock market is still, "The more things change the more they remain the same."

Market psychology, which is measured by a wide variety of "sentiment indicators," determines share prices and the market's direction along with other "real" factors, the most important of which are corporate earnings, interest rates, inflation rates, and actions of the Federal Reserve Board.

The relationship between interest and stock prices has become more complicated but is still quite simple to explain:

1. Interest is a cost of doing business, so higher interest causes lower earnings and lower stock prices.
2. Higher interest rates reflect a monetary supply imbalance—

more demand for money than supply—which is bad for companies that depend on borrowings to finance expansion.

3. Higher interest rates reflect Federal Reserve policy, indicating that in the Fed's opinion the economy needs slowing down. A slower economy is bad for business.

4. Higher interest rates draw investment capital away from stocks and into bonds, Treasury bills and money market funds.

5. Interest rates are a price of sorts, so higher interest implies increased inflation.

6. High interest rates attract money from foreign economies into our own. Unstable foreign economies, like those in the Pacific Rim in the late 1990s, can slow economic recovery in markets important to American producers.

Inflation is both good and bad for the stock market. Let's look at it.

As recently as the fifties and early sixties, inflation, which had been averaging under 2 percent, was simply not a major problem. To the extent that it did erode purchasing power, the popular wisdom had it that stocks were a hedge against inflation. Stocks represented ownership in companies that had a large percentage of their assets in real estate and machinery, the value of which would rise with the inflation rate and bring share prices with it. Companies, within limits, could also raise prices to customers, increasing sales and profits.

Then came the 1970s and a phenomenon labeled "stagflation," a combination of soaring inflation rates and stagnant economic growth brought about primarily by OPEC-driven oil prices that drove up the consumer price index while they slowed spending and business output.

With depressed corporate profits came a bear market. Precipitous declines in the Dow in 1970 and 1974 were matched by new peaks in the inflation rate, first to over 6 percent, then to over 12 percent.

So much, it seemed, for common stocks as an inflation hedge.

Indeed, until 1978 stocks ticked down whenever inflation ticked up and vice versa.

But then a crazy thing happened: Inflation soared, reaching a peak in 1980 of over 14 percent, and stock prices, led by small growth issues in energy and energy-related technology, soared with it. At the same time interest rates went into orbit as well (to put it mildly; this was when the prime rate got over 20 percent).

What to make of all this and what's happened since?

First, 74-year comparisons such as those cited at the outset of Chapter 2 and shown in Figure 1 on page 11 clearly show that stocks outperform inflation over the long run, and there is no reason to believe that won't be the case in the future.

The experience of recent years, however, would indicate that hyperinflation is bad for stocks because it affects *real* corporate profitability (for reasons having to do with depreciation and inventory accounting); because it means higher interest rates; and because it raises the specter of Federal Reserve action to slow the economy down by tightening credit.

The fact that stocks rose throughout the late 1980s despite relatively high interest rates is a comment on the respect we've gained for "controlling inflation" as the hallmark of a healthy economy.

When interest rates rise moderately, the market is inclined to see the increase as an indication that the Fed is heading off dangerous inflation and to treat it, if not as a positive, at least not as a negative.

We have also come to see relatively high rates as necessary to keep foreign capital invested in American financial markets.

A sharp rise in rates, however, is still enough to give the market the jitters. Any drop in rates will usually have the market feeling its oats. People believe what they want to believe, and are more apt to view a rate drop as good for profits than as a relaxation of the Fed's prudence with respect to inflation.

If all this confuses you somewhat, join the club. In 1989 and 1990, some economists were predicting a recession, while others bought into the Bush administration's promise of a "soft landing."

The market read it all as confusion and uncertainty and reacted by giving selected blue chips with demonstrated earning power higher than normal multiples and leaving the bargains alone.

When the recession was officially recognized in early 1991, investors returned to their more traditional pattern of buying depressed stocks in anticipation of economic recovery.

The rest of the 1990s was a story of robust economic growth and low inflation. Dubbed the Goldilocks economy because it was "not too hot, not too cold, just right," it spawned a record bull market that continues as this is written.

But the rising tide, in this case, wasn't lifting all boats. By mid-decade the raging bull began showing signs of schizophrenia. As the Dow skyrocketed at the rate of 1000 points a year, the market broke into two tiers, creating an interesting paradox.

A relative handful of overvalued high-capitalization growth stocks, bid up on the rationale that earnings growth without inflation justified a higher premium, got higher and higher in price and larger and larger in market capitalization. That phenomenon (remember our discussion in Chapter 5 of how averages are calculated) drove the blue chip averages to distorted levels even as the average stock contained in those averages languished or declined. Not surprisingly, the paradox was greatest in the price-weighted Dow.

More about the 1990s later. Let's look briefly at some history.

THE MARKET'S reaction to economic events and business cycles over the years has produced interesting investment cycles.

THE 1960S

Prior to the 1960s, a traditional rule prevailed that stocks should sell at 10 or 15 times earnings (P/E). With the "Soaring Sixties," also known as the "tronics boom," that old saw became history.

This was the decade when man set foot on the moon, and if a stock, especially an initial public offering, had the words space or electronics in its name (never mind what the company actually did), P/Es of 100 were not unusual. Some—Control Data in 1961, for example—sold briefly at twice that multiple.

In 1962, it all came tumbling down. The scapegoats varied. Some blamed President Kennedy's facing down of the steel industry. Others admitted that the market had excessively valued companies based on naïve speculation rather than demonstrated earning power.

Soon another craze had taken hold, this time in the name of "synergism." The theory was that the whole of an intelligently diversified company is worth more than the sum of its parts because divisions complement each other in various operational ways and benefit from a common source of financial support.

"Leisure time" was a big thing. Technology meant we were all going to be working short weeks and retiring early. A company that made surfboards and sold books somehow had synergy because both were "leisure-related."

"Conglomerates"—which included names like Litton, Ling-Temco-Vought, Gulf & Western, ITT, Textron, City Investing and Avco—also represented a management philosophy: by making divisions responsible in terms of the parent company's return on investment, divisions would be relatively autonomous and the entrepreneurial spirit would enjoy a revival in big companies. Mainly, though, the acquisition of companies added earnings per share, thus increasing the conglomerate's market value. That became the basis of new borrowing power with which to make further acquisitions, and so on.

But synergy was fool's gold, and the heads of the conglomerates, often financial men, proved largely incapable of managing the complex and still essentially vertical organizations under them.

When Litton Industries announced its first quarterly earnings disappointment in January 1968, following nearly ten years of 20 percent annual earnings increases, conglomerates as a group slipped 40 percent in market value.

The conglomerates continued to decline and never really recovered. Being generally highly leveraged, high interest rates compounded their profit problems. Tight money in the early 1970s put them at the mercy of frightened bankers who didn't really understand the companies they were lending to. Efforts to restructure organizationally in ways that made them seem less complex didn't fool an investing public that had become somewhat phobic about what Wall Street called "conglomeritis." "Deconglomeration" eventually became the "in" thing, ironically feeding the merger mania and leveraged buyout craze of the 1980s.

IN THE mid-sixties "concept stocks" hit the boards. By now, mutual funds had become important, performance was a big word, and names like Gerald Tsai of the Manhattan Fund had star quality.

By the latter part of the decade, the action was in names like National Student Marketing, Four Seasons Nursing Centers of America (bankrupt by 1970) and Performance Systems, the first two selling at multiples of over 100 times earnings, the third, a franchiser of fast-food chickens, believe it or not, having an infinite multiple because it had no earnings.

Run by promoters rather than real managers, overextended, too rapidly expanded and, in some cases, fraudulent in their accounting practices, the concept stocks joined the high-tech growth companies and the conglomerates in leading the steep market declines of 1969 and 1970, taking a good many of the "go-go" fund managers down with them.

THE 1970S AND THE NIFTY FIFTY

Wall Street entered the seventies like a bear with a bad hangover, pledging never to drink such heady stuff again. Only top shelf from now on—the solid, blue chip stocks with good growth records that could be relied upon not to come crashing down and that, because they would continue their steady growth, could be bought at any price without fear of loss, provided you held on.

By now mutual funds and institutional investors had become dominant. Such "one-decision" stocks appealed to the big guys for another reason: they were large-capitalization companies and the institutions could buy huge positions without upsetting the market.

There weren't all that many stocks around fitting such standards, and the four dozen or so that did became institutional favorites known as the nifty fifty, including IBM, Kodak, McDonald's, DuPont, General Electric, Westinghouse and other Dow stocks, plus names like Xerox, Avon Products, and Polaroid.

Again the institutional managers proved that expertise plus power does not equal sanity. As a general rule, the P/E of a company should equal its annual rate of growth; if the P/E of McDonald's is 18, earnings should be growing at the rate of 18 percent a year. But the pros ignored this rule of thumb and, by the end of 1972, *despite a general market decline,* had driven many of the nifty fifty to multiples nearing 100 times earnings, a far cry from any company's ability to sustain growth.

For a while there was a two-tier market, with the institutional favorites, benefiting from what today would be called a "greater fool" theory, going up while the market in general went down.

When the bear market of 1973–74 settled in, however, the growth stocks, small and large, had their comeuppance, or I should say come-downance; 27 of the nifty fifty dropped an average of 84 percent from their 1971–72 highs. The money managers looking best in those years were those holding cash, the "market timers."

When the market resumed an upward trend in 1975, growth issues lagged and cyclical stocks came into favor. Profiting from what analysts saw as a new era of "pricing power," the basic industries like steel, chemicals, aluminum, paper and copper had a glorious, if short-lived, revival.

By the end of the seventies, the cyclicals were back in a slump, the market was neither here nor there, and the market leaders were the energy issues, because of shortages and higher oil prices stemming from the Arab embargo in 1973; technology issues, including energy-related technology and small "biotech" issues; and defense/aerospace issues, reacting to the Iranian hostage crisis and anticipating a Republican administration.

THE 1980S

The 1979 market continued through 1980, but in 1981, anticipating recession, the market dropped, with energy and technology stocks the hardest hit.

Emerging from the recession, 1983 saw the height of the small-capitalization (often high-tech) stock craze and a flock of money to new issues that was reminiscent of the 1960s, all at the expense of high-capitalization stocks. At the peak, the price/earnings ratio of small stocks as a group enjoyed a premium of two and a half times the Dow's. But the small-stock boom was a flash in the pan, and lots of investors lost lots of money again. While the cyclicals enjoyed a brief rebound in 1983, the star performers in the early eighties were big companies whose "private market values" were low in relation to their market values—in other words, companies with understated book values, which became targets of a wave of hostile take-overs financed by the junk bonds made infamous by Michael Milken of Drexel Burnham Lambert. The buyout craze carried throughout most of the decade, finally winding down and then symbolically ending with Drexel Burnham's bankruptcy filing in early 1990.

Otherwise, the market from 1984 on was characterized by a blue chip rally led by noncyclical, consumer stocks like McDonald's, Coca-Cola, and Philip Morris. Up until midsummer 1990, the Dow continued to reach record levels within flirting distance of the magical 3000 mark. This was true even as the broader market was distinctly lackluster and some of the small-stock indexes were actually showing declines.

Nineteen eighty-nine was a freakish year. The institutions, not totally persuaded a "soft landing" could be pulled off, eschewed the bargains in the Dow, preferring to bid the blue chip growth stocks even higher.

Some market watchers saw in the two-tiered market that prevailed in midsummer 1990 a parallel to the early 1970s and the nifty fifty.

In August 1990 the United States was faced with crisis in the Middle East. The Dow dropped 150 points in two business days as gas lines, stagflation and war with Iraq loomed as serious possibilities. The oil stocks, rising on the prospect of higher prices, were an exception in a nervous market where transportation stocks, vulnerable to higher oil prices, and financial stocks, sensitive to higher interest rates, were especially under selling pressure.

We all know what happened early in 1991. We had and won our war in Iraq, quickly dispatched though it was. We also found ourselves in a certifiable recession, the ninth since World War II, proving that business cycles, deemed obsolete by economists of the "soft landing" school as late as the fall of 1990, were quite alive and well.

THE 1990S

As this is written in mid-1999, one is struck by how short memories are. "Goldilocks economy" may have replaced "soft landing" as the buzzword of the day, but the same complacency, after an unprecedented near decade of steady economic growth without significant inflation, impelled Fed Chairman Alan Greenspan recently to remind us that the economic laws explaining past business cycles had, to his knowledge, "not been repealed."

When *Beating the Dow* was last revised in 1991, I wrote, "Up until midsummer 1990, the Dow continued to reach record levels within flirting distance of the magical 3000 mark." If 3000 was magical, what do you call the 11,000 level at which the Dow sits today? A few thousand points ago, Mr. Greenspan called it "irrational exuberance," but when investors reacted with what looked for a minute like a return to rationality, Greenspan mellowed his rhetoric to keep the financial markets on an even keel. On it went.

It's interesting to look back at the previous summaries of market conditions during decades since the 1960s and see how history repeats itself.

The "tronics boom" in the early 1960s that sent stocks like Control Data to multiples of 200 clearly has its counterpart in today's Internet (or "internut," as one wag put it) craze that has seen companies without earnings trade at multiples over 1000. This market bubble, unfairly broad-brushed as "technology," seems to be collapsing, and to the extent it takes some of the market's overvaluation with it, that is good.

"Deconglomeration" in the late 1970s, which fed the merger mania of the 1980s, similarly has its analogy in the downsizing, back-to-basics, and consolidation trends of the 1990s. This round, however, is less concerned with undoing dubious "synergies" than with debt reduction, a management focus on market share rather than diversity, and consolidation in industries where overcapacity has resulted in price pressure and narrowed profit margins. That's also good, especially because it benefits the basic industry companies still substantially represented in the Dow.

The parallel most irresistible, though, has to be the 1970s and the "nifty fifty." It's worth turning a few pages back and reading that section again. Highly overvalued high-capitalization growth stocks leading a "two-tiered market" despite a general market decline—it's all eerily familiar.

Of course, there are important differences, too. While some of the nifty fifty were pushing multiples of 100 times earnings, the highest P/E in the Dow today is Coca-Cola's 47 times, followed by Wal-Mart's 40 and nine others in the 30s. And some of the similarities work in our favor. Then as now, values in the cyclicals and basic industry stocks were ignored as the nifty fifty became more overpriced. But when the correction occurred, those undervalued stocks became winners. My system actually made money in the worst bear market since the Great Depression.

But the stock market remains seriously overvalued, in my opinion. The Dow's overall P/E of 25 is way out of line with its historical average P/E of 15. Its price-to-book-value ratio of 6.7 is much too high, even adjusting for the fact that intellectual property now accounts for a much greater portion of overall asset value today than plant and equipment. Likewise, the overall Dow's dividend yield of 1.6 percent, when anything under 3 percent has traditionally signaled an overpriced market, is worrisome, even allowing for the more tax-efficient diversion of cash to stock buybacks.

Will we see another 40 percent–plus correction like we had when the nifty fifty collapsed in 1973? If you buy the concept of regression to the mean, and I do, it is certainly not out of the question.

Whatever happens, you should make out by following the strategies in *Beating the Dow*. In fact, it has been in lackluster markets that my methods have really shone brightest. From 1972 to 1984, when the Dow went virtually sideways with a total return of just 120 percent, my Basic Method (five-stock) portfolio returned 853 percent.

While we may see a sustained resurgence of the long-neglected small-capitalization stocks, there's no reason that has to be at the expense of the blue chips, which the institutions have to hold because their liquidity needs can only be met with high-capitalization stocks.

HOW DOES a contrarian like me look back at the years just discussed? With sweet nostalgia.

Some time back, I prepared for my clients, mainly for their information but also for fun, a piece based on my collection of headlines. The following will give you the idea:

In August 1982 the Dow Jones Industrial Average was at 780. Here were some of the headlines in the financial press:

Dark Days on Wall Street
Managers Skittish on Stocks
Wary Outlook for Stock Rise
A Time to Stay on the Sidelines
Running Scared from Stocks
An Analyst's Bearish View

In June 1983 the Dow had risen to 1250. Here were the headlines then:

Time Is Now for Playing Stock Market
Year of the Bull
Happy Birthday, Bull Market
Return of the Mutual Funds
Money Managers Still See Gains Ahead
Pension Funds Loading Up on Stocks

In June 1984 the Dow was down to 1079. The headlines:

Correction Expected to Continue
Wall Street Firms Retrench
What Happened to the Stock Market?
Few Stocks Pierce the Gloom
A Downtrend Seen for Prices
Bull Dead in a Gloomy Market

Within months the Dow began a record-breaking six-year advance that would take it to the brink of 3000. Following a short pause in 1990, it began its almost continuous ascent to over 11,000 in the first half of 1999.

PART IV

BEATING THE DOW

INTRODUCTION

"ENGINE CHARLIE" Wilson was only partly right when he said that what's good for General Motors is good for the country.

Competition, employment, productivity, quality—in these respects the business world and the world at large have the same agenda. Corporations try to analyze and anticipate how people will think and behave, and to varying degrees they succeed. But they will always fall short, have setbacks affecting their share prices and finances, and require some time to adjust.

At those junctures, the majority of investors overreact. A few, recognizing the difference between real and perceived risk, have the opportunity to profit.

Change is inevitable. Problems are inevitable. Companies are vulnerable, but the biggest and best of them also have survivability. The best stocks to invest in are of companies that know how to survive.

In the following chapters of *Beating the Dow,* I'll show you how to structure your own Dow stock portfolio.

The inevitability of individual stock price fluctuations and of market cycles raises two obvious questions: If companies are essentially sound and growing, isn't one way to beat the market simply to buy stocks and hold them? And since the stock market is cyclical, aren't there times when one should be in stocks and other times when one should be out? The answer to both questions is yes, but.

Buying and holding has the attraction of no ongoing commission expense, no management fees, deferred capital gains taxes, no risk of losing out on a stock dividend or a split, and no demands on your time.

But there are several problems with a buy and hold strategy. The first is your own possible need for liquidity. Although it would, of course, be unwise in the extreme to put your reserve for emergencies in common stocks, conceivably some circumstance could develop where you'd need to convert your stocks to cash. You might then find yourself faced with the choice of selling your best performers or taking a loss on stocks that are temporarily under-performing. A buy and hold strategy is an option only if you are prepared to do just that—to buy and hold and not to sell until some point fairly far in the future.

The second and more important problem is that even the most well-selected stocks would probably produce returns inferior to those possible with an actively managed portfolio.

Common sense would dictate that your buy and hold portfolio be chosen from quality stocks having the best earnings prospects. Earnings prospects are evaluated by those people having the greatest expertise and access to corporate information selection, namely Wall Street security analysts.

A fixed portfolio requires inhuman prescience to structure initially and is, by definition, unresponsive to changing market conditions. It is therefore vulnerable to significant deterioration of company prospects, a problem active portfolio management can avoid.

The following report in the May/June 1987 *Financial Analysts Journal* by Michelle Clayman of New Amsterdam Partners speaks of the futility of predicting earnings:

   The bestseller *In Search of Excellence* by Thomas J. Peters and Robert H. Waterman, Jr. profiled companies that had been identified as "excellent" on the basis of outstanding financial performance as ranked by several measures of profitability and growth. This article examines 29 of the companies and finds that their financial health—as measured by the same ratios—began to decline virtually across the board starting right from the date on which they were selected as "excellent." Furthermore, 39 companies ranked at the bottom by the same ratios showed widespread improvement over the next five years.

Over the next five years, a portfolio of 29 "excellent" companies wound up with 18 underperformers and 11 outperformers. It beat the S&P by 1% per year. A portfolio of the "unexcellent" companies ended up with 25 outperformers and 14 underperformers. It beat the S&P by over 12% per year.

So the "worst" companies did a whole lot better than the "best" companies! It's a comment on the value of Wall Street earnings forecasting, which somebody described as "a science that makes astrology look respectable." (I'd prefer to say that Wall Street analysts are highly professional people who work in a very inexact science.)

Beating the Dow–Basic Method outlines the simplest method of outperforming the Dow. It uses a combination of the highest-yielding and least expensive stocks to structure a five-stock portfolio. Its portfolio has done over five times better than the unmanaged Dow over the last 26 years, a period that included a bear market, a sideways market, and a bull market. Also described is a one-stock strategy that did over 17 times better than the Dow over the same period.

For more conservative investors, the Basic Method also includes a ten-stock high-yield portfolio that did better than three times the Dow over the same period. *Each of these three strategies involves reviewing and updating your portfolio once a year and fastidiously and deliberately ignoring it in between.*

Out-of-favor stocks in the Dow universe have produced superior returns. You can get these returns because you have two advantages over the pros. One is the freedom to operate in a universe as small as the Dow stocks. And you also have the freedom to take a truly disciplined approach. Discipline does not mean long-term. It means buying and selling on your time-table, not one dictated by clients.

Beating the Dow–Advanced Method is for those of you with a taste for thickening the plot. It should also fascinate stock followers with an interest in the research I have done on the Dow stocks, since it shows how contrarian strategies that have been applied successfully to other universes work out when applied to the Dow. Each of the advanced strategies produces superior returns and outperforms the Dow. Several reduce risk and variability of returns. But be prepared for some surprises. Complexity is *not* necessarily better; when dealing with the Dow stocks, the best strategy is simplicity itself.

CHAPTER 6

Beating the Dow—Basic Method

TEN SIMPLE STEPS TO SUPER RETURNS

HERE ARE ten simple steps to extraordinary returns:

Step 1: Determine Your Equity Fund

The very first order of business is deciding how much money you can set aside for investing in common stocks. Remember, stocks fluctuate even if they generally grow with time, so we're not talking about the food money, the cash set aside for emergencies, or even the money you plan to use for a child's college education if the need is short term (three years or less).

This is not a book about financial planning, critical though that subject is. You should be prepared either by yourself or with the help of a financial planning expert to:

1. analyze your circumstances—what you own, what you owe, what you have coming in, and what you spend;
2. determine your major financial goals—buying a home, financing education, starting a business, providing for vacations, your retirement;
3. prepare a budget—a *realistic* projection of income and

expenses that provides for *essential* needs, such as medical and life insurance, for a reserve for emergencies (one rule of thumb is two months' income), for savings toward your financial goals and—important, and the reason why most budgets are unrealistic—for the day-to-day *luxuries* you allow yourself.

When you have determined the amount of money that is *not* essential to the maintenance of your lifestyle, you have identified the amount of money appropriate for equity investments.

There is another, more subjective, consideration, which is your *emotional* ability to take risks. The fancy term for this is your "risk comfort level"; investment professionals like to measure it in terms of how "risk-averse" you are.

It's a very important concept, but like most things, it doesn't have to be as complicated as it sounds. I like to think of it as simply the sleep factor. You know yourself whether or not you tend to be a worrier. If you wear a belt and suspenders and still worry about your pants falling down, you'd be better off in government bonds or a money market fund. If you're a compulsive gambler, you'd be happier at the racetrack (but much better off getting help). If, like most of us, you're somewhere in the middle range, all it involves is deciding whether you are more comfortable with a one-stock, five-stock, or ten-stock Dow portfolio; greater diversification means more safety and somewhat lower returns.

Step 2: Open a Discount Brokerage Account

One of the beauties of the strategies we'll be using is that all the advice you need for your equity investments is in *Beating the Dow*. That means you can avoid the relatively high commission rates charged for full service at major brokerage firms by opening a discount brokerage account. The selection of brokers offering discount services is constantly widening. Traditional full-service brokers are getting into discounting. There are discount brokers and deep-discount brokers. There are Internet brokers who do nothing but electronic trades, and traditional discount brokers that offer a choice of Internet accounts, touch-tone telephone accounts, and broker-assisted accounts. Competition is fierce, and services are constantly being offered in different combinations. On-line broker commissions may be higher or lower depending on whether real-time quotes are offered free or at extra cost.

A handful of companies, including Exxon/Mobil, Procter & Gamble, and Wal-Mart, offer direct stock purchase plans as a part of their dividend reinvestment programs, making it possible to avoid brokerage commissions The drawbacks here are that you must already own at least one share to qualify (which is going to require a broker), the buy price is usually based on an average of the prices during a recent period (so it may not be the most favorable price), and there is a regular brokerage commission when you sell. These plans are designed to attract buy-and-hold investors, and are really not intended for trading strategies like ours.

Discount brokers offer no investment advice, although research can be obtained through many of them. Basically, they are all computerized operations, and where brokers are involved, they are on salary rather than commission. Most handle orders for Treasury and other bonds, options, and other securities. Many, but not all, will set up self-directed IRAs or Keoghs.

A listing with valuable information about discount brokers is available for $4 from the American Institute of Individual Investors, 625 North Michigan Avenue, Chicago, IL 60611, (312) 280-0170 (www.aaii.org). On-line brokers are rated by Gomez Advisors, a private membership organization, 55 Old Bedford Road, Lincoln, MA 01773, (978) 287-0095 (www.gomezadvisors.com).

They vary in the range of products they sell and in the extent of their basic service; some, for example, sell mutual funds, others do not; some accept telephone orders and provide quotes 24 hours a day, seven days a week, others do so only during regular business hours. Some allow you to request a specific account representative (unless you're a member of a lonely hearts club, you can probably do without this); others put you through to the next available representative.

Because of such differences in basic service, however, the rate structures of discount brokers vary widely. Since our strategies require only the most basic of service, you can choose from among the least expensive discount brokers.

Some Internet brokers advertise commissions that seem almost too good to be true. By all means check them out, but just make sure they aren't charging you extra for services that are free elsewhere. A $4 fee for postage and handling, for example, can make a $14 transaction cost $18. There can also be a hidden cost in the form of poor executions. Trades executed on a primary exchange like the New York Stock Exchange can save ⅛ per share over trades routed through the "third market." That's $0.125 per share, or $1.00 for every eight shares traded. Some on-line brokerages use the third market exclusively. Others that may charge a little more go to pains to find the best price available. Charles Schwab and Company, for example, has an electronic system that "works the order" to ensure it gets the best execution.

A larger question about Internet brokers concerns their ability to execute orders in a market crash. Normally, orders are executed in seconds, but a sudden correction of 10 percent or more might cause Web site freezing and costly trading delays in some cases. The nascent Internet trading industry simply hasn't been put to that test.

Most discounters have minimum commissions ($25 or more). Ironically, if you plan to spend less than $1,000 on a particular stock, you may be better off at a full-service broker! They generally don't have minimums and their higher commission rate plus the usual extra charge for odd-lot trades (under 100 shares) may actually amount to less than the discount broker's minimum charge.

It pays to shop!

Commissions decline as volume increases. The cost of transacting 5,000 shares of a $50 stock would cost from $150 to $750 or more at firms on the list of the least expensive discount brokers. That's quite a difference, but the typical full-service broker would charge much more—close to $2,000 for that $250,000 trade.

Another thing to note is that the cheapest broker in one transaction category (number of shares at a particular price level) is not necessarily the same firm as the cheapest broker in another transaction category.

You should figure out in advance how much money you expect to spend on how many shares and shop a list of discounters to see who's cheapest in that category.

The annual turnover (number of stocks bought and sold) will vary with the different strategies we'll be discussing. But you can figure that if you are spending a total of $5,000 on five stocks, you should be able to keep your annual transaction cost down around 3 percent, or $150.

When you get under $5,000, commission costs become a higher percentage of the value because of the minimums that apply. You might consider getting a group of friends or relatives together and pooling your funds to get the benefit of lower transaction costs.

A few other tips on discount brokerage accounts:

• Verify that the broker is SIPC-insured. That stands for Securities Investor Protection Corporation, an organization funded by member broker–dealers that insures customer accounts up to $500,000 (there's a limit of $100,000 on cash) against loss due to failure of the discount broker. The law requires that brokers have this insurance; it's a good way to verify that the broker is legitimate.

• Most discount brokers prefer that securities left with them be registered in "street name"—that is, in the name of the firm as opposed to your own name. This is simply a practical procedure to facilitate buying and selling and presents no problem, assuming the broker has SIPC insurance.

• You may be asked to choose between a cash account and a margin account. The latter, which typically requires a deposit of $5,000 in cash or securities, enables you to borrow up to 100 percent of the value of your stock to buy additional stock.

The cost of borrowing on margin is as little as ½ percent to 1 percent above the "broker call loan rate" listed in the financial pages. Moreover, it is fully tax-deductible. There is a risk, since if the market value of your collateral declines more than 25 percent, you will be forced to come in with more cash or sell enough stock to bring the margin to the minimum maintenance level (which can be higher than 25 percent, depending on the firm's policy). This is the dreaded margin call.

Buying on margin can make a lot of sense if you know what you're doing but can be a real trap if you don't. You can make twice as much or lose twice as much. If you already know about margin buying, you probably don't need any caveats from me. If it's coming as news to you, do yourself a favor and wait a while before you get into margin buying.

You may have no choice but to open a margin account, since many brokers won't accept cash accounts. That doesn't mean, however, that you have to use it to borrow. There may be times when you will want to use the privilege just as a convenience, to facilitate a transaction that you are planning to settle in cash.

Margin borrowing privileges are also available for general borrowing needs as a feature of *asset management accounts* offered by some firms. Such accounts, which usually require minimum account balances, also typically provide credit card and checking privileges as well as automatic crediting of income and sales proceeds to an interest-paying money market account.

• Find out what the firm does with cash that flows into your account, either from the sale of stock or from dividends. Discounters will usually pay interest on credit balances, but they may require minimum balances before they do so. Ask.

Our investment return calculations assume full investment of principal and reinvestment of dividends, but in practice you may have the option of being paid out cash on request, having dividends paid to you according to some weekly or monthly payment arrangement, reinvesting cash, or keeping a cash balance in a cash management account of some sort. You should decide what you want done and make sure the firm is equipped to accommodate you.

To open an account just dial the 800 number of the broker and ask for the forms. Or use the Internet.

Discount Brokerage Firms

Below is a sampling of discount brokers and their rates. All are SIPC-insured. They were selected at random among several hundred discount brokerage companies around the country. It is quite possible your local bank offers discount brokerage services. Each broker has its own commission structure and range of services. Rates and services are subject to change and should always be confirmed. As I said, it is quite possible that the broker least expensive for a transaction of a given number of shares and dollar amount would not be the least expensive for a transaction involving different quantities and dollars. The brokers below were asked three questions: What would be your commission to buy or sell 20 shares of a $50 stock? How about 5000 shares of a $50 stock? What is your minimum charge?

		Price per Share: $50.00		
Broker		*20 Shares*	*5000 Shares*	*Minimum*
Brown & Company	BA	$12.00	$12.00	$12.00
One Beacon Street	TT	5.00	5.00	5.00
Boston, MA 02108	I	5.00	5.00	5.00
(800) 225-6707				
Fidelity Brokerage				
Services, Inc.	BA	59.00	250.00	59.00
161 Devonshire Street	TT	38.35	162.50	38.35
Boston, MA 02110	I	25.00	105.00	25.00
(800) 533-8666				
Quick & Reilly, Inc.	BA	37.50	332.00	37.50
120 Wall Street	TT	33.75	298.80	33.75
New York, NY 10005	I	30.38	268.92	30.38
(800) 221-5220				

(Continued)

| | | Price per Share: $50.00 | | |
Broker		20 Shares	5000 Shares	Minimum
Charles Schwab & Co.				
Inc.	BA	47.00	430.00	39.00
101 Montgomery Street	TT	42.30	387.00	35.10
San Francisco, CA 94104	I	29.95	149.95	29.95
(800) 435-4000				
Muriel Siebert & Co. Inc.	BA	37.50	150.00	37.50
444 Madison Avenue	TT	33.75	135.00	33.75
New York, NY 10022	I	14.95	94.95	14.95
(800) 221-3154				
Waterhouse Securities,				
Inc.	BA	35.00	583.70	45.00
100 Wall Street	TT	31.50	525.33	31.50
New York, NY 10005	I	12.00	12.00	12.00
(800) 934-4430				

BA = Broker Assisted
TT = Touch Tone Phone
I = Internet

Step 3: Prepare a Portfolio Planning Worksheet

For this you'll want to buy a pad of accounting paper at your stationery store.

As pictured in Figure 2, list the Dow stocks alphabetically next to their symbols in the lefthand columns numbered (1) and (2). The symbols will help you make sure you're looking at the right stock when you turn to the newspaper stock tables. We'll also be using them as shorthand from time to time as we discuss the different stocks.

FIGURE 2

1 Symbol	*2* Dow Stock	*3* Closing Prices	*4* Yield	*5* Hi-10	*6* Lowest Price
T	AT&T	75¾	1.7		
ALD	AlliedSignal	44 5/16	1.4		
AA	Aluminum Company of America	74 9/16	1.3		
AXP	American Express	102½	0.9		
BA	Boeing	32⅝	1.7		
CAT	Caterpillar	46	2.6	✓	X
CHV	Chevron	82 15/16	2.9	✓	
C	Citigroup	49 11/16	1.4		
KO	Coca-Cola	67	0.9		
DIS	Disney	30	0.7		
DD	DuPont	53 1/16	2.6	✓	X
EK	Eastman Kodak	72	2.4	✓	
XON	Exxon	73⅛	2.2	✓	
GE	General Electric	102	1.4		
GM	General Motors	71 9/16	2.8	✓	
GT	Goodyear Tire & Rubber	50 7/16	2.4	✓	XX
HWP	Hewlett-Packard	68 5/16	0.9		
IBM	International Business Machines	184⅜	0.5		
IP	International Paper	44 13/16	2.2		
JNJ	Johnson & Johnson	83⅞	1.2		
MCD	McDonald's	76 13/16	0.5		
MRK	Merck	147½	1.5		
MMM	Minnesota Mining & Mfg.	71⅛	3.1	✓	X
JPM	J.P. Morgan	105 1/16	3.8	✓	
MO	Philip Morris	53½	3.3	✓	X
PG	Procter & Gamble	91 5/16	1.2		
S	Sears, Roebuck	42½	2.2		
UK	Union Carbide	42½	2.1		
UTX	United Technologies	108¾	1.3		
WMT	Wal-Mart Stores	81 7/16	0.4		

(The illustration includes two stocks, AlliedSignal and Union Carbide, that were in the Dow as of December 31, 1998, but were involved in pending mergers as this was being written. AlliedSignal was slated to merge with Honeywell Inc. (HON) to become Honeywell International, and Union Carbide was acquired by Dow Chemical Co. (DOW). The original stocks are shown because they would have been used as the basis for your 1999 portfolio selection, and once selected, would have been held throughout the year. Obviously a Portfolio Planning Worksheet prepared now would include the current list.

In addition, seven stock splits and one spin-off occurred (so far) during the year and would have to be taken into account when tallying the results at the end of the year. AT&T split three-for-two and Alcoa, IBM, McDonald's, Merck, United Technologies, and Wal-Mart all split two-for-one. In late May 1998, General Motors spun off Delphi Automotive Systems, Inc. (DPH), with GM shareholders receiving 0.69893 percent of a Delphi share for each share of GM. That proportionate value of Delphi became a part of the GM total return for the year.

None of the above, however, affects the worksheet being illustrated, which would have been based on values as they appeared December 31, 1998.)

Following the form used in Figure 2, label column (3) "closing prices," column (4) "yield," column (5) "Hi-10," column (6) "lowest price" and column (7) "execution price."

This worksheet is your annual overhead equivalent of Merrill Lynch Pierce Fenner & Smith's brokerage, research, and economics departments, so keep it away from the dog and kids.

Step 4: List the Closing Prices

Open the *Wall Street Journal,* the *New York Times,* or another paper with a comprehensive business and financial section and turn to the New York Stock Exchange Composite listings. All the Dow industrials are listed on the New York Stock Exchange except Microsoft and Intel which are listed under NASDAQ National Market Issues.

Figure 3 shows the *Wall Street Journal* listings in its January 4, 1999, edition, which reported closing prices as of the last trading day of 1998. The research material we will be reviewing in the next chapter that documents total returns for Beating the Dow–Basic Method is based on year-end to year-end closing prices.

(The calendar year-end cutoff needn't be used unless it happens to satisfy your sense of organization. There may actually be an advantage to avoiding the ends of quarters, which is when unit investment trusts based on the system tend to do their buying and selling. The important thing, as we'll see, is the discipline of buying stocks that meet certain criteria at a given point in time, and replacing them 12 months later (adding a few days to make sure you meet the 12-month holding period required to benefit from the more favorable long-term capital gains tax rate) with whatever stocks meet the criteria then, ignoring anything that happens in the interim. This discipline explains the outperforming returns. It shouldn't matter what 12-month period is used.

With a highlighter, underline or circle each of the Dow stocks (using the stock symbol to be sure you're not confusing Coca-Cola Enterprises with Coca-Cola Company or that sort of thing) so you can easily find them for later reference.

Now transfer the closing prices (those in the newspaper column headed "last") to column (3) of the worksheet next to the appropriate stock.

These are the prices you will use as the basis for your portfolio selection after we have performed the next few steps.

Step 5: List the Yields

Transfer the numbers in the newspaper column under the heading"Yld" (1.4 for AlliedSignal, 1.3 for Alcoa, and so on) to column (4) of the worksheet.

FIGURE 3

NEW YORK STOCK EXCHANGE COMPOSITE TRANSACTIONS

Stock	Symbol	Div	Yld	Sales 100s	Hi	Lo	Last	Net Chg	Pct Chg
AlliantTech	ATK		...	144477	83 1/16	55	82 7/16	+ 26 11/16	+ 47.9
AlldHldg	AHI		...	44810	24	10	14 3/8	− 4 3/4	− 24.8
AlldIrishBk	AIB	1.76e	1.6	71222	110 3/4	57	110 3/8	+ 52 3/8	+ 90.3
AlldPdts	ADP	.16	2.5	68630	25 3/16	5 7/8	6 5/16	− 17 5/8	− 73.7
AlliedWaste	AW		...	f28896	31 5/8	16 1/8	23 5/8	+ 5/16	+ 1.3
AlldSgnl	ALD	.60	1.4	f36810	47 9/16	32 5/8	44 5/16	+ 5 1/2	+ 14.2
AllmericaFnl	AFC	.20	.3	442737	75 1/4	38 3/8	57 7/8	+ 7 15/16	+ 15.9
AllmrST	ALM	.80	7.2	17135	11 3/8	10 5/16	11 1/8	+ 5/16	+ 2.9
Allstate	ALL	.54	1.4	f41209	52 3/8	36 1/16	38 1/2	− 6 3/4	− 14.9
Allstate QUIBS		1.78	7.0	64831	26 1/4	24 1/2	25 3/8	+ 7/16	+ 1.8
AllstFng QUIPS		1.99	7.7	53646	26 3/4	25 1/16	26	...	...
Alltel	AT	1.22f	2.0	f15398	61 3/8	38 1/4	59 13/16	+ 18 3/4	+ 45.7
Alltel pf		2.06	.7	8	292	250	292	+ 55	+ 23.2
Alltrista	ALC		...	30882	29 1/4	19	24	− 4 3/8	− 15.4
Alpharma A	ALO	.18	.5	261101	36 15/16	18 15/16	35 5/16	+ 13 9/16	+ 62.4
AlpineGp	AGI		...	130504	22 1/4	13 1/8	15	− 3 3/4	− 20.0
Alstom ADS	ALS		...	52309	34 1/16	19	23 1/4	− 10 3/4 h	− 31.6
AltosHrn ADR	IAM		...	4457	12	2 7/8	3 7/16	− 8 3/16	− 70.4
Alcoa	AA	1.00a	1.3	f24175	81 1/4	58	74 9/16	+ 4 3/16	+ 6.0
Alza	AZA		...	f19213	54	30 13/16	52 1/4	+ 20 3/8	+ 64.2
AmbacFnl	ABK	.40	.7	608321	65 15/16	40 7/8	60 3/16	+ 14 3/16	+ 30.8
Ambac deb	AKB	1.77	7.0	47882	26 1/8	24 1/4	25 3/16	+ 7/16 h	+ 1.8
AmcastInd	AIZ	.56	2.9	68309	24 1/2	13 7/8	19 1/8	− 3 13/16	− 16.6
Amdocs	DOX		...	312683	17 1/2	8 3/16	17 1/8	+ 3 1/8 h	+ 22.3
AmerHess	AHC	.60	1.2	861206	61 1/16	46	49 3/4	− 5 1/8	− 9.3
Amerco pfA		2.13	8.2	25217	27 1/4	24 5/8	26	− 1/2	− 1.9
Ameren	AEE	2.54	6.0	756723	44 5/16	35 9/16	42 11/16	− 1/8 h	− .3
AmFstMtg	MFA	.80e	17.5	34351	9 15/16	4 5/16	4 9/16	− 4 9/16 h	− 50.0
AmOnline	AOL		...	f164490	160	20 5/8	155 1/8	+ 132 1/2	+ 585.6
AmWestAir wt			...	155342	19 1/8	3	7 1/2	...	...
AmWstHldg B	AWA		...	f11237	31 5/16	9 9/16	17	− 1 5/8	− 8.7
AmAnnuity	AAG	.10	.4	29834	25 1/4	21 3/4	23	+ 1	+ 4.5
AmAnuty TOPrS		2.32	9.0	6198	27	25	25 7/8	− 7/8	− 3.3
AmBkNtHolo	ABH		...	183316	18 7/16	4 3/4	17 1/2	+ 9 h	+ 105.9
AmBkrsIns	ABI	.48f	1.0	f12211	66 1/16	30 1/8	48 3/8	+ 2 7/16	+ 5.3
AmBkrsIns pf		3.13	3.1	55716	133 7/16	65 1/2	100	+ 6 5/8	+ 7.1
AmBknote	ABN		...	117765	5 1/4	1 1/4	1 7/16	− 3 13/16	− 72.6
AmBusnPdts	ABP	.66f	2.8	51860	24 1/8	16 1/16	23 1/2	+ 1 7/8	+ 8.7
AEP	AEP	2.40	5.1	f10196	53 5/16	42 1/16	47 1/16	− 4 9/16	− 8.8
AmExpress	AXP	.90	.9	f42680	118 5/8	67	102 1/2	+ 13 1/4	+ 14.8
AmExpress pfA		1.75	6.9	130994	26	24 1/4	25 5/16	+ 3/8 h	+ 1.5
AmFnlCap TOPrS		2.28	8.7	10449	27 1/8	25	26 1/8	− 15/16	− 3.5
AmFnl	AFG	1.00	2.3	179183	45 3/4	30 1/2	43 7/8	+ 3 9/16	+ 8.8
AmGen	AGC	1.50	1.9	f12385	79	52 5/16	78	+ 23 7/8	+ 44.3
AmGen pf		2.57	4.0	7678	65	45	65	+ 18	+ 38.3
AmGenl MIPS A		2.11	8.1	24774	26 9/16	25 5/8	26 1/16	− 1/4	− 1.0
AmGenl MIPS B		2.03	7.9	18946	26 1/2	25 1/4	25 11/16	− 1/4	− 1.0
AmGenDE MIPS		3.00	3.0	33324	98 3/4	67 1/2	98 3/4	+ 27 3/4	+ 39.1
AmGreetgs	AM	.76	1.9	622278	53 3/4	35	41 1/16	+ 1 15/16	+ 5.0
AmHlthProp	AHE	2.18	10.6	108367	29	19 7/8	20 5/8	− 6 15/16	− 25.2

Step 6: Identify the Hi-10

Now put a checkmark in column 5 beside the ten highest yields in column 4. Here you may find several stocks with the same yields competing to make the cut. This happens because the newspapers round yields to the first decimal. Thus, in Figure 2, Exxon, International Paper, and Sears all have yields of 2.2, but only Exxon is checked as one of the ten highest yielders. The apparent tie was resolved by doing the arithmetic for the three stocks. Here's how that is done:

Yield is the annual dividend divided by the price. You'll find the annual dividend in the same newspaper table where you found the yield. In *The Wall Street Journal,* it is in the column headed "Div," just to the left of the column headed "Yld." For example, in Figure 3, AlliedSignal's annual dividend is shown as .60 (60 cents). To get ALD's exact yield, we want to divide 60 cents by ALD's price, which is 44⅚₆.

But first we have to convert ALD's price into dollars and cents. The dollar part is easy—$44—but the ⅚₆ has to be converted from a fraction into a decimal by dividing 16 into 100, then multiplying by 5. In this example, ⅚₆ comes out to .3125. ALD's yield is thus its annual dividend—.60—divided by its price—$44.3125—which comes out to 1.3540197. *The Wall Street Journal* rounded that off to 1.4, but if ALD were in contention for the Hi-10 (which it wasn't) and tied with others, we'd have to use the figure carried out to additional decimals.

Figure 4 will save you the trouble of converting fractions to decimals.

FIGURE 4

Conversion of fractions to cents (decimals)

$\frac{1}{16}$ = .0625	$\frac{9}{16}$ = .5625
$\frac{1}{8}$ = .125	$\frac{5}{8}$ = .625
$\frac{3}{16}$ = .1875	$\frac{11}{16}$ = .6875
$\frac{5}{16}$ = .3125	$\frac{13}{16}$ = .8125
$\frac{3}{8}$ = .375	$\frac{7}{8}$ = .875
$\frac{7}{16}$ = .4375	$\frac{15}{16}$ = .9375

Getting back to our worksheet, we have to determine which of the three stocks, Exxon, International Paper, or Sears, all sharing the same rounded yield of 2.2, was actually the highest.

Exxon's annual dividend, according to the newspaper stock tables, was $1.64. Its price was 73⅛. Using Figure 4 to convert the fraction, XON's price is $73.125. Dividing that into $1.64, we get 2.242735.

International Paper's annual dividend was $1.00 and its price 44¹³/₁₆, which converts to $44.8125. Dividing dividend by price, we get 2.231520.

Sears's dividend was $0.92 and its price 42½; $42.50 divided into $0.92 equals 2.164705.

The winner? Exxon. In this case, the others didn't make the cut, so we didn't check them off.

What if two or more stocks were to remain tied even after doing the arithmetic? In that unlikely event, choose the stock with the lowest price. If the prices are the same, it's your call.

Step 7: Identify the Lowest-Priced High Yielders

In column (6), put an X next to the five checked stocks with the lowest closing prices. You have now identified the five stocks combining the highest yield with the lowest price.

Put a second X next to the second lowest-priced high yielder. You have now identified the Penultimate Profit Prospect, or PPP (penultimate means next to last), which I'll get more into later.

Step 8: Select Your Portfolio

You now have your choice of three strategies.

1. *Ten highest-yielding stock portfolio* This portfolio of the ten stocks identified with checks is the most conservative alternative since it provides the most diversification. The more stocks there are, the less vulnerable the portfolio is to a decline in one or more individual stocks.
2. *Five high-yield/lowest-priced stock portfolio* Identified by single Xs, this portfolio offers five- rather than ten-stock diversification. It has the incidental advantage of requiring less capital because of fewer stocks and lower prices.
3. *Penultimate Profit Prospect (PPP)* This is not, strictly speaking, a portfolio, but rather a single stock, the second lowest-priced high yielder. There is method in this seeming madness, but you'll have to wait until the next chapter to see it.

Step 9: Place Your Order

Once you have decided which of the above suits your wallet and temperament, placing your order is as simple as picking up the phone and dialing your discount broker's 800 number or turning on your computer and accessing your on-line broker. Most brokers will accept payment on purchases by check between the trade date and the "settlement date," which is five days later. Some firms, however, require that sufficient funds be in your account at the time your order is executed. You should check into this.

However many stocks you buy, you should buy an equal dollar amount of each. This is conventional practice in portfolio management and is the assumption underlying the returns we'll be looking at, but it also enhances returns, since lower-priced stocks, which tend to register greater gains, are bought in greater quantity.

The simplest and easiest way to order stock is to place a market order, in effect instructing the broker to make the transaction at the prevailing market price—the best price the broker can get for you at that time.

You may, however, want to consider placing a limit order. This can protect you against the order being executed (actually transacted on the floor of the stock exchange) at an unfavorable price (as could happen in a volatile market), but you run the risk that the order will go unexecuted if the market price fails to hit the price specified in your order.

For example, if you look at the sample worksheet (Figure 2), Caterpillar turns up in the five high-yield/lowest-priced portfolio at a closing price of 46. You decide to go with that portfolio and thus will be buying Caterpillar, or CAT. But already a few days have passed since CAT closed at that price, and who knows what will happen to its price today?

There are two things you can do. In both cases, you would ask the broker for a quote on CAT. If it's currently still trading at around 46 or so or at a price that is acceptable to you, you can place a market order and be pretty well assured that in the few minutes it normally takes to execute a Dow stock trade it will be executed at or near that price.

If, however, the price has risen or you have reason to think you'll get a poor execution (if the market is going haywire when you call), you can place a limit order instructing the broker to execute the order only if the price dips to 46 or better. Limit orders can be placed for a day, a week, a month or can be placed on a "good till canceled" basis. They can be used on the sell side as well, in which case you tell the broker to execute only if the price rises to the limit price or better.

My feeling is that the degree of protection against volatility afforded by limit orders is not significant enough, and our returns are significant enough, that the risk of a market order is preferable to the risk of having the order not executed.

You may be tempted to place a *stop-loss* order, but I strongly advise against doing so. A stop-loss order, which becomes a market order to sell when a stock's price declines to a level specified by you, is designed to protect against losses, but you may find yourself selling out a stock that is merely fluctuating and that will have a net gain for the period over which returns are being measured. The dramatic returns we will soon be reviewing were achieved using discipline and no such tampering. Let's keep it simple.

Whatever type of order you place, you should get confirmation to ensure there is no misunderstanding.

Normally, a broker will confirm the price while you are still on the telephone or on-line. The execution price should be entered in column (7) of your worksheet. That will be your basis for calculating price changes a year later.

Step 10: Take Stock and Revamp

Here's where we fast-forward to a year later, reach again for the worksheet, take the newspaper and list the closing price at period's end in column (8). The difference between the prices at which the order was originally executed and the closing prices at the end of the period (the selling prices of stocks replaced) plus dividends received during the year equals your total return for each stock.

About restructuring and rebalancing:

You're now ready to structure your portfolio for the coming year by starting a new Portfolio Planning Worksheet and following the same steps just described. Normally you can expect to replace two or three of the stocks in the five-stock portfolio and half the ten-stock portfolio. The others will still qualify as high yielders.

The question now arises, how do I start the new 12-month period with equal dollar amounts without getting eaten alive with transaction costs to cover odd lots? Ideally, the capital gains and dividends from the stock you sell should enable you to start the new 12-month period with equal dollar amounts in all five or all ten stocks. Chances are, though, it won't work out that way. Here I advise being practical. Aim for rough dollar equality, but don't get obsessive-compulsive about it. It's not important that the dollar amounts be exactly equal.

To get the portfolio return, the totals for each stock are then added and the sum divided by the number of stocks.

How have the three Beating the Dow–Basic Method strategies performed historically?

For the 26 years from 1973 through December 31, 1998, the three strategies produced the following cumulative total return, excluding commissions and taxes:

1. Ten highest-yielding stocks:	7264%
2. Five high-yield/lowest-priced stocks:	13279%
3. Penultimate Profit Prospect	43177%
Cumulative total return of the Dow Jones Industrial Average for the same 26-year period:	2408%

No magic was performed here. These are the actual cumulative total returns assuming annual review and replacement with stocks meeting the high-yield criteria.

The key to these remarkable returns is discipline—putting the 30 Dow stocks to the same tests year in and year out, selling stocks when they fail to measure up, buying those that do. Come hell or high water.

The low incidence of negative returns is remarkable.

On average, between three and four stocks were replaced each year in the ten-stock portfolio and the turnover in the five-stock portfolio averaged 50 percent. The PPP turnover was 100 percent, with the exception of four zero turnover years.

I don't know about you, but for my money that kind of return from a bunch of stuffy old dividend-paying blue chips ain't bad.

CHAPTER 7

Why High Yield
and Low Price
Work

BEFORE WE consider why high-yield stocks outperform the Dow—and why adding the element of low price enhances your portfolio even more—let's look at a breakdown of our three Basic Method strategies:

TOTAL RETURN* COMPARISONS

Year	PPP	Five High-Yield/ Low-Priced	Ten Highest-Yield	DJIA
1973	73.4%	19.6%	3.9%	−13.1%
1974	−41.7	−3.8	−1.3	−23.1
1975	157.2	70.1	55.9	44.4
1976	55.1	40.8	34.8	22.7
1977	4.3	4.5	0.9	−12.7
1978	1.0	1.7	−0.1	2.7
1979	−10.1	9.9	12.4	10.5
1980	50.6	40.5	27.2	21.5
1981	27.3	0.0	5.0	−3.4
1982	95.3	37.4	23.6	25.8
1983	36.1	36.1	38.7	25.7
1984	−2.8	12.6	7.6	1.1

203

TOTAL RETURN* COMPARISONS *(Continued)*

Year	PPP	Five High-Yield/ Low-Priced	Ten Highest-Yield	DJIA
1985	26.4	37.8	29.5	32.8
1986	29.6	27.9	32.1	26.9
1987	3.3	11.1	6.1	6.0
1988	19.5	18.4	22.9	16.0
1989	12.9	10.5	26.5	31.7
1990	−17.4	−15.2	−7.6	−0.4
1991	185.6	61.9	39.3	23.9
1992	69.1	23.1	7.9	7.4
1993	39.1	34.3	27.3	16.8
1994	−37.4	8.6	4.1	4.9
1995	21.7	30.5	36.7	36.4
1996	28.1	26.0	27.9	28.9
1997	51.8	20.5	21.9	24.9
1998	21.9	12.3	10.6	17.9
Cumulative	43177%	13279%	7264%	2408%
Average Annual	26.3%	20.7%	17.9%	13.0%

*Excluding commissions and taxes, as throughout book.

First, some observations on our two portfolios, leaving aside the PPP momentarily:

The five-stock portfolio outperformed the Dow in 18 out of 26 periods, better than two-thirds of the time. It lost money only in 1974, when it was down just 3.8 percent while the Dow was off 23.1 percent in the midst of an historic bear market, and in 1990, when Iraq invaded Kuwait, the single instance where it lost more than the Dow.

Of the eight years it underperformed the Dow, two—1978 and 1979—were virtually even (within a percentage point or so) with the average.

In only six years, 1989 and 1990 and 1995 through 1998, did the five-stock portfolio significantly underperform the Dow. In

1989 consumer stocks that had seemed fully valued going into the year surprised everybody: Coca-Cola was up 73 percent, Philip Morris 64 percent, and Procter & Gamble 61 percent, for example. So it wasn't that the yield strategy didn't work in 1989. It in fact produced a very respectable 10½ percent return. It was that the Dow in general went through the roof, with stocks like the aforementioned leading a 32 percent return!

Same thing in 1995 through 1998. As observed earlier, a handful of dangerously overpriced growth stocks elevated the price-weighted Dow to an average gain of 27 percent, while our undervalued (translate "low-downside") high-yielders turned in a mere 22.3 percent. As the late ivory tickler Liberace used to say, we cried all the way to the bank.

Continued economic uncertainty was compounded by impending war in the Persian Gulf in 1990, making it an aberrational year. The Dow, especially our economically sensitive cyclicals, began declining after the Middle East crisis erupted in late summer. The exceptions were the same consumer growth issues that had led 1989, now bid even higher, plus the oil issues, which of course rose because of the crisis.

But after Stormin' Norman did his good work, our 1991 portfolios, 70 percent carried over from 1990, turned in the second-best performance in our history. Both the decline and the rebound were led by Goodyear, which plunged 52.5 percent in 1990 and gained a staggering 185.5 percent as 1991's PPP.

THE TEN-STOCK (Hi-10) portfolio produced less dramatic returns than the five-stock portfolio but was generally equal in the consistency of its outperformance.

In the losing years, 1974 and 1990, the ten-stock portfolio was down less than the five-stock portfolio and in 1974 substantially less than the Dow's overall 23 percent decline. It underperformed in only eight of the 26 periods (including a negligible loss in 1978). In the 1995–1998 period, the ten outperformed the five with a 24.3 percent return.

In both portfolios, but especially in the five-stock portfolio, there were years when the outperformance was particularly striking (see Appendix B).

A WORD about the Penultimate Profit Prospect, which I've defined as the second lowest-priced stock of the ten highest yielders.

Here's the detail on it, with the Dow's performance noted as a comparison:

Year	PPP Stock	Total Return	DJIA
1973	Allied Chemical	73.4	− 13.1
1974	Chrysler	− 41.7	− 23.1
1975	Woolworth	157.2	44.4
1976	International Harvester	55.1	22.7
1977	American Can	4.3	− 12.7
1978	Goodyear	1.0	2.7
1979	U.S. Steel	− 10.1	10.5
1980	U.S.Steel	50.6	21.4
1981	Goodyear	27.3	− 3.4
1982	Sears	95.3	25.8
1983	Exxon	36.1	25.7
1984	Chevron	− 2.8	1.1
1985	Goodyear	26.4	32.8
1986	Texaco	29.6	26.9
1987	Union Carbide	3.3	6.0
1988	Primerica	19.5	16.0
1989	AlliedSignal	12.9	31.7
1990	AlliedSignal	− 17.4	− 0.4
1991	Goodyear	185.6	23.9
1992	Union Carbide	69.1	7.4
1993	Union Carbide	39.1	16.8
1994	Woolworth	− 37.4	4.9
1995	Chevron	21.7	36.4
1996	Chevron	28.1	28.9
1997	AT&T	51.8	24.9
1998	Philip Morris	21.9	17.9
Cumulative		43177%	2408%

First of all, I wouldn't put my grandmother in one stock. But I'm not doing this just for fun, either; I present this research quite seriously.

It dramatizes that an out-of-favor Dow stock priced low enough has very favorable odds of becoming a winner.

If you have unessential funds, a good set of nerves, and iron-clad discipline, to the extent history is a guide, you can make out with the PPP strategy as the above results clearly show. You might want to consider having two or three portfolios, including the PPP stock.

Why not simply the lowest-priced high yielder? Why select the second lowest? Am I just playing with numbers? No. On the few occasions over the years when a Dow stock got into real financial difficulty, its price tended to drop precipitously before dividend action was taken by the company. That has made it the lowest-priced high yielder. Chrysler, Johns-Manville, Westinghouse, and most recently, Woolworth, are examples. Because of this, the lowest-priced stock has a lower average annual return than the other nine high yielders historically.

So the PPP has tended to optimize the combined dynamics of high yield and low price, while historically avoiding the major disasters, however few and far between.

Why not drop the lowest-priced stock altogether? Because in 22 of the last 26 years, it has outperformed at least one of the other stocks in the ten-stock portfolios, and in 17 it has outperformed the other four stocks in the five-stock portfolios. (In over 25 percent of the years, one of the other stocks has been the PPP.)

WHY HIGH YIELD PRODUCES
OUTPERFORMING RETURNS

Bear with me for a quick review of Equities 101.

A stock's dividend yield—what I'm calling simply yield—is the annual dividend paid by a company as a percentage of its market price. A stock selling for $100 that pays $1 each quarter in dividends has a yield of 4 percent. The major newspaper stock tables give the anticipated yield—that is, they show the latest quarterly dividend multiplied by four and calculate the yield on the assumption that the same dividend will be paid for the ensuing year. We're of course using the same yield and the assumptions that go with it for our purposes.

Not all companies pay dividends, so not all stocks have yields. Stocks that don't pay dividends tend to be either growth companies that plow their earnings back in to finance their faster growth rates or companies that are short on cash. The usual reason for being short on cash is lousy earnings. Earnings, and the anticipated future levels thereof, are the prime determinant of stock prices, whether a company pays dividends or not.

But earnings and cash flow are not the same thing. Earnings are just part of cash flow, or the cash a company actually generates from all its activities (mainly operations, but also borrowed money, or new stock issued and other things done to raise cash).

Earnings and cash flow also differ because accounting rules permit companies to make certain deductions from earnings, such as depreciation of plant and equipment, depletion of natural resources (like an oil well), and the establishment of reserves for bad debts and often contingencies. Because these charges reduce earnings (and therefore taxes) but do not require the expenditure of cash, they are an important factor in differentiating between earnings and cash flow.

Professional stock analysts make a big thing of cash flow per share. Particularly since the law forbids the payment of dividends from capital—that is, it limits dividend payments to earnings or retained earnings—net cash flow (cash left over after obligations requiring cash are satisfied) is important in predicting a company's ability to pay or increase dividends in the future. That has obvious relevance to the value of the stock.

Cash flow explains a reality that is key to the dividend yield strategy: earnings can go down and dividends can go up. What I'm saying, simply, is that stock prices fluctuate with earnings expectations—the investing public has a short-term obsession with earnings—but are ultimately sustained by dividend payments made possible by cash flow. The significance of this will become clearer in a minute.

High yield is a contrarian indicator—a way to identify bargains—because it is telling us that the investing public has doubts about the stock, usually doubts about the company's immediate earnings prospects or about whether it's still eating nails for breakfast financially. What is happening is that the stock price has gotten low in relation to the dividend.

You might ask why, if such uncertainty exists, a company doesn't lower or discontinue its dividend, thereby conserving cash and addressing whatever the problem might be. If we were looking at the London stock market we'd find that is exactly what happens. Even their blue chips regularly adjust their dividends to reflect their earnings.

But American companies have a thing about consistent dividend payment. Annual reports boast of x years of consecutive (if not increased) dividend payments. When real financial problems cause a company to suspend its common stock dividend, it can take years to live it down, to restore the investment community's confidence in the stock as a solid investment.

In the United States the dividend is a sacred cow. A company would do almost anything to avoid lowering or suspending a dividend.

What does all this mean to us? First, the risk of earnings and stock price fluctuations is far greater than the risk of a suspension or lowering of dividends. Historically, dividends have accounted for 40 to 50 percent of the total return on the Dow stocks as a group, so this cherished continuity of dividends is of more than passing importance to Dow stockholders.

In the 26-year period we've been focusing on, none of the Dow stocks in the average as of December 31, 1998, has ever suspended a dividend. Twelve stocks have reduced dividends, in four cases after spin-offs that more than compensated shareholders, and in virtually all cases in cash-saving restructurings that produced

higher capital gains, on average, than high-yield stocks that
didn't cut dividends. The majority have a record of continuous and
usually rising dividends.

This relationship—or nonrelationship, in most cases—of dividends and earnings can be seen by comparing the two statistics as
they are shown for each year in the stock charts that accompanied
our discussions of individual companies.

Look at Boeing, for example. In 1985 BA made 84 cents per
share and paid out 23 cents. In 1995 it made 58 cents, 31 percent
less, and paid out 50 cents, or more than twice the dividend ten
years before. J.P. Morgan's earnings in 1996, 1997 and 1998 were
$7.63, $7.17, and $4.71, respectively. Its dividend payout for the
same years was $3.24, $3.52, and $3.80, respectively. There are
many other examples.

The point can be dramatically illustrated in a larger way.
Barron's has a table each week showing the return on the Dow
Jones Industrial Average as a whole—in other words, treating the
aggregate of 30 stocks the way you'd look at a single company.

It shows that for the period between 1974 and 1985 earnings
went down from 99.04 to 96.11. The Dow Jones Industrial
Average rose, however, from 616 to 1547 during the same
period—not quite tripling, but a major gain.

The key to this seeming contradiction? Dividends. Dividends
nearly doubled during the period, rising from 37.72 in 1974 to
67.04 in 1985. Dividends were driving the market!

The Dow earnings in 1988 were 215.46. During the week of
May 28, 1990, Dow earnings were 207.84. The DJIA at the end of
1988 was 2168.57. It closed at the end of May 1990 at 2820.92—
up 30 percent. Crazy? Not really. Dividends for the period rose
from 79.53 to 113.07—up 30 percent.

As the 1990s have progressed, corporations increasingly have
been using their cash to buy back stock rather than pay out more
in dividends. With fewer shares bidding for the same corporate
earnings, earnings per share increase, giving a boost to share
prices. Instead of getting paid out in dividends, which are taxable
at ordinary rates as they are paid, the investor thus gets compen-

sated in the form of a capital gain that, if it is realized after a year or more, is subject to the favorable 20 percent long-term capital gains tax rate.

This recent development obviously complicates traditional relationships among dividends, earnings, and stock prices, and makes dividends a less important part of total return. It affects our type of stocks because it assumes a large number of shares outstanding, makes most sense when shares are undervalued by the market, and uses cash that otherwise would be paid out in dividends rather than reinvested in growth.

And it has generally been a positive for Beating the Dow portfolios. In raging bull markets led by high-capitalization growth stocks, value stocks, like ours, tend to get sidelined. Massive buybacks in the traditional industrials sector have been a major factor in the strong returns our portfolios have continued to turn in during this two-tiered market period.

But the buyback fad owes its existence to the expansionism of the 1980s combined with the Goldilocks economy and bull market of the 1990s. Downsizing and divesting—getting back to basics—have been the 1990s' reaction to the diversification trends of the 1980s. With robust corporate earnings and proceeds from divestitures providing the funds, and lagging prices of value stocks versus the index leaders providing the incentive, the stock buyback strategy, particularly given its tax efficiency, became a timely if temporary development.

But dividends will resume their traditional importance. Corporations pay and raise dividends to compete for capital. And there is a limit to the amount of stock available for repurchase. Moreover, both cash and stock will be needed to finance the consolidation taking place in industries, such as paper and aluminum, where overcapacity is pressuring profit margins.

The fact that dividends are the driving force in the blue chip segment of the market and that there tends to be a high level of constancy to dividend payments by such companies explains why our yield strategies are not only singularly effective but quite conservative.

WHY LOW PRICE ENHANCES HIGH YIELD

Wall Street has a concept known as the small firm effect. It essentially observes that small stocks register higher percentage gains on average than large stocks.

Small and large refer to market capitalization, but it happens also to be true that smaller-capitalization stocks generally have lower prices than higher-capitalization stocks. That was why, you'll recall, the price-weighted DJIA tended to perform like the broad market value-weighted indexes; big-cap stocks had the highest prices and small-cap stocks the lowest prices, generally speaking.

Much of what is involved in the small firm effect has limited, if any, relevance here: the tendency of smaller firms to have more growth potential; the tendency of smaller companies as a group to include a higher proportion of financially distressed firms, whose price gains are dramatic when their fortunes recover; and the tendency of small firms, again as a group, to be neglected by the analytical community, with dramatic price gains when they are "discovered."

Another factor, and the one of most relevance here, is simply the phenomenon that the less expensive a stock is, the more it is prone to greater percentage moves:

TOTAL RETURN COMPARISON

Year	10 Lowest-Priced	5 Lowest-Priced	DJIA
1973	1.9%	29.0%	− 13.1%
1974	− 14.0	− 3.4	− 23.1
1975	50.7	70.1	44.4
1976	42.3	48.1	22.7
1977	− 9.6	− 12.7	− 12.7
1978	− 8.7	− 3.7	2.7
1979	12.4	13.9	10.5
1980	27.6	32.8	21.4

TOTAL RETURN COMPARISON *(Continued)*

Year	10 Lowest-Priced	5 Lowest-Priced	DJIA
1981	−7.3	4.7	−3.4
1982	23.4	13.2	25.8
1983	55.3	68.0	25.7
1984	−7.9	−20.0	1.1
1985	20.1	13.0	32.8
1986	−3.2	−24.7	26.9
1987	33.6	58.7	6.0
1988	22.1	23.6	16.0
1989	15.9	4.6	31.7
1990	−20.6	−21.0	−0.4
1991	43.3	46.8	23.9
1992	25.5	22.0	7.4
1993	22.2	17.4	16.8
1994	7.7	11.4	4.9
1995	30.4	19.7	36.4
1996	19.5	15.3	28.9
1997	17.6	12.8	24.9
1998	16.8	25.3	17.9
Cumulative	2825.7%	3368.6%	2383.8%

The column showing ten stocks is really there to assure you that we're not just playing with statistics. Ten stocks over a 26-year period is a meaningful sample. And when the five most expensive of those are taken out, the improvement in total returns is formidable.

1. Pick the ten highest-yielding Dow stocks if you want to protect yourself against the remote possibility of three Manville Corporations occurring in one year. (Manville Corporation, formerly Johns-Manville and a Dow stock until August 1982, was the world's largest producer of asbestos. Faced with massive lawsuits alleging the company was responsible for debilitating and often fatal lung diseases, it declared bankruptcy in 1982. Manville stock, which had been as high

as $150 in 1977 (retroactively adjusted), plunged to under $20. The Manville story and its current status is discussed in Appendix A.)

2. Pick the five of the ten high yielders with the lowest prices if you want the cheapest way to buy in to a portfolio providing the highest returns.

And if you're looking for income as well as the safety of blue chips, with the exception perhaps of the PPP in some years, that comes as an automatic part of any basic method.

3. Consider the PPP if you are comfortable without portfolio diversification and want even higher returns and minimal price of admission.

CHAPTER 8

Beating the Dow– Advanced Method

UP FOR something a little chewier? In the following pages I will share some advanced methods of beating the Dow. These strategies are interesting for different reasons.

Several, such as those based on market timing and seasonal phenomena, enhance the Basic Method on a risk-adjusted basis. They would have you invested in stocks only part of the time and in risk-free or lower-risk investments the rest of the time. The advantages include less period-to-period variability of returns, and the virtual elimination of negative returns. Although absolute dollar returns may be lower when compared to a fully invested position, they become superior when adjusted mathematically for the lesser exposure to risk.

Another advanced strategy—investing in stocks with the lowest price to book value ratios—appeals to investors who feel more comfortable relating a stock price to underlying asset values than to earnings or dividends.

Other contrarian strategies that have had well-publicized success in broader stock universes, such as low price to earnings ratios, low price to sales ratios, and prior year poor performers, have, when applied to the Dow universe, beaten the Dow but by lesser margins than high-yield strategies. The explanation for this has been the historical stability of Dow stock dividends and their percentage importance as a part of total returns. Were U.S. companies ever to go to a system (such as that in the U.K.) whereby dividends float with earnings, these strategies could be more effective than those based on dividend yield.

To show that a strategy of investing in stocks with the worst analysts' earnings forecasts not only beats the Dow but beats a strategy based on the best earnings estimates is just too much fun to resist—and it's useful as well. You'll see what I mean.

Investing in Dow stocks with the greatest relative strength is another advanced method that has been highly effective. As we will see, however, it involves trading off some of the peace of mind a larger portfolio would provide.

As a final exercise, I subjected the ten highest yielders to a series of Dow-beating screens in an effort to get the best of all worlds. Such complexity has to enhance our simple methods, right? Well, you'll see.

Read on.

AT THE beginning of *Beating the Dow,* I introduced O'Higgins' Law—there is a natural human tendency to complicate things in direct relationship to their importance.

Look at weight control, to take an example outside the realm of finance and investment. Hundreds of books have been written on complex methods of weight reduction and control. We all know that the way to lose weight is to eat less and exercise more. (Remember the old joke: Place your hands against the dining room table and push.) But who wants to hear it?

The way to accumulate wealth is to work hard and spend less than you make. But who wants to hear that? People would rather pay millions to buy books, tapes and videos and attend expensive seminars claiming to reveal the secret road to riches. The investment field is no exception. In fact, because so many people are worried about money, we probably have more con artists pitching miracle cures for your investment ills than in any other field.

Thousands of stockbrokers, financial planners, investment letter writers, financial columnists, securities analysts, mutual fund salespeople and investment advisers live off an unsuspecting public's belief that the world of finance and investing is beyond their comprehension. Nothing could be further from the truth. The truth is that, for the most part, the activities of investment "experts" are detrimental to investment success.

For those who may still disbelieve, perhaps a brief look at what the investment experts do will show what a waste of time it is to use complex strategies to beat the Dow.

INVESTMENT RESEARCH

Back in 1971, because the company I worked for, Spencer Trask, was considered the number one research firm in the country, there were thousands of institutional investors eager to pay big bucks for the privilege of listening to our analysts. Being young and gullible at first, I bought the party line and went busily around propagating the gospel according to Spencer Trask. There were fifty high-quality growth stocks, the gospel went, that could be bought and held forever regardless of price.

You'll recognize what I'm talking about. It's our familiar nifty fifty, the "one-decision" investment approach that had worked very well since the late sixties and continued to work well through 1972, my first full year in the business. But the past, as I've observed more than once in these pages, is seldom heeded in the investment business, and one should reserve a special wariness for trends of such long duration that they have become confused with permanent reality.

So it was that the 1973–74 bear market went after the nifty fifty with a vengeance. While the Dow Jones Industrial Average lost 47 percent of its value in under two years, many of our "one decision" glamour growth stocks declined by 75 percent or more. Table 8.1 illustrates the debacle.

TABLE 8.1

PERFORMANCE OF TEN ONE-DECISION STOCKS
IN THE 1973–74 BEAR MARKET

Company	1972–73 High	1974 Low	% Decline
American Express	64.75	17.38	− 73.2%
Avon Products	140.00	18.63	− 86.7%
Disney	112.38	15.63	− 86.1%
Honeywell	170.75	17.50	− 89.8%
Howard Johnson	34.88	4.00	− 88.5%
Polaroid	149.50	14.13	− 90.6%
RCA	45.00	9.25	− 79.4%
Simplicity Pattern	176.63	18.00	− 89.8%
Westinghouse Electric	54.88	8.00	− 85.4%
Xerox	171.88	49.00	− 71.5%
		Average	− 84.1%

The shellacking my clients' portfolios took in 1973 and 1974 made me wonder: if we were the best research firm in the country, how did the clients of the worst one make out?

PREDICTING EARNINGS

Most stock analysts believe the way to beat the Dow is to forecast a company's earnings per share. There are different ways of doing this. Some analysts use the top-down or macro method, which looks first at the overall world economy, then at particular countries where the company's products are sold, then at the industry, finally focusing on the individual company. Other analysts prefer a bottom-up or micro method looking only at particular companies without regard to the outside world. In either case, the record of the analytical community is generally pretty dismal.

Looking at the 1973–74 period again (Table 8.2), we see that instead of the continued growth trend so confidently predicted in 1972 to justify price earnings ratios of 46.9, seven of ten "desert island stocks" (as the nifty fifty were also called, because you could be stranded for ten years or more without having to worry about your stock portfolio) had earnings declines of 10 to 45 percent, while the group as a whole saw earnings plummet almost 10 percent. So much for predictable growth.

TABLE 8.2

EARNINGS AND P/ES FOR TEN GLAMOUR GROWTH STOCKS,
1972–74

	1972–73 High	EPS 1972	P/E 1972	1974 Low	EPS 1974	P/E 1974	EPS % 1972–74
AXP	64.75	5.16	12.55x	17.38	6.54	2.66x	26.7 %
AVP	140.00	2.16	64.81x	18.63	1.93	9.65x	− 10.7 %
DIS	112.38	2.62	42.89x	15.63	3.06	5.11x	16.8 %
HON	170.75	4.38	38.98x	17.50	3.93	4.45x	− 10.3 %
HJ	34.88	.90	38.75x	4.00	.81	4.94x	− 10.0 %
PRD	149.50	1.30	115.00x	14.63	.86	17.01x	− 33.9 %
RCA	45.00	2.05	21.95x	9.25	1.45	6.38x	− 29.3 %
SYP	176.63	3.21	55.02x	18.00	1.77	10.17x	− 44.9 %
WX	54.88	2.24	24.50x	8.00	1.57	5.10x	− 29.9 %
XRX	171.88	3.16	54.39x	49.00	4.18	11.72x	32.3 %
	Average		46.89x			7.72x	− 9.32%

In a study we did of analysts' projections for the 30 DJIA stocks between 1973 and 1990, we found an *average* margin of error of 47.5 percent per year (Table 8.3) when comparing what the analysts predicted the Dow companies would earn and what those companies actually reported a year later.

It is not as though we were looking at statistics biased by inexperienced or incompetent analysts. Why do Wall Street analysts, who earn six-figure salaries ranging upwards of $500,000 and have computers and large staffs at their service, do so badly? There seem to be several reasons.

TABLE 8.3

IBES CONSENSUS EARNING ESTIMATES
ANNUAL MARGIN OF ERROR

Year	Margin of Error
1974	off 36.6%
1975	54.1
1976	46.7
1977	25.3
1978	24.2
1979	74.8
1980	42.5
1981	38.4
1982	153.3
1983	42.1
1984	28.0
1985	56.3
1986	60.2
1987	23.5
1988	33.7
1989	26.2
1990	41.0
17-Year Average	off 47.5%/year

One is that, at year end, the analysts don't even know what the accountants will ultimately determine earnings were for the year just ended. In a recent ten-year period, they were off an average of 18 percent, with only two weeks left in the year. How can they accurately predict where earnings are going if they don't know where they've been?

Another reason is their tendency to extrapolate trends from historical earnings experience. This problem has been greatest in the case of cyclical, basic manufacturing companies. Analysts have a poor record of anticipating cyclical downturns and recoveries over the years.

A third, and perhaps most important reason, has essentially to do with conflict of interest. We have had the dramatic example of Donald Trump managing to get an analyst who was negative on the Trump enterprises fired from his brokerage firm—an extreme case, but it serves to point up a more subtle yet pervasive problem, which is summed up well by Thornton O'Glove in *Quality of Earnings:*

> The pressure on analysts to "be positive," particularly when writing up firms which the investment banking part of the firm is wooing, can be intense. This is especially so when the analyst has earlier been positive on the stock. Being negative makes enemies of managements; switching positions can be murder on the brokers and institutional salesmen, those people and fiduciaries with whom customers deal. "If you put out a negative on the stock, people who own the stock hate you. And the people who don't own the stock don't care," was the conclusion of one analyst, while another, who claims never to have issued a sell recommendation in his 20 years of experience in the business, added, "It's very, very difficult to go before fifteen or twenty salesmen at 9:00 A.M. Monday morning and tell them to sell something you were recommending."

The conflict that exists between the brokerage firm as researcher and as investment banker was well illustrated during the high-tech, new issue craze in 1983. According to Zacks Investment Research, a Chicago organization similar to the International Broker's Estimate System (IBES), the balloon burst then not because profits were bad but because they came in so far under expectations. O'Glove quotes Zacks as saying, "The analysts just started out way too optimistic, possibly because they are pushing stocks or have investment banking relationships with their companies."

Analysts also tend to become enamored of the companies they follow. They develop close personal relationships with executives and financial public relations people, who, of necessity, are their prime sources of information.

Analyst company relations are a key factor in the generally

mediocre record the profession has. The Securities and Exchange Commission requires that the same information be available to all analysts, and one way companies protect themselves is to channel a party line through an investor relations representative.

With everybody getting the same numbers, the consequences when the numbers happen to be wrong are obvious.

ADVANCED METHOD #1:
THE TEN WORST EARNINGS ESTIMATES

Where to get the information you need: December Investment Outlook issue of *Business Week* magazine.

What to do:

1. Using extra columns (or pages) in your portfolio planning worksheet, calculate the percentage earnings gains expected by the consensus of Wall Street analysts for each Dow stock.
2. Rank the stocks from 1 to 30, giving a 1 to the stock with the highest estimated percentage gain.
3. Buy the ten *lowest* ranking stocks.

The results: See Table 8.4.

The significance: You outperform the Dow rather impressively, wouldn't you say? But you'd do better with any of the Basic Methods. The significance of this exercise is that it proves the fallibility of fundamental analysis as a tool to predict stock performance. It bears out the value of keeping it simple.

TABLE 8.4

THE TEN DJIA STOCKS WITH THE
LOWEST EPS ESTIMATES

Year	Total Return	DJIA
1973	− 14.51	− 13.12
1974	− 10.52	− 23.14
1975	39.21	44.40
1976	39.15	22.72
1977	− 3.50	− 12.71
1978	− 1.82	2.69
1979	7.99	10.52
1980	29.48	21.41
1981	1.32	− 3.40
1982	9.54	25.79
1983	55.25	25.65
1984	3.91	1.08
1985	42.96	32.78
1986	27.38	26.92
1987	− 14.27	6.02
1988	20.59	15.95
1989	25.34	31.71
1990	− 15.15	− 0.40
1991 (6 mos.)	18.13	12.12
Cumulative	731.05%	559.31%

UPDATE: *Beating the Dow* newsletter tracked the same IBES earnings estimates for the period between 1993 and 1998, with the following results:

Year	Total Return	Annual Margin of Error	DJIA
1993	17.1	NA	16.8
1994	2.6	NA	4.9
1995	49.1	35.1	36.4
1996	18.4	15.7	28.9
1997	30.5	26.1	24.9
1998	4.6	15.1	17.9

Although the analysts turned in a somewhat better showing on average during this most recent period, the annual margin of error, where figures are available, is still unacceptably high. The earnings that analysts have the most difficulty predicting are those of the cyclical stocks and the more traditional industrials. In the 50 percent of time (vs. 42 percent historically) that the strategy underperformed the Dow, the Dow itself was elevated artificially (because of its price weighting) by growth stocks, whose earnings are inherently easier to predict. There is no evidence that analysts' ability to predict earnings has improved.

PREDICTING P/E'S

But even if earnings were predictable, it still wouldn't help us much, because the key variable in the price of a stock—the price to earnings ratio—is even more unpredictable than its earnings.

Let's look at two examples of how useless it would be to know future earnings from either a macro (total stock market) or a micro (individual stock) point of view.

Let's imagine ourselves gazing into our crystal balls at the end of 1965 to determine what the DJIA as a whole would be earning nine years later. Starting with 1965 earnings of $53.67, we see earnings remaining fairly flat until mid-1972 ($58.87) and then taking off—rising 69.4 percent to $99.73 by September 1974, a mere 1¼ years later!

If you had known that the Dow's earnings were going to rise by 85.8 percent over a nine-year period or, even better, by 69.4 percent in only 2¼ years, couldn't you have assumed that stocks were a pretty safe bet with that kind of fundamental support?

Look at what in fact happened. Instead of rising from December 31, 1965, to September 30, 1974, the Dow dropped 37.3 percent from 969.26 to 607.87. In the 27-month period between June 30, 1972, and September 30, 1974, the loss was an almost identical 34.6 percent.

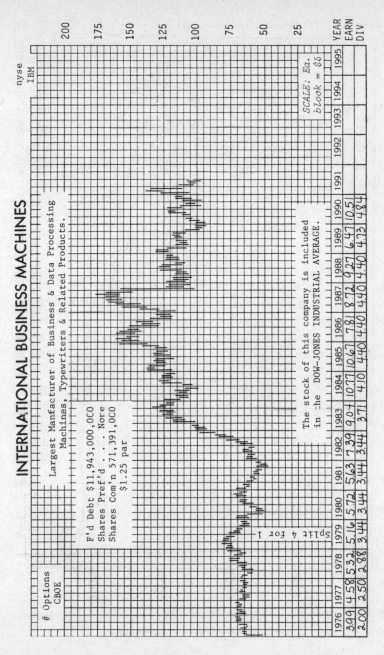

CHART 1

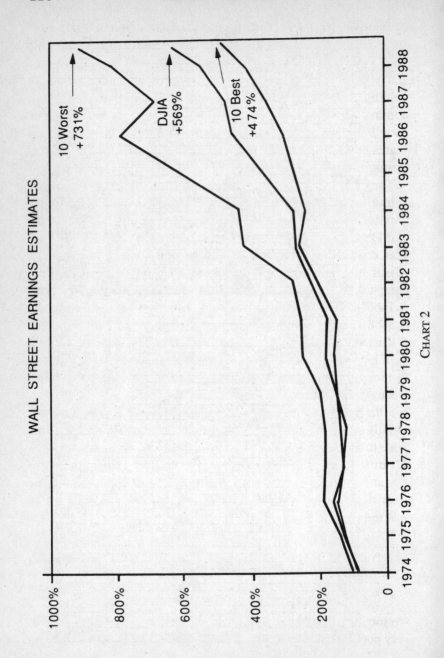

WALL STREET EARNINGS ESTIMATES

10 Worst +731%

DJIA +569%

10 Best +474%

CHART 2

Taking it down to individual stocks, suppose that in early 1973 someone had told you that the earnings for the bluest of blue chip stocks, IBM, were going to more than triple over the next ten years. Wouldn't you have felt pretty comfortable about buying or holding shares in such a fast-growing, high-quality company, one dominating a very attractive industry? As Chart 1 shows, however, poor IBM and its hapless shareholders would have seen their shares erode by 23.8 percent by 1982 in the face of a 235 percent earnings jump!

They say a compass pointing south is as useful as a compass pointing north, as long as you're onto it. The only way I have found to make constructive use of analysts' research is to take the mid-December Investment Outlook issue of *Business Week* each year, compute the percentage earnings gains expected by the consensus of Wall Street stock analysts, then buy the stocks these overpaid soothsayers predict will do worst in the coming year!

Table 8.4 shows what an investment strategy based on analysts' worst estimates would have produced in total returns.

Chart 2 shows that if you had applied the erroneous analysts' indicator between 1974 and 1988, a period that includes a range of economic conditions, you would have made almost twice as much money betting against the experts as betting with them.

Still, however, even though you would have beaten the Dow handily (and 75 percent of the pros), you wouldn't have come close to the returns shown in Beating the Dow–Basic Method.

I trust I've demonstrated the futility of trying to predict earnings and, more importantly, price earnings ratios. How about some other methods we sophisticated investment professionals use to beat the Dow?

VALUE INVESTING

We touched briefly on this approach to investing in Chapter 4. Very popular among analytical types, fundamental value investing is the method made famous by Graham and Dodd, whose book *Security Analysis* is a widely read classic on fundamental analysis.

Value investing attempts to determine the basic value of a company and to compare it with the current market price of the company's stock. "If you can buy a dollar for 40 cents," Ben Graham used to say, "you don't have to worry about what the stock market's going to do." Graham is said to have been fascinated by the fact that the worth of private companies is evaluated in terms of book value, but once a company goes public, attention shifts away from book value to earnings.

The problem with this approach is that value, like beauty, is sometimes in the eye of the beholder. One analyst's bargain may be another's overvalued sale candidate.

One quick way to discover "value" is to look at the ratio of a stock's market price to the value of its net assets, or book value per share.

Unlike the dividend yield and ratio of price to earnings, book value is not shown in the newspaper stock tables. It is, however, easily found in the reports of popular stock services, such as Standard & Poor's and Value Line Investment Survey, which most public libraries have. It is also in *Barron's* and highlighted in corporate annual reports.

Book value per common share is the value of a company's assets less what it owes to various kinds of creditors and less the par value of its preferred stock, divided by the number of its outstanding common shares. The significance of book value is that it is an indication of what the common shareholders, as owners, would have left over for themselves after all the assets were sold or converted to cash and everybody with a prior claim was satisfied. I say "an indication" because book value, when it comes to property, plant and equipment, does not pretend or even intend to measure market value. Such fixed assets are shown at their original cost less accumulated annual depreciation charges. Depreciation is an accounting concept. The government, to encourage companies to keep their facilities modern, allows them to "recover" the cost of such assets by taking annual deductions from their income and thus paying less in taxes.

So the original purchase price of fixed assets is continually reduced until it is either replaced, starting the whole process over again, or gets down to a figure representing salvage value.

My point is that book value, to the extent it reflects fixed assets, is unreal. The resale value of the assets, called liquidation value since such assets are normally sold at auction, could be less if, say, the equipment is obsolete or in really bad shape. On the other hand, with inflation, it may be worth now what it originally cost, or even more. Real estate, particularly, is typically worth much more than its book value because it has actually appreciated while, for accounting purposes, it has been depreciated.

Assets other than property, plant and equipment tend to have book values more closely approximating their market values. Cash is cash, accounts and notes receivable are adjusted for potential losses, so they should be worth pretty close to the book figure. Inventory can be tricky, depending on what it is and the accounting valuation method used, but it has to be reflected at the lower of cost or market value, so it can usually be viewed as a conservative figure.

The bottom line is that book value is not just a meaningless accounting figure. It is, in fact, a pretty good clue to what a company would be worth in liquidation and, where assets have appreciated during the time they were being depreciated, can represent substantial hidden values.

That having been said, it is also true that computerization has made it possible for companies to improve productivity while relying less and less on traditional fixed assets. With companies' ability to generate earnings becoming more reliant on intellectual property and less reliant on physical property, book-value ratios have been allowed to rise much higher than historical levels. Simultaneously, book and liquidation value have to an important extent given way to "breakup" value as the tool that value analysts use to identify stocks that are bargains.

Breakup value, which is also called private market value and takeover value, looks at the aggregate market value of a company if each of its parts operated independently and had its own stock price. The usefulness of the concept does not assume the actual breaking up of companies, although that occasionally happens. Nor does it necessarily assume a company will become a takeover target, although companies whose parts, valued at appropriate multiples, total more than the market capitalization of the company frequently do become takeover targets that attract substantial premiums.

What really gives breakup value its everyday usefulness as an analytical tool is that such possibilities always exist, and also that it is within management's power to unlock hidden value through such commonly used strategies as initial public offerings, spin-offs, split-offs, tracking stock, asset sales, and other strategies.

Unfortunately, determining breakup value involves complex analysis and doesn't easily reduce to a simple ratio like price to book.

Anyway, a portfolio of Dow stocks selected because their price-to-book-value ratios are relatively low has historically beaten the Dow. Table 8.5 shows how the ten Dow stocks with the lowest ratios of price to book value compared with the Dow from 1973 through mid-1991.

Once again, though, we find ourselves with an advanced strategy that beats the Dow impressively but is left in the dust by Beating the Dow–Basic Method.

HALLOWEEN INDICATOR

I'm a golf nut, and maybe that's one reason I'm so fond of a seasonal technique we call the Halloween indicator, so named because it would have you in the stock market starting October 31 and through April 30 and out of the market for the other half of the year. For me it means I can spend half the year working on my slice, and the other half worrying about the market.

ADVANCED METHOD #2:
PRICE TO BOOK VALUE

Where to get the information you need: You will find book value per share in *Barron's* (separate from the stock tables), in corporate annual reports and in the reports of popular stock services, such as Standard & Poor's and Value Line Investment Survey, which most public libraries have. Stock prices, of course, are in the New York Stock Exchange Composite Listings of daily newspapers.

What to do:

1. If a price-to-book-value ratio is not provided, you must compute it. It is simply the market price of the stock divided by the book value per share of that stock.
2. Using a column of your portfolio planning worksheet, list the price-to-book-value ratio of each Dow stock.
3. Rank the stocks from 1 to 30, giving the highest ratio a 1.
4. Buy the ten *lowest* ranking stocks.

The results: See Table 8.5.

The significance: This strategy produces one of the better margins of outperformance, more than doubling the Dow's cumulative total return over the period shown.

Low price to book does not produce returns comparable to our high-yield strategies, but some investors find comfort in the knowledge that the market price of a company is low in relation to the value at which its assets could probably be liquidated

TABLE 8.5

THE TEN DJIA STOCKS WITH THE LOWEST
PRICE-TO-BOOK VALUE RATIOS

Year	Price/Book	DJIA
1973	5.71%	− 13.12%
1974	− 7.15	− 23.14
1975	51.18	44.40
1976	45.22	22.72
1977	− 13.82	− 12.71
1978	− 6.05	2.69
1979	12.45	10.52
1980	22.03	21.41
1981	− 2.40	− 3.40
1982	21.78	25.79
1983	56.91	25.65
1984	− 6.39	1.08
1985	19.79	32.78
1986	6.91	26.92
1987	29.39	6.02
1988	33.36	15.95
1989	21.07	31.71
1990	− 5.00	− 0.40
1991 (6 mos.)	32.67	12.12
Cumulative	1283.39%	559.31%

I ran a series that compared the annual gains in the Dow
Industrial average from 1925 through 1989—just capital gains,
not dividends—for the six months between October 31 and April
30 and for the full year. It revealed that 85 percent of all capital
gains occurred from November to May. The figures, on a compounded annual basis, were 4 percent versus 4.63 percent.

I then took the ten highest-yielding Dow stocks and did calculations that assumed you were invested in them for the six months
between November and May and had your money in Treasury bills
for the other six months of the year. The Treasury bill rate is a

widely available statistic, which is why I used it instead of a money market fund. As a practical matter, money market funds would pay a higher rate, so the figures would look even better.

For the 22 years from November 1977 through June 30, 1998, the ten highest yielders bought and sold on that seasonal basis and including two dividends would have produced a cumulative total return of 3077.9 percent, or 16.9 percent per year. The comparable in-and-out return for the DJIA was 1990.8, or 14.6 percent per year.

Interestingly, the total return on the DJIA if you had simply held it for 12 months each year and not switched to Treasury bills would have been an almost equal 2033.2 percent, or 14.7 percent per year for the same period. What that tells us is that you would not only have gotten your gains from November through May, but you'd have been virtually risk free by being in T-bills for the other six months.

Running the same exercise for a five high-yield, low-priced stock portfolio, our return would have been 4122.9 percent, or 18.4 percent per year, significantly better than the ten high-yield stock portfolio.

Table 8.6 shows a summary of the above data. Significantly, the period covered is one when the DJIA itself rose more sharply than in any period in history.

There are several notable observations to be made about these results, especially when compared with the calendar-year returns shown earlier for the high-yield portfolio alternatives. First, with the exception of 1990, you would have had positive returns in every year, including years when the DJIA had negative returns. Second, there is less volatility—that is, a lesser degree of variance between annual returns. (Statisticians use the term standard deviation.) Third, and perhaps most important: your money is at risk only half the time—T-bills and money market funds are just about risk-free.

Statisticians use mathematical means to make returns comparable on a risk-adjusted basis, and if those methods were applied

TABLE 8.6

HALLOWEEN STRATEGY
INVESTED 11/1–4/30 / T-BILLS 5/1–10/31

Year	DJIA Full Year	DJIA Using Halloween Strategy	10 High-Yield Using Halloween Strategy	5 High-Yield/ Low-Price Using Halloween Strategy
1977	− 12.7%	.9%	15.0%	19.0%
1978	2.7	9.0	11.1	9.8
1979	10.5	16.7	22.6	28.2
1980	21.4	8.0	6.2	6.3
1981	− 3.4	19.5	38.6	32.4
1982	25.8	8.3	9.1	16.0
1983	25.7	32.0	35.3	40.2
1984	1.1	2.9	8.1	17.6
1985	32.8	10.8	13.1	19.4
1986	26.9	36.1	25.5	20.0
1987	6.1	27.2	24.3	17.5
1988	16.0	7.2	10.6	8.7
1989	31.7	19.6	20.4	12.4
1990	− 0.4	1.3	2.6	− 3.2
1991	23.9	22.2	26.1	32.7
1992	7.4	16.2	12.7	25.8
1993	16.8	10.8	20.5	28.3
1994	4.9	5.6	4.5	10.1
1995	36.4	17.8	17.2	18.9
1996	28.9	21.0	24.4	27.8
1997	24.9	19.8	16.0	9.3
1998	<u>17.9</u>	<u>21.4</u>	<u>18.4</u>	<u>20.1</u>
Cumulative	2033.2	1990.8	3077.9	4122.9
Average Annual	14.7	14.6	16.9	18.4

here there would be an astounding benefit to the returns you'd gain using the high-yield strategies (or any of the other strategies we have covered) from November through April and being out of the stock market the rest of the year.

What explains the Halloween phenomenon?

Before I attempt to answer that question, let me explain that market analysts, most notably Yale Hirsch, publisher of the *Stock Traders Almanac* and author of a popular book about seasonality and market timing, *Don't Sell Stocks on Monday,* have exhaustively established that certain months have historically been significantly better for the market than others, some being egregiously bad.

For example, Hirsch has determined that in the 49 years through December 31, 1998, the hottest month has been January, with 1617.19 Dow points gained, and the worst month October, with 604.54 Dow points lost during the same period.

March has historically been lousy but November, December and January consecutively good. And so on. But it would be too hard to switch in and out of all these months. If you kept ducking in and out of the market to avoid months in which the probabilities are against you and took advantage of those with a favorable history, you'd be like a one-armed paper hanger trying to keep track of it all and you'd get eaten alive by commission expense.

I've determined that the best half-year to be in the market is November through April—that period encompasses the best months and avoids the worst months.

Why are some months better than others? There are different but logical theories to explain each month. November, December and to a lesser extent January are good months for capital gains because it is then that new money is put into corporate and private pension funds in lump sums. That money is dollar-averaged into the market over a period of months, creating more buying than selling and thus lifting prices.

April has always been a good month for the market, but it was especially favorable between 1981 and 1987, when everybody could take a tax deduction for money put into Individual

Retirement Accounts (IRAs). Since the 1986 Tax Reform Act was passed, only certain taxpayers are allowed deductions. Everybody can still enjoy the tax deferment of IRA income, though, so there is still a big influx of cash into the market before the April 15 deadline.

What's the bottom line? Using the Halloween strategy every year since 1976, combined with the five high-yield/lowest-priced strategy, would have produced 21 years of steady gains and just one losing year. Over 22 years, you would have done twice as well as the Dow. But it still would have underperformed our fully invested strategies outlined in Beating the Dow—Basic Method.

ADVANCED METHOD #3:
THE HALLOWEEN INDICATOR

Where to get the information you need: This is a market timing method, which can be used with any strategy, although for the best returns you would probably want to combine it with the Basic Method high-yield portfolios.

You would thus find your prices and yields in the newspaper stock tables as of November 1.

From May 1 through October 31, you will be out of the stock market and invested in a money market fund. The yields of such funds are published in the financial sections of newspapers, usually on Thursdays or Fridays.

What to do:

1. Simply perform the same exercise outlined in the Basic Method, except that instead of buying and selling annually, your portfolio is structured as of November 1 and sold as of April 30.
2. An account with a money market mutual fund can be

opened easily, and it is quite likely one is offered as part of your existing discount brokerage arrangement.

The results: Table 8.6 shows the results of applying this seasonal approach to the ten highest-yielding stocks portfolio and the five high-yield/lowest-priced portfolio.

The significance: This method has several advantages over the Basic Method portfolios held for 12 months.

1. With the single exception of 1990, you would have had positive returns in every year, including years when the Dow had negative returns.
2. There is less variability when returns are compared from year to year.
3. Your money is at risk (a money market fund is assumed to be risk-free) only half the time. Although your absolute returns were higher historically on a fully invested basis, your returns on a risk-adjusted basis were much higher using the Halloween strategy.

PRESIDENTIAL ELECTION CYCLE

One of the most reliable market indicators over the years has been the presidential election cycle, and there's an obvious reason why: presidents do their dirty work in the first 1½ years of their administrations and spend the latter 2½ years softening up the electorate for the next election. Since it's the pocketbook issues that usually make the difference, the implications for the stock market are clear.

Figure 5 compares the Dow stocks' performance for the respective stages of presidential administrations going back to the 2½ years at the end of the last Truman administration. It shows that in virtually every administration the market was

FIGURE 5

PRESIDENTIAL CYCLE

Time Period	2½ Yrs In/1½ Yrs Out	D.J. Ind Avg
June 1950–Dec 1952	+39.6%	+39.6%
Dec 1952–June 1954		+14.3
June 1954–Dec 1956	+49.8	+49.8
Dec 1956–June 1958		−4.3
June 1958–Dec 1960	+28.8	+28.8
Dec 1960–June 1962		−8.9
June 1962–Dec 1964	+55.7	+55.7
Dec 1964–June 1966		−0.5
June 1966–Dec 1968	+8.5	+8.5
Dec 1968–June 1970		−27.6
June 1970–Dec 1972	+49.2	+49.2
Dec 1972–June 1974		−21.3
June 1974–Dec 1976	+25.2	+25.2
Dec 1976–June 1978		−18.5
June 1978–Dec 1980	+17.7	+17.7
Dec 1980–June 1982		−15.7
June 1982–Dec 1984	+49.2	+49.2
Dec 1984–June 1986		+56.2
June 1986–Dec 1988	+14.6	+14.6
Dec 1988–June 1990		+32.8
June 1990–Dec 1992	+14.6	+14.6
Dec 1992–June 1994		+9.8
June 1994–Dec 1996	+77.9	+77.9
Dec 1996–June 1998		+38.8
	+3387.3	+4179.2%

weak in the first 1½-year period and strong in the latter 2½-year period.

The exceptions, such as the beginning of the Eisenhower administration and the latter Reagan/Bush period, had their explanations in unusual economic circumstances. From 1952 to 1954—the postwar period—industrial capacity was increasing to meet high consumer demand, and a figure of unprecedented popularity,

Eisenhower, was generating high optimism about almost everything. The strong market in the first years of the second Reagan administration and Bush administration reflect the thrust of a raging bull and confidence that the government had finally mastered the art of managing economies and mitigating the effects of unfavorable economic cycles.

Prior to the Eisenhower era, the only bad presidential year in 175 years was 1931, when the market slide that had begun in 1929 was nearing its bottom.

But now we've had this unprecedented stretch of economic growth, low inflation, and rising stock prices under President Bill Clinton, and as this is written in the summer of 1999, there seems to be no stopping it.

I'm certainly not convinced that we've seen the end of economic cycles, and neither is Fed Chairman Alan Greenspan, who's being credited for adept stewardship. But it's sure done a number on our presidential cycle strategy. Back in 1990 the middle column totaled +1610.5 percent and the right-hand column totaled +1277.2 percent. That's the way it would look under normal conditions.

ADVANCED METIIOD #4:
PRESIDENTIAL ELECTION CYCLE

Where to get the information you need: This is another market timing method that uses the same information and produces the best results when applied to the Basic Method high-yield strategies.

What to do: Simply follow the procedures for structuring the high-yield portfolio you prefer, but be invested in the stock market only in the last 2½ years of a presidential administration.

In the other (first) 1½ years, put your money in a money market fund.

The results (pre-Clinton): See Table 8.7

The significance: This method has the advantages of consistently positive years (only one was negative) when the ten- and five-stock yield portfolios are used. Although returns beat the Dow impressively, they are inferior on an absolute basis to the fully invested strategy. Again, however, you are at risk only a portion of the time. On a risk-adjusted basis, you are better off with this seasonal method.

TABLE 8.7

TOTAL RETURN COMBINING PRESIDENTIAL CYCLES
WITH BASIC METHOD, 1973–1991

Year	PPP (2nd Lowest Price of 10 (PPP) High-Yield)	5 High-Yield/ Low-Priced	10 High-Yield
1973	6.93%	6.93%	6.93%
1974	8.00	8.00	8.00
1975	157.24	70.07	55.87
1976	55.08	40.79	34.81
1977	5.12	5.12	5.12
1978	7.18	7.18	7.18
1979	−10.08	9.91	12.37
1980	50.57	40.53	27.23
1981	14.71	14.71	14.71
1982	10.54	10.54	10.54
1983	36.05	36.11	38.73
1984	−2.82	12.64	7.64
1985	7.72	7.72	7.72
1986	6.16	6.16	6.16
1987	3.33	11.06	.61
1988	19.46	21.43	26.14
1989	8.37	8.37	8.37
1990	−17.42	−15.22	−7.58
1991 (6 mos.)	78.28	37.63	21.25
Cumulative	2506.16%	1707.58%	1192.36%

YEAR-END TAX LOSS VICTIMS AND THE JANUARY EFFECT

Year-end tax selling is another opportunity to profit with the Dow stocks. Taxable investors look for stocks to sell at year end in order to create tax-deductible losses, and they ain't about to sell their best performers.

That means you can make out by identifying the year's poorest performers (the 12-month high-lows in the newspaper stock tables are a quick way of doing it, but it's better to track them from the end of the last calendar year) and buying these tax-loss "victims" before the final day on which, for tax purposes, profits can be taken for the year.

My studies show that for the last 24 years, the Dow's five worst losers rose an average of 4.9 percent during the two-week period between that December deadline and the fourth trading day in January.

There are other factors, in addition to tax selling, that explain this phenomenon. Since most corporations and money managers operate on a calendar-year basis, the end of the year is also the time for "window dressing" done by realizing capital gains or simply getting stocks with poor results out of the year-end portfolios. Corporations and individuals also tend to sell stock for the purpose of raising holiday cash for bonuses and for holiday spending. Since such seasonal selling depresses prices without altering the fundamentals of the stocks concerned, bargain hunters (like you and me) are there in early January to take profits.

ADVANCED METHOD #5:
YEAR-END TAX LOSS VICTIMS
AND THE JANUARY EFFECT

Where to get the information you need: Most stock tables show 12-month highs and lows along with daily prices.

Actually, the tax deadline was changed to year-end a few years ago, so what we've been doing is identifying the losers as of November 30, buying them on December 15, and selling them in on the first business day of the new year or thereabouts.

What to do:

1. Using your portfolio planning worksheet, rank the stocks in order of how far they have dropped from their 12-month highs or how badly they've performed between January 1 and November 30.
2. Buy the five worst losers around December 15.
3. Sell these stocks before the fourth business day of January.

The results: For the last 24 years, the Dow's five worst losers rose an average of 4.9 percent during the above two-week period. Annualized, that's some return!

The significance: This seasonal timing technique has a history of producing profits in the Dow universe. The tendency of stocks to decline in late December and rise in the first days of January can also be used to time purchases and sales when using the Basic Method strategies.

MEDIA INDEX

When headlines scream bull or bear or magazine covers picture one or the other, you are well advised to run in the opposite direction. In June 1990 *Barron's* ran a picture of two bears with a headline that read: "Endangered Species: Bears in a Bull Market." The only thing I could make of that was confusion and uncertainty, which did seem accurately to describe the market's mood then.

Of course, like almost everything else, the media index has lost some of its relevance during the momentum-driven bull market of the 1990s. Which isn't to say investment advisors are unanimously bullish. As somebody put it, this market has a lot of fully invested bears. But nobody wants to be accused of missing the train, so ads have tended to be noncommital rather than negative.

In January 1999, *Barron's* cover showed a bull and a bear anxiously holding a crystal ball. The headline was simply "Outlook '99." No help there.

I get a lot of magazines and all the financial newspapers, so I have made something of a game of using them as a contra-indicator. For example, back in October 1983, I happened to notice one Saturday morning that seven publications had headlines announcing the bankruptcy of the airline industry. I could hardly wait until Monday morning. I bought four airline stocks when the market opened. Between October 3, 1983, and February 27, 1985, I had made 57 percent on the four stocks. The Dow in the same period had gained 4 percent.

In 1984 headlines proclaimed doomsday for the nuclear utilities industry. I bought the best nuclear plays and between October 25, 1984, and February 27, 1985, gained 16 percent while the Dow gained 4.5 percent.

In November 1980, the name of the game was oil. Buy, buy, buy said one headline after another. I did a little short selling on that occasion and was rewarded with a 25.3 percent decline between November 21, 1980, and April 26, 1983. While the oils were plummeting, the Dow was gaining 21 percent.

The October I booked my short-sale profits, the headlines almost to a fault said get out of oil. I bought. Between October 26, 1983, and February 27, 1985, my oil stocks gained 10.3 percent and the Dow gained 5.9 percent.

I could go on and on. Headlines announcing the Death of Equities in August 1979 were followed by a 57.7 percent gain in the Value Line composite index between then and April 30, 1983. When Rebirth of Equities was the headline in April 1983, the Value Line started a decline of 6.6 percent until December 31, 1984.

In his bestseller *Winning on Wall Street,* analyst and adviser Martin Zweig describes his *Barron's* ads indicator. He counts the number of bullish and bearish ads that appear weekly in *Barron's,* the most popular medium for ads placed by investment advisers.

Actually it's more a matter of keeping track of how many or how few bullish ads there are, since advisers know that bearish ads don't pull. Zweig figures if you can count as many as 20 bullish ads, you're probably looking at a bear market. If you count seven or fewer bullish ads and any bearish ads, consider buying. The ads are a reflection, he reasons, of two important areas of sentiment: the advisers themselves, and the investing public as the advisers read it.

ADVANCED METHOD #6: MEDIA INDEX

Summary: This contrarian timing method relies on such indicators as magazine covers, newspaper headlines and ads placed by investment advisers, primarily in *Barron's.*

It is the least scientific of our advanced methods, but if it gives you a clear reading of market psychology you can make out like a bandit by acting the opposite way.

TACTICAL ASSET ALLOCATION

This strategy had been very much in vogue in the years leading up to the first edition of *Beating the Dow,* having gotten a boost when most asset allocators avoided the October 1987 crash. It involves shifting percentages of portfolios among stocks, bonds or cash, depending on the relative attractiveness of the respective markets.

For example, if the tactical asset allocator's model indicates that stocks are expensive relative to bonds or Treasury bills, he will sell some or all of his stocks and put the proceeds into bonds and/or T-bills.

A relatively easy way for an investor to assess the relative attractiveness of those three markets would be to compare current rates on high-grade bonds to the earnings yield of the DJIA. These figures are all published in *Barron's.*

A strategy using this calculation at every year-end since 1972 and shifting 100 percent of the portfolio from stocks to bonds when *Barron's* 10 Best Grade Bonds yielded more than the earnings yield of the DJIA and then reversing the procedure when the opposite was true would have outperformed the Dow but (you guessed it!) underperformed Beating the Dow–Basic Method. Table 8.8 tells the story as it was in 1990 and I am leaving it intact.

I have since done considerable research into the question of using bonds, zero coupon Treasury bonds (which are a fairly recent development), Treasury bills, and stocks as part of an individual investment strategy aimed at maximizing return and minimizing risk under different market conditions.

I have developed an approach that produces remarkable returns when back-tested, and it is the subject of my second book, *Beating the Dow With Bonds,* published by HarperCollins in 1999. Since the approach discussed in that book would come under the rubric of tactical asset allocation, I take this opportunity to refer interested readers to it.

TABLE 8.8

TACTICAL ASSET ALLOCATION COMBINED WITH BASIC
METHOD, 1972–1991

Year	2nd Lowest Price of 10 High-Yield (PPP)	5 High-Yield/ Low-Priced	10 High-Yield Total Return
1973	1.14	1.14	1.14
1974	− 41.70	− 3.75	− 1.28
1975	157.24	70.07	55.87
1976	18.65	18.65	18.65
1977	4.29	4.47	.93
1978	1.01	1.65	− .13
1979	− 10.08	9.91	12.37
1980	50.57	40.53	27.23
1981	27.25	.01	5.02
1982	95.26	37.36	23.58
1983	4.70	4.70	4.70
1984	16.39	16.39	16.39
1985	30.90	30.90	30.90
1986	19.85	19.85	19.85
1987	− .27	− .27	− .27
1988	10.70	10.70	10.70
1989	16.23	16.23	16.23
1990	6.78	6.78	6.78
1991 (6 mos.)	6.10	6.10	6.10
Cumulative	1659.29%	1116.87%	846.57%

ADVANCED METHOD #7:
TACTICAL ASSET ALLOCATION

Where to get the information you need: Barron's will give you
the figures you need: 1) the current earnings yield on the Dow
Jones Industrial Average; 2) current rates on high-grade corporate bonds.

What to do:

1. Compare the two above figures at the end of each year.
2. If *Barron's* 10 Best Grade Bonds are yielding more than the DJIA, put your entire portfolio in bonds.
3. If the Dow is yielding more than the best-grade bonds, put your money in the Basic Method strategy of your choice.
4. Repeat the exercise the following year.

The results: See Table 8.8. Where the return is the same for all three Basic Method strategies in a particular year, the portfolio was in bonds.

The significance: You outperformed the Dow, but not the Basic Method fully invested in stocks. To the extent that bonds are safer than stocks, there is an advantage in terms of risk.

OTHER CONTRARIAN STRATEGIES

Almost every investment professional claims to be a contrarian. That's because we all know that in the investment business, at least, it pays to be contrary. I have alluded to contrarianism throughout *Beating the Dow*. A contrarian tries to figure out what the majority are thinking and doing so the opposite path will be clear to see. Since the majority is usually wrong (crowds are stupid, is another way of putting it), a contrarian is more likely than not to beat the Dow. There are, however, some serious practical problems with contrarianism. One is that it's not always that easy to determine what one should be contrary to. It's not as if contrarians had polls or surveys to give them readings on matters of interest. Another is that the majority can be right for a long time before its sheeplike behavior is brought to task. If a majority is right long enough, most contrarians will either be wiped out, lose faith, or lose clients. Usually it is all of the above.

Three easy ways to take a contrarian position successfully are to invest in 1) stocks that have performed poorly, such as a group of the ten Dow stocks that performed most poorly the previous year; 2) the ten DJIA stocks with the lowest P/E ratios; or 3) the ten DJIA components with the lowest price-to-sales ratios. (Price to sales can be viewed as a variation on price to earnings, the rationale being that sales are more constant and less vulnerable to ephemeral "glitches.")

As Table 8.9 shows, all three strategies beat the Dow by a long shot. But they can't lay a glove on Beating the Dow–Basic Method.

TABLE 8.9

THREE CONTRARIAN STRATEGIES 1972–1991

Year	10 Stocks with Lowest Price/Sales Ratio	10 Stocks with Worst Price Performance the Previous Year	10 Stocks with Lowest P/E Ratios Total Return
1973	−18.55%	14.33%	18.29%
1974	−3.54	−7.48	−6.16
1975	57.91	52.30	54.35
1976	47.82	36.99	27.24
1977	−6.14	−16.31	−7.10
1978	1.81	−5.38	2.00
1979	7.60	15.27	15.27
1980	18.14	15.04	21.54
1981	−4.34	−5.55	5.67
1982	18.09	14.40	9.16
1983	59.32	55.31	37.77
1984	−2.77	.05	12.56
1985	21.14	20.29	30.52
1986	1.68	5.45	35.18
1987	16.71	30.94	−16.08
1988	37.00	30.91	30.72
1989	17.96	28.99	14.04
1990	−19.67	−17.02	−18.79
1991 (6 mos.)	29.26	34.83	19.66
Cumulative	836.54%	802.98%	669.85%

ADVANCED METHOD #8:
OTHER CONTRARIAN STRATEGIES

Where to get the information you need:

1. Price earnings ratios are part of the stock tables in the *Wall Street Journal,* the *New York Times,* and other newspapers with comprehensive financial sections.
2. Price-to-sales ratios may have to be calculated. The ratio relates the share price (daily newspaper) to sales per share—the most recently available sales figure divided by the number of shares outstanding.
3. Previous year's performance is calculated by taking the difference between the market price of a share at the beginning of the previous year and the price at the end of the year.

What to do:

1. On your worksheet, rank the Dow stocks in terms of P/E, P/S, and previous year's performance.
2. Structure portfolios comprising the *low* ten stocks in each category.
3. Repeat the exercise the following year.

The results: See Table 8.9.

The significance: These three contrarian strategies have been demonstrated to produce superior total returns in different universes of stocks and are shown here, applied to the Dow stock universe, as a matter of interest.

Again, all outperform the Dow, but none comes close to the Basic Method.

RELATIVE STRENGTH

The flip side of contrarianism is relative strength, also called momentum analysis. This approach to investing monitors potential investments and their price action relative to one another or to some other benchmark or index.

The momentum buyers aim to jump aboard just as the stock is taking off. Unlike the contrarians or the value investors, they want to be where the action is. They don't want to be sitting in dull, listless stocks while other people are thriving on the hot stocks of the moment.

Although there are various ways of measuring relative strength, the easiest method appropriate for the Dow universe is simply to compute the previous two years' percentage changes for each Dow component and then, after adjusting for splits and spin-offs, ranking them in descending order. You would thus wind up with two lists, one for each of the two immediately preceding years. On each list, the stock with the greatest gain would be number 1 and the stock with the greatest loss number 30. A stock that gained in rank from one year to the next would have relative strength percentage changes for each Dow component and then rank them in descending order.

By identifying the stocks in the 5 high-yield/lowest-priced portfolio that were gaining relative strength, I obtained the results shown in Table 8.10.

The total return, a cumulative 16,175 percent for our 26-year period, is the best any advanced strategy has produced. Its limitation is that because we are applying the relative strength test to five stocks, not all of which necessarily had gains, it results in portfolios ranging in size from one to three stocks. Again, you may prefer the greater security of a larger portfolio.

An investor willing to risk single stock exposure for any length of time would probably prefer the significantly higher return of the Penultimate Profit Prospect discussed in Beating the Dow–Basic Method.

TABLE 8.10
RELATIVE STRENGTH ANALYSIS

Year	Total Return 1 to 3 Strongest of 5 High-Yield/ Low-Priced	DJIA
1973	51.02%	− 13.12%
1974	8.00	− 23.14
1975	77.48	44.40
1976	39.10	22.72
1977	3.21	− 12.71
1978	− 6.72	2.69
1979	− 12.09	10.52
1980	39.23	21.41
1981	27.25	− 3.40
1982	95.26	25.79
1983	42.71	25.65
1984	13.92	1.08
1985	15.53	32.78
1986	32.22	26.92
1987	5.92	6.02
1988	10.93	15.95
1989	5.52	31.71
1990	6.08	0.40
1991	29.7	23.9
1992	40.6	7.4
1993	25.8	16.8
1994	11.2	4.9
1995	7.8	36.4
1996	22.2	28.9
1997	10.8	24.9
1998	<u>13.7</u>	<u>17.9</u>
Cumulative	16175%	2408%

ADVANCED METHOD #9:
RELATIVE STRENGTH

Where to get the information you need: Relative strength rankings are published in the stock tables of *Investor's Daily* but are related to all stocks and are not as useful as other methods for ranking the Dow stocks relative to each other. Our method simply uses the beginning and ending prices for each year, available in newspapers and stock guides.

What to do:

1. Compute the previous two years' percentage changes for each Dow component, ranking them in *descending* order. Stocks that gained in rank between the two years have relative strength.
2. Referring to the portfolio planning worksheet where you did your Basic Method calculations, identify those stocks in the five-stock, high-yield/low-priced portfolio that were gaining relative strength.
3. Structure a portfolio of the identified high-yield/low-priced/relative strength stocks.

The results: See Table 8.10.

The significance: This portfolio produced a cumulative total return of 16.175 percent, the best return of any strategy we have considered, with the exception of the Basic Method PPP.

The drawback here is that by the time you have purified a five-stock portfolio in terms of relative strength, you wind up with a portfolio ranging in size from one to three stocks.

Since this means there will be years when you have no diversification, isn't PPP with its 43.177 percent return preferable?

MULTIPLE SCREENING

It is natural to wonder what would happen if the portfolio strategies that have beaten the Dow most impressively were combined, theoretically taking the best of each world and creating sort of a contrarian cocktail, with a twist of relative strength.

I did this exercise by taking the ten highest yielders each year, screening them using price to book, price to earnings, price to sales, worst earnings estimates, and relative strength, and giving each stock a score.

For example, take General Motors in 1989, which had a score of 4. In addition to being a high yielder, it also qualified in terms of worst earnings estimates (one point), low price to book (two points), low price to earnings (three points), and low price to sales (final score, 4 points).

Tallying everything up for the 18½ years, I took the five top scorers for each year. Since I included ties that occurred in some years, I wound up with portfolios ranging from five to seven stocks.

Table 8.11 shows the result—a cumulative total return nearly four times the Dow.

But Beating the Dow–Basic Method, put through the wringer, emerges victorious.

The final lesson of *Beating the Dow* is that analysis beyond a point becomes counterproductive. In investing, simplicity beats complexity.

ADVANCED METHOD #10:
MULTIPLE SCREENING

Where to get the information you need: This method combines six separate strategies already covered, so the data you need have been compiled.

What to do:

1. Start with your basic list of the ten highest-yielding Dow stocks.
2. Refer to your price-to-book value portfolio, and put a checkmark next to the high yielders that also appear as low P/B stocks. Any stock with a checkmark now has a score of 1.
3. Refer to your price-to-earnings portfolio and put a checkmark next to the high yielders meeting the ten lowest P/E criterion.
4. Do the same thing with your price-to-sales portfolio.
5. Check off any high yielder that was gaining relative strength.
6. Refer to your ten worst earnings estimates portfolio and put a checkmark next to any high yielder appearing on it.
7. Identify the five highest scorers (the highest possible score is 5), including additional stocks where there are ties.

The results: See Table 8.11.

The significance: Although it produces the small advantage of a sixth or seventh stock in some years, the total return on this most complex of portfolio strategies—one that theoretically should combine the best of worlds—is inferior to our Basic Method five-stock high-yield/low-priced portfolio.

TABLE 8.11

5–7 SURVIVING
HIGH-YIELDERS* 1972–1991

Year	High-Yield+ Total Return
1973	18.36%
1974	−5.96
1975	56.26
1976	37.76
1977	4.47
1978	−.05
1979	5.56
1980	33.09
1981	2.11
1982	31.70
1983	43.36
1984	3.53
1985	31.12
1986	30.98
1987	4.88
1988	30.61
1989	22.96
1990	−21.92
1991 (6 mos.)	<u>34.25</u>
Cumulative	2022.42%

*Ten highest yielders were screened using five additional criteria. Highest scorers (including ties) produced a portfolio of five to seven stocks.

Conclusion

HAD YOU invested in super-safe 30-year U.S. government bonds between 1972 and 1974, the worst bear market since 1932, your portfolio would have declined 16.57 percent.

Had you been holding the Beating the Dow–Basic Method five-stock high-yield/low-priced portfolio during that historic bear market, you would have had a positive total return for the two years of 12.50 percent.

The blue chip companies with their vast resources and profit incentive were making the adjustments required to survive and prosper in difficult times.

IT'S WIDELY acknowledged that the investment alternative with the greatest wealth-building potential is common stocks. But common stocks have discouraged many individual investors because of their volatility, particularly in recent years, and because the professional establishment has led people to believe that investing is too complex a business to be left to the average person.

The result has been that individuals seeking the returns available only through common stocks have flocked to mutual funds and investment advisers of various sorts.

But as we have seen, 95 percent of these professionals fail to match, much less beat the market.

In *Beating the Dow,* I have demonstrated how the individual investor can consistently outperform the market and most professionals by rather awesome margins using the simplest investment methods with the most conservative common stocks.

The key to these returns has been buying these stalwart stocks when they are inexpensive relative to each other—when the institution-dominated investing public has, as is typical, over-reacted to an earnings forecast or a news development and made a strong stock cheap. Of equal importance has been the individual investor's ability to follow a disciplined approach rather than having to respond to the quarterly expectations and liquidity requirements of a client community.

Beating the Dow has demonstrated the efficacy of its simple strategies going back to 1973, a 26-year period that has encompassed bear, bull and sideways markets, as well as moments of frightening volatility. This historical experience has proved that buying the highest-yielding Dow stocks year in and year out outperforms the Dow in all kinds of markets. Indeed, by automatically enforcing a contrarian discipline, the strategies in *Beating the Dow* actually capitalize on the volatility institutional trading causes.

Mutual funds and other professional investors, who must operate in a larger universe of stocks and have high overhead and limited flexibility, cannot enjoy the rich benefits of my simple, conservative investment approach.

In turbulent economic times, there is always talk of a flight to quality, referring to a movement of funds from investments of a more speculative character to those offering greater safety. With equities, this means the blue chips. *Beating the Dow* doesn't fly to quality; it begins and ends there.

While the long-range investment potential of these viable companies is virtually certain, short-term profit opportunities can be exploited by playing these stocks against each other using the simple methods we have described.

At a time when even banks are looking shaky, *Beating the Dow* provides a safe and highly effective way for individual investors not only to participate in the wealth-building potential represented by the stocks of these vital multinational enterprises but also to benefit from their enormous adaptability and resilience.

John Neff, one of the great living contrarian investors, had a pithy bit of wisdom when he said, "Get 'em while they're cold."

Beating the Dow is unique in bringing these worthy ideas into the gilt-edged world of the 30 Dow Jones industrials. Like an exclusive club, the silver is heavy, the linen starched, and the leather soft. But there's no lack of action in the squash courts. There's plenty in this venerable club to keep the investment heart pumping.

The ultimate lesson of *Beating the Dow* is Keep It Simple. The investment world has become complex to the point where analysis can be counterproductive. It's like a photograph blown up so you see detail you never imagined—but where you can't recognize the faces.

So it has become for the analysts trying and failing to predict corporate earnings, the economists divided on whether we are headed for recession or continuing recovery, and the technical analysts trying to predict the direction of the markets, only to discover ever-new support and resistance levels.

Sometimes the best way to read the weather is to stop studying the barometer and look out the window.

The investment returns we achieved with the strategies outlined in Beating the Dow–Advanced Method were, by any conventional standard, superior. In several cases, they reduced risk.

But the best returns—I don't mind calling them phenomenal returns—were obtained by methods ingenious for their simplicity. *Beating the Dow* is proof that in investing, simplicity can beat complexity.

APPENDIX A

Recent Deletions and Substitutions in the Dow

A BRIEF review of changes and substitutions in the average since August 1976 is useful. It focuses our attention on exceptional situations, of which two are particularly notable: the greatest turnaround in Dow history and the most dismal *non*-turnaround in Dow history. I'm talking about Chrysler and Manville Corporation, respectively.

Here, first, are the facts:

Date	Deleted	Substituted
August 9, 1976	Anaconda	Minnesota Mining
June 29, 1979	Chrysler	IBM
June 29, 1979	Esmark	Merck
August 30, 1982	Manville Corporation	American Express
October 30, 1985	General Foods	Philip Morris
October 30, 1985	American Brands	McDonald's
March 12, 1987	Owens-Illinois	Coca-Cola
March 12, 1987	Inco Limited	Boeing
May 6, 1991	Navistar International Corporation	Caterpillar, Inc.
May 6, 1991	Primerica Corp.	J.P. Morgan
May 6, 1991	USX Corporation	The Walt Disney Company

(Continued)

Date	Deleted	Substituted
March 17, 1997	Bethlehem Steel	Hewlett-Packard
	Texaco	Johnson & Johnson
	Westinghouse	Travelers Group
	Woolworth	Wal-Mart Stores
November 1, 1999	Chevron	Home Depot
	Goodyear	Intel Corp.
	Sears	Microsoft Corp.
	Union Carbide	SBC Communications

It's probably worth noting that the Dow Jones Company doesn't hire a hall and send out invitations when it makes a change in the average. To the contrary, it all takes place very quietly. According to the *Wall Street Journal:*

> A company is selected for the list by the editors of the *Journal.* The selection is made from companies with large market value, extensive ownership by individuals and institutional investors, consistent earnings and dividends and a leading position in an important industry. The idea is that each of the 30 stocks serves as a proxy for other companies in the same market sector and therefore that the 30-stock index serves as a proxy for the market as a whole.

It can be inferred, with the obvious exception of Dow companies that merge with each other, that the policy guiding deletions uses the same criteria as that determining selections. We can often only surmise what the *Journal* editors had on their minds in any particular case.

ANACONDA

Anaconda Company, an old and leading producer of copper in the United States and Mexico, operated mining, smelting and refining facilities. It also mined lead, zinc, silver, gold and uranium. Through its subsidiaries, Anaconda Wire & Cable Company and the American Brass Company, it was a leading fabricator of copper and brass. Anaconda was also among the nation's largest producers of aluminum.

It joined the Dow in 1959, replacing American Smelting, which was essentially in the same industry.

On March 31, 1976, 27 percent of Anaconda was bought in a cash tender offer by Atlantic Richfield (ARCO) and on January 12, 1977, the company was merged into a subsidiary of Atlantic Richfield pursuant to a Plan and Agreement of Reorganization dated July 26, 1976.

Before its deletion from the Dow, Anaconda had been having trouble. In 1971 its Chilean investments were expropriated, causing a $350 million writeoff net of insurance claims. A relatively high-cost producer in a cyclical industry, its profit margins were highly volatile. Low copper and aluminum prices, operating problems in uranium, and generally poor operating conditions caused a loss in 1975, and Anaconda stock had dropped from a 1969 high of $66 to a 1975 low of $14.

With analysts projecting recovery, Anaconda was the object of takeover attempts by Crane and Tenneco until Atlantic Richfield emerged. With the stock selling at $21, ARCO paid $27 a share for 27 percent of Anaconda, then subsequently exchanged stock and cash for the remaining shares in a transaction that worked out to $32 a share.

ARCO thought it had acquired an inflation hedge in Anaconda, but poor copper conditions persevered and ARCO ultimately restructured it out of its system.

CHEVRON

Chevron was deleted from the Dow November 1, 1999, probably because the editors of the *Wall Street Journal* thought the oil industry would be well enough represented by the newly combined Exxon Mobil.

They all had a common ancestor in John D. Rockefeller's Standard Oil Company, Chevron being the divestiture that became Standard Oil of California (Socal). It later changed its name to make peace with other Standard Oil offspring operating in the same territories.

Chevron was also the white knight that in 1984 saved Gulf Oil from the legendary corporate predator T. Boone Pickens. Up until then, a lot of people thought Gulf was too big to eat. At the time, it was the biggest corporate acquisition in American History. Chevron is now one of the world's largest oil companies, with international operations that include exploration and production of oil and natural gas, crude oil refining, marketing and transportation, and petrochemicals.

Through its acquisition of Tenneco's natural gas properties in Mexico, Chevron is in good shape to benefit from projected increases in the volume and prices of natural gas sold in North America. Its core market continues to be southern California, where environmental activism has been an ongoing challenge for Chevron.

In another development prospect with extraordinary potential, Chevron was the first American oil company to pursue joint ventures with the former Soviet Union as a member of the American Trade Consortium. That gave the company an inside track on having a part in the drilling of the vast (25 billion barrel) Tengiz oil field in Kazakhstan. Construction of a 900-mile pipeline that will connect the huge field to a worldwide export market through the Russian port of Novorossiysk on the Black Sea is expected to be completed in mid-2001.

In early 1999, a combination of slackened demand from the Asian/Pacific markets, a mild winter, and failure of OPEC producers to observe quotas caused crude oil prices to plunge 20 percent to the lowest levels in twenty years. This caused share prices to fall off substantially. Although subsequent production curtailment by OPEC brought crude prices back into the mid-

$20 range later in the year, there remained an overhang of supply on the oil market that caused a consolidation trend in the industry.

Although Chevron was on both sides of takeover rumors in 1999, its especially effective job of cutting costs and expenses prompted its CEO to comment, "We have the financial strength to deal with low oil prices, poor economic conditions in Asia, and other financial challenges over the next few years."

At the time of its deletion, CHV was trading at $91.31. It has paid dividends since 1912.

CHRYSLER

Chrysler's near death and revival (with an assist from the United States government) have become a part of America's industrial folklore and made its scrappy saviour Lee Iacocca a legendary symbol of tough, no-nonsense management.

A Dow stock between 1928 and 1979, Chrysler became one of the original "big three" after Walter Chrysler quit GM to turn around the failing Maxwell Motor Car Company and rename it after himself. But the 1970s were bad times for the American auto industry, and Chrysler, always the weak sister, was the hardest hit. The decade had begun with the oil embargo and gas shortages. GM was quick to respond with smaller cars and gained market share, as did imports. But Ford and Chrysler still offered gas guzzlers, the latter with unappealing designs to boot, and lost market share. A series of price increases further aggravated the situation. New car sales dropped 20 percent in 1974 alone.

By 1978 Chrysler was on the verge of bankruptcy when it turned to Iacocca, recently fired from Ford after a personal feud with Henry Ford II. Iacocca took his considerable persuasive powers to Washington, where he convinced the Carter administration that a Chrysler bankruptcy would exacerbate an already troubled economy. Washington responded with $1.2 billion in loan guarantees in 1979 which, together with labor and lender concessions, gave Chrysler a new lease on life.

By the mid-1980s, with well-received new models, an improved economy, voluntary export restraints by the Japanese competitors and cost cutting combined with industrywide price increases, Chrysler was well on its feet and making advance payments on its government-backed loans.

Although it was dropped from the Dow June 29, 1979 (replaced by IBM, returning for the second time since its own 1956 deletion), investors who held on to their Chrysler saw it peak at just under $50 before the 1987 market crash. On a split-adjusted basis, the stock had seen a low of under $2 from a 1973 high of $20. It resumed paying dividends in 1984. In 1998 Chrysler merged with Daimler-Benz AG of Stuttgart, Germany, to form Daimler-Chrysler AG, which trades on the New York Stock Exchange under the symbol DCX.

ESMARK

In 1973 Esmark Incorporated, the new name of Swift & Company, a Dow stock since 1959, acquired Playtex, a maker of bras and other women's undergarments. In 1979, Esmark was deleted from the Dow.

The old Swift & Company, the nation's leading meat packer, had already become a conglomerate, with interests in petroleum (Vickers Energy Company), fertilizers, adhesives, specialty chemicals, dental equipment, automotive additives and sound systems and, of course, undergarments and personal products.

And it was just warming up. Before he sold Esmark to Beatrice Foods in 1984 for $60 a share, Donald Kelly, the colorful Chicago Irishman who was Esmark's chairman between 1977 and 1984, had made some 50 acquisitions. The last one was Norton Simon, itself a conglomerate with interests in cosmetics and apparel (Halston), foods (Hunt, Wesson), beverages (Canada Dry), liquor

(Johnny Walker Scotch, Tanqueray gin) and publishing *(McCall's, Redbook)*.

Meanwhile the food industry in general was both consolidating and diversifying, a trend that culminated in the late 1980s with Philip Morris/General Foods/Kraft and RJR Nabisco.

Esmark, as noted, was bought out by Beatrice, which finally was taken private by Kohlberg Kravis Roberts & Company in the largest such leveraged buyout ($6.2 billion) until then.

I suppose the Dow Jones Company figured Esmark had lost its identity, that the food industry was undergoing fundamental changes, and that since the Dow had no real representation in the growing health care field, the substitution of Esmark with Merck made sense.

Esmark stockholders had nothing to worry about. The shares, in the high teens (split-adjusted) before the deletion, rose quite steadily following the 1981–82 recession to the $60 level at which Esmark was tendered to Beatrice.

JOHNS MANVILLE CORPORATION

Johns Manville Corporation, I think, was put on earth to prove that no rule is pure. Huge companies, even Dow stocks, can go down for the count. Johns Manville, though, seems finally to be struggling to its feet as I write in 1999.

In the mid-1970s *Moody's Handbook of Common Stocks* said of Johns-Manville, "Earnings tend to move with changes in the national economy, but diversification has helped to stabilize results. The stock is high-grade."

Johns Manville, a Dow stock since 1930, was the world's largest producer of asbestos, which was widely used for insulation and as a fire retardant in the construction industry and had a variety of industrial applications. Although diversified in such areas as fiberglass and plastic pipe, asbestos was its core business.

Asbestos also happened to be extraordinarily profitable,

earning three times the operating margin of any other Manville activity. That may have had something to do with management's obliviousness to mounting evidence that asbestos was the cause of severe, even lethal diseases, mainly of the respiratory system.

Although Manville had been putting warning labels on its asbestos products since 1964 and had won earlier lawsuits, by the early 1980s suits were being filed against the company at the rate of 425 a month. In August 1982 Manville Corporation, having changed its name the previous year, filed for Chapter 11 bankruptcy and the stock was deleted from the Dow.

The stock, which (retroactively adjusted for capital restructuring done as part of its release from bankruptcy) had been as high as $150 in 1977, plunged to under $20.

The bankruptcy reorganization plan provided that Manville transfer 80 percent of its stock to a Personal Injury Settlement Trust, which it also funded with cash and a promise to pay $75 million a year starting in 1991. In addition, the trust had the right after 1992 to 20 percent of Manville's profits if it needed the money to settle claims.

In exchange for that, Manville received court protection from claims against the corporation and was allowed to emerge from bankruptcy in November 1988. In 1989 the company netted $173 million from sales of fiberglass, forest and specialty products.

In 1992 Manville Corporation changed its name to Schuller Corp., but in May 1997 changed it back to the original Johns Manville.

In 1996 the company eliminated a substantial obligation to the trust by issuing 32.5 million common shares in exchange for the trust's right to 20 percent of net profits.

As of April 1999 the trust, which owns 79 percent of Johns Manville, and Johns Manville were exploring options that included a secondary public offering by the trust of a portion of Johns Manville stock, as well as a buyback of stock by Johns Manville.

In September 1999 Standard & Poor's gave JM's outlook a

rating of 4 (1 = lowest, 5 = highest) and estimated its fair value at $21.25. JM had been under $10 between mid-1987 and mid-1996 and was at $14.125 at the time of the S&P report.

Let Manville be a reminder that with stocks, risk is always present, which is what makes a portfolio so important. With Dow stocks, the probability of long-term losses is small. Small but, as Manville proves, not nonexistent.

GENERAL FOODS

General Foods was deleted from the Dow because it was acquired in October 1985 by Philip Morris. General Foods stock, which prior to takeover speculation had been selling at $40 to $60 a share, was tendered at $120. Not a bad deal at all for holders of General Foods.

AMERICAN BRANDS

At the time of the above substitution, *The Wall Street Journal* ran an article pointing out that the combination of Philip Morris and General Foods would overweight the average in the tobacco products and processed food sectors.

The *Journal* therefore deleted American Brands, formerly American Tobacco. American Brands is best known for Lucky Strike and Pall Mall cigarettes and Jim Beam bourbon, but it also makes Swingline staplers and owns Franklin Life Insurance Company. It was a Dow stock from the very beginning.

The substitution of McDonald's increased the Dow's representation in the service sector.

American Brands disposed of its tobacco operations in two transactions. In December 1994 it sold its American Tobacco

Company to Brown & Williamson Tobacco Corporation, a subsidiary of B.A.T. Industries p.l.c., and in May 1997 it spun off Gallaher Group p.l.c. In both cases it gained idemnity from tobacco-related health claims.

Following the Gallaher spin-off, American Brands changed its name to Fortune Brands, which began trading on the New York Stock Exchange June 2, 1977.

OWENS-ILLINOIS

This leading producer of glass containers, plastic bottles, corrugated boxes and other packaging products, a Dow stock since it replaced National Distillers in 1959, was taken private for $2.1 billion in March 1987 by Kohlberg Kravis Roberts, the same gang that did the Beatrice Foods deal. Holders were offered $60.50 for shares that had traditionally been high at half the price (adjusting for a two-for-one split the previous year).

INCO LIMITED

This venerable Canadian company is best known as the world's leading producer of nickel, but it also produces copper, silver and platinum and has other metals processing activities.

Under its former name, International Nickel Company, it became a part of financial folklore by raiding ESB, Inc. (formerly Electric Storage Battery) in 1974. Considered an ungentlemanly act at the time and the more surprising because Inco was aided by the indisputably white-shoe Morgan Stanley & Company, the move started the modern wave of hostile takeovers.

Inco, which has a virtually exclusive franchise on nickel in the free world (as Peter Lynch says, nobody in Japan or Korea can invent a nickel mine), has nonetheless ridden the roller coaster of commodity and precious metals prices through the years.

Since its replacement in the Dow, in March 1987, by Boeing, which brought needed transportation sector representation to the average, Inco, after a $10 special dividend, emerged from the 1987 market crash to soar to a 1989 high of $38 ($48 if you were still holding and counted your special dividend). It saw high $30 levels several times in the nineties, but was back in the single digits in 1998. In late summer 1999, with commodity prices recovering, N trades in the mid-$20 range.

NAVISTAR INTERNATIONAL CORPORATION

Navistar, with about $9 billion in sales, is the truck part of the old International Harvester Company, one of the original 30 Dow stocks. International Harvester, for many years the country's leading manufacturer of farm equipment, got into trouble in the late 1970s and early 1980s when a six-month strike compounded problems caused by high interest rates, President Carter's embargo on grain sales to the Soviet Union and growing levels of food imports. In 1985, it sold its agricultural equipment division and the name International Harvester to J.I. Case, a subsidiary of Tenneco, Inc.

Renamed Navistar, the company has since been focusing on the heavy- and medium-duty truck business, but its road has been a rocky one. Despite a rigorous cost cutting and plant modernization program, the stock, adjusted for a one-for-ten reverse split in 1993, declined to a low of $9 in 1996.

In 1994 the company showed a profit after four consecutive years of losses, but its recovery stalled again in 1996. In 1998 profits were double 1997's and the president's letter in the annual report proclaimed, "In 1998, we gained back a belief in ourselves and in Navistar."

NAV hit a high of $56.25 in 1999.

USX CORPORATION

On May 6, 1991, the same day USX Corporation was deleted from the Dow, shareholders approved a recapitalization plan whereby each share of USX was exchanged for one share of USX-Marathon Group and one fifth of a share of USX-US Steel Group. Both securities are listed on the New York Stock Exchange. USX Corporation's $0.35 quarterly dividend was continued by Marathon Group. Steel Group initiated a $0.25 quarterly dividend in July 1991. At the end of 1990, a share of USX was worth $30.50. Two months later, the Marathon share was trading at $31.25 and the one-fifth Steel share was worth $5.65—total value $36.90.

USX Corporation was the new name given to United States Steel Corporation in 1986 by its biggest shareholder, Carl Icahn. "Big Steel," founded in 1901 by banker J.P. Morgan and one of the original Dow 30, had acquired Marathon Oil, a fully integrated, medium-sized oil and gas company with international activities and extensive North Sea holdings. That was in 1982 and the idea was to use Marathon's strength to counter the cyclicality of the steel business. In 1986 U.S. Steel augmented its energy holdings, especially in natural gas, by paying $4 billion plus for Texas Oil and Gas.

But then low crude oil prices and poor steel conditions conspired to depress the stock, which caught the predatory eye of Mr. Icahn. First attempting a $7 billion takeover of the whole company in October 1986, Icahn was rebuffed by a poison pill defense, but he wound up with a 13.3 percent interest and began immediately trying to split steel and energy into separate businesses. Icahn pressed the argument that the profits and cash flow of the energy operations were propping up the capital- and labor-intensive steel activities and that the two divisions would be worth more to shareholders as separate entities. The original Icahn plan was voted down in a proxy fight in May 1990, but his determination to get the stock price higher registered on USX management and a year later the present restructuring was done at management's initiative.

In the years since USX was deleted, USX-Marathon followed the upward climb of the oil stocks, peaking at about $41 in 1998. When crude oil prices fell in early 1999, MRO dropped to under $20 and has since recovered to low $30 levels.

The United States steel industry has fought an uphill battle against more efficient foreign producers, and USX-United States Steel Group, having seen the mid-$40 range in 1993 and 1994, was trading in 1998 at 1990 levels.

BETHLEHEM STEEL

When it was deleted from the Dow, Bethlehem was its cheapest stock, selling at just over $8.

Although it eked out a profit in 1998 and a somewhat larger one in 1997, the company lost money in five of the last ten years and paid its last dividend in 1991.

Reflecting an industry whose cycles parallel the construction and auto industries, Bethlehem has been up and down since it peaked at just under $30 in 1989. But the steel industry has also been under relentless competition from foreign producers and been faced with increasing competition in automotive applications from other industrial materials, such as aluminum and plastics.

But Bethlehem has struggled valiantly to make itself profitable despite depressed industry conditions. It has closed unprofitable plants, laid off thousands of employees, spent billions modernizing facilities, and greatly reduced its debt.

In October 1996, the company began an extensive restructuring to improve profitability and narrow its focus to three core steel businesses. As a result of the restructuring, it ceased the manufacture of wide flange beams and no longer operates any nonsteel businesses. In May 1998, it acquired Lukens Inc. for about $750 million in order to improve its product mix.

Although BS is selling at $7.875 as this is written in September 1999, a Standard & Poor's August report predicts the company will return to profitability in 2000 and that "the positive change we foresee is predicated on the belief that the steel industry is in the early stages of a solid recovery following the sharp downturn that began in 1998's second quarter."

Among positive factors was a ruling in early May that upheld domestic industry complaints that certain foreign producers were guilty of dumping.

TEXACO, INC.

Texas Company was one of the original thirty Dow Jones industrials. It became Texaco when the company adopted its cable address as its corporate name in 1959. It remains one of the world's largest integrated international oil companies, known in the trade as the majors.

The company's extensive international interests include 50 percent–owned Caltex (Chevron holds the other 50 percent), which operates in 58 countries. In 1988, Texaco and Saudi Arabian Oil Co. formed Star Enterprises, a U.S.-based joint venture that refines, distributes, and markets Texaco-brand petroleum products in twenty-six Eastern and Gulf Coast states and the District of Columbia.

In January 1998 Texaco and Shell Oil merged their midwestern and western U.S. refining and marketing businesses, creating Equilon Enterprises. Shell owns 56 percent and Texaco owns 44 percent.

In July, the two companies and Saudi Refining Inc. merged Star Enterprises, forming Motiva Enterprises.

Unlike its peers, Texaco does not have chemicals operations.

In the mid-1980s Texaco was ordered to pay $10.3 billion to Pennzoil Company, which it had outbid in a successful move to acquire Getty Oil. Pennzoil had sued, charging Texaco with tortious interference with a contract it already had with Getty. After losing an appeal, Texaco declared bankruptcy to avoid having to post a bond to cover the award. Corporate raider Carl Icahn, who owned 12 percent of Texaco, got Texaco and Pennzoil to settle for $3 billion and Texaco emerged from bankruptcy in 1988.

Texaco was again in the news in 1996 when it agreed to pay $176.1 million to settle a racial discrimination lawsuit brought by six black officials in the company's finance department. The case received wide publicity, including transcripts of audio tapes of managers belittling black employee grievances.

Texaco stock, which was selling at just under $110 before the discrimination suit, dropped to the nineties before the settlement. It recovered, split 2-for-1 in 1997, dipped on lower oil prices in late 1988, then went to an all time high of over $70 in the spring of 1999 on news that Texaco and Chevron were having merger talks. The talks failed, but merger speculation still surrounds Texaco and that, plus higher oil prices, has TX in the low-sixties range in the fall of 1999.

WESTINGHOUSE ELECTRIC CORPORATION

Westinghouse was formed in 1866 to manufacture and promote alternating current (AC), a revolutionary technological improvement on direct current (DC) that permitted greatly increased voltage to carry far greater distances and could be reduced to safe levels at the point of use. Its founder, George Westinghouse, held the first patent on a lightbulb, a variation of Thomas Edison's invention.

Before the turn of the twentieth century, Westinghouse had a contract to install three AC generators at Niagra Falls, which became the first big hydroelectric project and made AC the industry standard.

In 1957, Westinghouse designed and developed the first nuclear power plant, in Shippingport, Pennsylvania, and then went on to lead the world in nuclear reactors.

By the mid-1990s, 19 percent of total revenues were derived

from the company's Group W and other radio and TV broadcasting activities, 50 percent of revenues were from power systems for electrical utilities, 18 percent from Thermo King temperature control equipment for the transportation industry, and the balance from assorted industrial, communications, and financial activities.

In October 1995, the company paid $5.4 billion to acquire CBS Corp. and began divesting its industrial businesses. By year end 1966, some 60 percent of revenues derived from broadcasting activities. Broadcasting became the focus of the company, which became CBS Corp. in December of 1997. CBS was trading at around $50 in late summer 1999, more than twice the approximately $20 price of a Westinghouse share when CBS was acquired.

On September 8, 1999 Viacom Inc. agreed to acquire CBS for about $36 billion in stock. Assuming regulatory approval, Viacom's fast-growing cable-TV networks and the CBS broadcasting and outdoor advertising assets are considered a good strategic combination.

Viacom-CBS would have annual sales of about $21 billion and $4 billion in annual cash flow.

WOOLWORTH CORPORATION

Woolworth Corporation was started in 1894 and was one of the original 30 Dow Industrials. Best known for its inner-city variety stores, it expanded in the 1980s into mall-based specialty stores, such as Northern Reflections, Kinney Shoes, Foot Locker, Champs Sports, and others.

At fiscal year end January 1991, Woolworth operated more than 8,600 stores in the United States, Canada, West Germany, Australia, Belgium, and the Netherlands—including some 7,000 specialty units and 1,600 general merchandise stores. It was celebrating its eighth consecutive year of increased operating earnings.

The 1990s, however, began with lackluster sales from recessionary economies in the United States and abroad. In addition, Woolworth's volume leader, its Footlocker chain of athletic shoes and accessories, began showing signs of maturity with level, then declining, sales and profits. In 1993, the company announced it would close 970 stores in the United States and Canada, eliminate 13,000 jobs, and take a $480 million charge, citing unfavorable economic conditions, increased competitive pressures, and depressed consumer spending.

In the spring of 1994, the company stunned the investment community with the announcement that it had appointed a directors' committee to investigate accounting irregularities, that it would be restating its earnings for the fiscal year ending January 1994, and that its chief executive officer and chief financial officer would step down pending the outcome of the investigation. When concluded, the investigation found that "senior management had failed to create an environment in which it was clear to employees at all levels that inaccurate financial reporting would not be tolerated." This led to the resignations of the CFO and, in October, the CEO. In the meantime Woolworth shares had plunged from the mid $30 range in 1993 to around $12.

Hopes of a turnaround were raised in spring 1995 when Roger N. Farah, former president of Macy's, came abroad as CEO. Farrah suspended the company's annual dividend, sold off some unprofitable units, and made some operational progress, but he was preoccupied with financial matters and unable to address the company's main problem: It was in the wrong businesses in the wrong places.

By early 1999, the company, now renamed Venator Group, had two consecutive loss years behind it and was selling at under $5 a share. But it has restructured its athletic footwear operations, and apparently put the worst behind it. Value Line's May 21, 1999 report concludes, "As the market leader (in athletic footwear) at retail, Venator stands to benefit handsomely from a recovery."

GOODYEAR

Goodyear earned a place in the *Beating the Dow* Hall of Fame in 1991, when it produced a total return of 185.5 percent, following a restructuring that reduced debt and cut costs.

After that, the tire and rubber industry, a cyclical business anyway, had more than the usual ups and downs. When it was deleted from the Dow November 1, 1999, GT was selling at $41 and change. By the end of that month, it was at $28 and a fraction, after announcing a disappointing third quarter.

Goodyear, whose 1998 sales were $12.6 billion, derives 96 percent of its sales from automotive products, mainly tires, but also hoses, belts, tubes, foam cushioning accessories, and repair services. The balance includes chemicals, plastics, shoe products, roofing materials, and industrial products. Replacement tire volume, which tends to be countercyclical, is significantly higher than sales to the original equipment market. The company produces in thirty-four plants in the United States and thirty-nine plants in twenty-four other countries. It also operates six rubber plantations.

With the domestic auto industry enjoying a boom period in the late 1990s, you'd expect Goodyear's sales to up too. But the tire industry has been one of those basic industries suffering from worldwide overcapacity. As a result, even as tires have become more advanced and durable, the consumer is paying less in absolute dollars today than was the case ten years ago.

Compounding a pricing problem has been the fact that troubled economies in Asia and Latin America have reduced demand there and increased supply domestically. The good news is that conditions have forced companies to become more efficient and to consolidate.

In February of 1999, Goodyear announced an alliance with Sumitomo Rubber Industries Ltd. of Japan that will extend its global reach and make it the world's number one tire maker. Sumitomo and Goodyear will swap ownership stakes in each other and Goodyear will pay $936 million for the value of Sumitomo's contributions to a series of joint ventures. Analysts estimate the savings from the Sumitomo ventures could add $1 to $1.30 a share to Goodyear's bottom line within three years.

Goodyear's financial goals, as stated early in 1998, are to grow sales at twice the industry rate, generating $20 million to $23 billion by the end of 2003; to reduce selling, general, and administrative expenses to below 12 percent of sales; and to produce a return on sales of 6.5 percent to 7.5 percent annually.

SEARS

Sears, Roebuck & Company, Inc. was one of the original 30 Dow Industrials designated in 1928. Its unique identification with Americana (the old Sears catalog had been a fixture in American houses, the out variety included, for many decades) made its deletion in November 1999 a sad event.

But times change, and so did Sears, but it was all too little and too late.

Sears started as a mail order operation. When the automobile made America mobile, Sears began opening retail stores, eventually becoming America's largest retailer and later yielding that honor to Wal-Mart. In 1972, Sears' sales amounted to 1 percent of the United States gross national product

In the 1980s, Sears, having owned Allstate Insurance since 1921, caught the financial supermarket bug. It acquired Dean Witter Financial Services, engaged in securities brokerage, investment banking, consumer finance, and mortgage banking; bought Coldwell Banker Real Estate, a developer manager and broker of real estate; and introduced the Discover credit card.

While these businesses never produced the synergies envisioned, they nonetheless accounted for 55 percent of 1992 profits, which says something about the sorry state Sears' primary retail business had reached. Sears Merchandising had stopped expanding and was stuck in regional shopping malls when strips were the trend. Its catalog operations were losing money. It had women's dresses hanging next to lawnmowers. Its cash registers were out of date, its sales people surly, its executive organization bloated.

But then began one of the great turnaround stories in American business. In September 1992, Sears suddenly announced plans to shed its financial services and real estate activities, reversing its ten-year "socks and stocks" strategy. It hired an outsider, Arthur Martinez of Saks Fifth Avenue, to revitalize its merchandising group and change its image from a general merchandiser to a department store. Meanwhile, it spun off Dean Witter and Discover in 1993, discontinued its catalog, and in 1995 spun off Allstate, giving investors that year a total return of 71.5 percent.

After hitting an all-time high of $63 in June 1997, Sears plunged to $41 the following October. Seems that a lot of its booming sales were charged to Sear's credit cards distributed indiscriminately to shoppers who were not paying their bills. By the spring of 1998, credit card problems were under control and the stock again hit $63. But slow apparel sales combined with reduced revenues from scaled-back credit operations produced lackluster results. Sears dropped again and was at $28 when Home Depot replaced it in the Dow.

Argus Research says, "Driving 1999 results are a revamped credit operation, a continued focus on an already strong hard line business, and a revitalized strategy for recapturing the core middle market apparel constituency. In addition, the company has a growing online business that could prove highly successful. We reiterate our buy recommendation."

UNION CARBIDE

Along with Sears, Union Carbide (UK) had been one of the original Dow 30 before its deletion in 1999 at $61. The precipitating factor seemed to be its 1999 acquisition by Dow Chemical, although there's no relationship between the Dow Chemical and Dow Jones. Anyway, Union Carbide's shares jumped 22 percent on August 4, 1999, the day Dow Chemical offered 0.537 of its shares for each share of UK, in a deal expected to close early in 2000.

The combined company would have $24 billion in revenues, ranking number two globally behind DuPont and ahead of Germany's BASF AG.

Union Carbide is a good example of the "back to basics" trends of the 1990s. For sixty-odd years through the 1970s, it had been a stolid producer of chemicals, rolling with the punches of a cyclical industry. Then came the recession in the early 1980s, which hammered the industry in general and Union Carbide in particular.

To hedge the cyclicality of commodity chemicals, and using advantages from its strength in basic chemicals, the company diversified and gained significant market share in such products as antifreeze, batteries, and plastic wrappings, including Glad Bags.

Then came the infamous Bhopal, India, disaster in 1984, when deadly gas leaked from a 51 percent–owned pesticide plant, killing more than 3,000 people. Litigation on behalf of Bhopal victims exceeded $4 billion.

That was followed a year later by a hostile takeover attempt led by Samuel Heyman, head of GAF Corporation. To ensure the loyalty of shareholders, Carbide sold its consumer products division, its agricultural division, and its sybaritic Connecticut headquarters for $3.5 billion and paid shareholders $4.5 billion in special dividends and other payments. It had preserved its independence, but at the price of heavy debt and the loss of its most promising activities.

In 1989, UK realigned into a holding company and three separate operating companies. The first of those, UCAR Carbon, was 50 percent sold off in 1990 to Mitsubishi Corp. of Japan and carried thereafter as an investment. In mid-1992, Union Carbide Industrial Gases, Inc., was spun off to shareholders, who got a

share of a new company called Praxair, and racked up a 69.8 percent total return for that year.

After that Union Carbide, back to basic chemicals, rode an
industry upcycle to a record high of $57 in mid–1997. When signs
of another downcycle began appearing in late 1997, UK began taking strict cost-control measures aimed at minimum "trough" earnings of $4 a share.

For its part, Dow Chemical has sold off Ziplock bags, Fantastik
cleaner, and other products to refocus on chemistry-related businesses. It has also reduced costs and expanded geographically. The
merger is generally viewed as a good fit that expands Dow's performance businesses while strengthening its commodity businesses. The industry is looking up once again and the combined
company would appear to have excellent prospects.

As a general comment on stocks that were deleted from the Dow
prior to 1997, it is clear that anybody left holding them would have
made out quite nicely.

When Navistar, Primerica and USX were replaced by
Caterpillar, Disney and Morgan in 1991, *Money* magazine, noting
that the three substitutions had risen initially on the news, asked if
I thought they should be bought simply by virtue of their having
been added to the Dow. I responded by pointing out that in the preceding twelve years, with the exception of Manville, the stock that
was dumped fared better than its successor. Since the 1997
changes, however, the reverse seems to be true.

APPENDIX B

A Look at the Major Outperformers

ALTHOUGH WHAT I said about it taking four Manvilles to lose money with a five-stock high-yield/low-priced portfolio in 1982 is absolutely true, I must admit I lucked out again. I certainly don't want to make light of anything as serious as the risk of stock ownership and the value of diversification.

Sears, Roebuck, the cheapest stock after Manville, gained 95.26 percent that year, and Woolworth, the next cheapest, gained 53.75 percent—two retailers starting from the bargain basement of a stock market that was anticipating recovery from one of the worst recessions in history.

It is entirely within the realm of possibility that a five-stock portfolio under other circumstances would have lost heavily, although the previous year (1981) Manville dropped over 34 percent and the five-stock portfolio gained 5.02 percent, still outperforming a Dow that went underwater by −3.02 percent.

The fact that in recent years there is no example to dramatically illustrate the greater safety of the ten-stock alternative doesn't change an indisputable fact: stocks are vulnerable to risk, and diversification helps reduce that risk. It's a question of how well you sleep at night. As long as that's clear, the choice is yours.

There were several years when high-yield stocks outperformed the Dow to an exceptional extent, and it will be both useful and fun to take a close-up look at them.

The first example were the years 1973 through 1976, when, to recap the results summarized on page 202, the five high-yield, low-priced stock portfolio outperformed the Dow as follows:

Year	5 High-Yield/ Low-Priced	DJIA Total Return
1973	19.64%	− 13.12%
1974	− 3.75	− 23.14
1975	70.07	44.40
1976	40.79	22.72

The individual five-stock portfolios in those years and the performance of their components is shown below:

Year	Stock	Total Return
1973	American Can (Primerica)	− 10.04%
	U.S. Steel	28.62
	General Foods	− 11.75
	Allied Chemical (Allied-Signal)	73.41
	Bethlehem Steel	17.96
Average:		19.64%
1974	Chrysler	− 41.70
	United Aircraft (United Technologies)	48.75
	Johns-Manville (Manville Corp.)	25.45
	Goodyear	− 8.82
	Woolworth	− 42.42
Average:		− 3.75%
1975	Chrysler	39.66
	Woolworth	157.24
	Westinghouse	43.55
	Anaconda	32.41
	Goodyear	77.48
Average:		70.07%

(Continued)

Year	Stock	Total Return
1976	Texaco	27.27
	International Harvester (Navistar)	55.08
	Westinghouse	39.10
	Standard Oil of California (Chevron)	46.95
	International Nickel Company (Inco)	<u>35.54</u>
Average:		40.79%

The years 1973 and 1974 were bad years for the market as a whole. The Dow, which closed 1972 at 1020.02, closed 1973 at 850.86 and 1974 at 616.24 before beginning its recovery the following year. In 1973 only eight of the 30 Dow stocks rose, and in 1974 only seven, and they were different stocks.

Our 1973 portfolio was led by U.S. Steel, then exclusively a steel company, Bethlehem Steel and Allied Chemical, then still a chemical company. That these three companies led the group reflected a short-lived market theory known at the time as the shortage thesis.

Somewhat simplistically put, the economic boom that began in 1963 and continued through 1966, before leveling off, left supplies of basic raw materials such as chemicals and steel in short supply. Prices began rising in the early 1970s and earnings of these companies peaked in 1974.

The other two companies in the 1973 portfolio, American Can and General Foods, both being "defensive" food or food-related stocks, were simply off less than other stocks that affected the average negatively.

In 1974, the economy began sliding into stagflation, with unemployment over 7 percent and inflation over 10 percent. The Arab oil embargo had gone into effect in 1973, creating fuel shortages and causing factory closings.

Two companies in our 1974 portfolio benefited from the fuel crisis—Johns-Manville, which sold fuel-saving insulation materials, and United Aircraft, whose jet engines were in demand from an aircraft industry that was switching to fuel-efficient planes. These gains, of 25.45 percent and 48.75 percent, were enough in a generally depressed Dow to offset the dismal results of Chrysler and Woolworth, which both lost over 40 percent. Goodyear raised its dividend that year despite lower earnings, and was off only 8.82 percent.

Nineteen seventy-five brought raging inflation, but by midsummer the market had turned around. Chrysler and Woolworth, the prior year's worst losers, bounced back. The latter, an inflation-sensitive stock, gained 157 percent and was clearly the dominant factor in the outperformance.

Westinghouse, which, as we saw in an earlier chapter, had almost gone under and was the worst-performing of all the Dow stocks in 1974, showed a 43.55 percent gain as the market took note of its survival. Anaconda was the object of several suitors and rose on takeover speculation as well as anticipated higher metals prices. Goodyear's earnings were up, and it was doubtless still benefiting from the prior year's dividend increase.

In 1976 the Dow broke 1000. Jimmy Carter had been elected to bring the economy and inflation under control. Instead inflation went to even higher levels in the next three years, giving us our first double-digit prime rate.

Our five-stock portfolio that year was led by International Harvester (now Navistar), which was anticipating a cyclical recovery that never materialized. The anticipated recovery also explains the rise in International Nickel (Inco). Westinghouse continued to recover. Otherwise, the action was in the oil stocks, namely Texaco and Chevron, which were now benefiting from the higher prices resulting from the Arab embargo of 1973.

As a general comment on the 1970s, the bull markets were led by the nifty fifty, which were seen as solid investments offering sure growth potential. The bear markets were caused by depressed basic industry stocks that were caught in the shift to a service economy.

In 1980, our five-stock portfolio returned 40.53 and the Dow returned 21.41.

At the onset of the 1980s, everyone was obsessed with energy and the technology required to produce or save it. Oil prices, which had gone from $18 a barrel in 1976 to $35 in 1980 (spurred by the Iranian revolution in 1979), were about to tumble.

Texaco, which was putting less of its profits into exploration than its competitors, was anticipating higher earnings in 1981 (when other oil companies were looking at declines) and led the portfolio in 1980 with a 74.72 percent gain.

Manville, with its fuel-saving insulation, gained 10.55 percent. U.S. Steel, which had suffered a deficit in 1979 of nearly a half-billion dollars, came back in 1980 and was up 50.57 percent. Bethlehem Steel, anticipating higher 1981 earnings, was up 32.43 percent. Goodyear, down in 1979 on earnings, recovered and was up 34.37 percent.

In 1982 the five-stock portfolio outperformed the Dow 37.36 percent to 25.79 percent.

The retailing stocks, Sears and Woolworth, were characteristically strong in a market anticipating economic recovery. Sears soared 95.26 percent to offset Manville's 26.52 percent decline.

Westinghouse, having increased its dividend the previous year, enjoyed a 59.51 gain as it continued its steady recovery. The outperformance was also helped by the fact that Bethlehem Steel and United States Steel took major writeoffs in a year that they figured couldn't be much worse anyway; that depressed their stocks and curbed the exuberance of a Dow that otherwise was up on favorable economic forecasts.

In 1983 and 1984, the DJIA peaked out in mid-1983, moved sideways until year end, corrected sharply into the summer of 1984 and then built a bottom springboard for the upward explosion of 1985.

Our five-stock portfolio beat the Dow handily both years—by

41 percent in 1983 and 116 percent in 1984—due to its 60 percent weighting in high-yielding oils (Chevron, Exxon and Texaco) and help from American Can (+83.7 percent), American Express (+19.3 percent) and Woolworth (+42.7 percent).

The 1987 and 1988 outperformance of 11.06 percent and 21.43 percent compared to the DJIA's return of 6.02 percent and 15.95 percent, respectively, can be attributed to the portfolio's heavy weighting in import-sensitive cyclicals which were hurt so badly by the strong dollar from 1980 to 1985, but bounced back strongly and led the Dow in 1987 and 1988.

By December 31, 1991, our five stocks had again knocked the cover off the ball by returning 61.86 percent while the Dow's total return was a very respectable but far inferior 23.91 percent. The common thread in 1991's winners was their sensitivity to signs of economic recovery, which promised a revival in earnings and continuity of the fat dividends that got us to buy them in the first place.

But there were other explanations: Goodyear, which had a stunning total return of 185.49 percent as the PPP, reflected the combined effects of a recovering economy and a dramatic operational turnaround under CEO Stanley Gault, who had performed similar miracles in his previous capacity as CEO of Rubbermaid. Goodyear's remarkable gain more than offset a 31.93 percent negative return of Westinghouse Electric, whose main businesses would not benefit until late in the recovery cycle and whose financial and office furniture businesses were adversely affected by a weak commercial real estate market.

Union Carbide, up 29.73 percent, and AlliedSignal, up 68.44 percent, had been double-digit losers the previous year, when the crisis in the Persian Gulf affected stock values. Sears, which gained 57.13 percent, was an internal recovery story as well as an economic story. It had announced plans to divest of its financial and real estate activities and get back to basics.

In 1992 the five-stock portfolio returned 23.22 percent compared with the Dow's 7.4 percent. The leader that year was Union Carbide, whose 69.78 percent return included the value of Praxair, a new company formed when Union Carbide's industrial gases division was spun off to shareholders.

GM and Sears contributed 16.10 percent and 25.08 returns, respectively, as GM reported operational progress and Sears announced the hiring of CEO Arthur Martinez, formerly of Saks Fifth Avenue, to head its retail operations. American Express, up 26.99 percent, was "holding talks" aimed at divesting of its Shearson Lehman subsidiary as a step toward refocusing on its core travel-related services.

Gains in these four stocks offset a 21.85 percent loss in Westinghouse, whose financial losses due to bad real estate investments were spurring talk of bankruptcy.

In 1993 the five stocks returned 34.26 percent versus the Dow's 16.80 percent. Sears led the group with a 50 percent return after making good on its promise to spin off Dean Witter Discover. Eastman Kodak followed with a 43.90 percent return after spinning off Eastman Chemical, reducing debt and demonstrating a resolve to focus on core photography activities. American Express gained 28.10 percent after hiring CEO Harvey Golub, who sold Shearson to Primerica for $1.5 billion and promised other concrete actions to put AmEx back on track. Union Carbide gained 39.10 percent on increased profits, and Westinghouse produced a positive 10.3 percent return as it began showing the results of the economic recovery and hired its first outside CEO in 64 years.

Nineteen ninety-four saw a series of Federal Reserve rate increases and the Dow gained only 4.90 percent, but the five-stock portfolio returned 8.60 percent despite a negative 37.4 percent turned in by Woolworth. Union Carbide and DuPont, both late-cycle recovery stocks, led with gains of 34.60 percent and 20.10 percent, respectively.

In the years 1995 through 1998 a raging bull market was paced by overpriced, high-capitalization growth stocks, which had disproportionate influence in the price-weighted Dow. The result, an aberration, was that our ten-stock portfolio did slightly better on average than the five-stock portfolio, while both underperformed the Dow. The returns in both our basic portfolios continued to be superior to professionally managed portfolios but underperformed the Dow and the S&P 500 indexes, which were inflated by a relative handful of high-priced stocks with dangerously high price-earnings ratios.

Bibliography

Arbel, Avner. *How to Beat the Market with High-Performance Generic Stocks*. New York: New American Library, 1986.

Blamer, Thomas, and Shulman, Richard. *Dow Three Thousand: The Investment Opportunity of the 1980s*. New York: Simon & Schuster, 1982.

Bruck, Connie. *The Predator's Ball: The Inside Story of Drexel Burnham and the Rise of the Junk Bond Raiders*. New York: Penguin Books, 1989.

Cobleigh, Ira U. *Happiness Is a Stock That Lets You Sleep at Night*. New York: Donald I. Fine, 1989.

Downes, John, and Goodman, Jordan Elliot. *Dictionary of Finance and Investment Terms*. 5th ed. Hauppauge, N.Y.: Barron's Educational Series, 1998.

Dreman, David. *Contrarian Investment Strategies: The Next Generation*. New York: Simon & Schuster, 1998.

Fisher, Kenneth. *Super Stocks*. New York: McGraw-Hill, 1991.

Glassman, James K., and Hassett, Kevin A. *Dow 36,000: A New Strategy for Profiting from the Coming Rise in the Stock Market*. New York: Random House, 1999.

Graham, Benjamin. *The Intelligent Investor*. 4th rev. ed. New York: HarperCollins, 1985.

Hirsch, Yale. *Don't Sell Stocks on Monday: An Almanac for Traders, Brokers and Stock Market Investors*. New York: Penguin Books, 1986.

Knowles, Harvey C., and Petty, Damon H. *The Dividend Investor: A Safe and Sure Way to Beat the Market with High-Yield Dividend Stocks*. Chicago: Probus Publishing, 1995.

Lynch, Peter, with Rothchild, John. *One Up on Wall Street*. New York: Simon & Schuster, 1989.

Malkiel, Burton G. *A Random Walk Down Wall Street*. rev. ed. New York: W.W. Norton & Company, 1999.

Mattera, Philip. *Inside U.S. Business: A Concise Encyclopedia of Leading Industries*. Homewood, Ill.: Dow Jones-Irwin, 1987.

Naisbitt, John, and Aburdene, Patricia. *Megatrends 2000: 10 New Directions for the 1990s*. New York: Avon, 1991.

O'Glove, Thornton L., with Sobel, Robert. *Quality of Earnings: The Investor's Guide to How Much Money a Company Is Really Making*. New York: The Free Press, 1987.

O'Higgins, Michael B., with John McCarty. *Beating the Dow with Bonds: A High-Return, Low-Risk Strategy for Outperforming the Pros Even When Stocks Go South*. New York: HarperBusiness, 1998.

O'Neil, William J. *How to Make Money in Stocks: A Winning System in Good Times and Bad*. New York: McGraw-Hill, 1994.

Peters, Thomas J., and Waterman, Robert H., Jr. *In Search of Excellence: Lessons from America's Best-Run Companies*. New York: Warner Books, 1988.

Rosenberg, Claude N., Jr. *Investing with the Best: What to Look For, What to Look Out For in Your Search for a Superior Investment Manager*. New York: John Wiley & Sons, 1993.

Siegel, Jeremy J., and Peter L. Bernstein. *Stocks for the Long Run: The Definitive Guide to Financial Market Returns and Long-Term Investment Strategies*. 2nd ed. New York: McGraw-Hill, 1997.

Stillman, Richard J. *Dow Jones Industrial Average: History and Role in an Investment Strategy*. Homewood, Ill.: Dow Jones-Irwin, 1986.

Train, John. *The Money Masters: Nine Great Investors: Their Winning Strategies & How You Can Apply Them*. New York: Harper-Business. 1994.

———— *The New Money Masters: Winning Investment Strategies of: Soros, Lynch, Steingard, Rogers, Neff, Wanger, Michaelis, Carret*. New York: HarperBusiness, 1994.

Walden, Gene. *The 100 Best Stocks to Own in America*. 5th ed. Chicago: Dearborn, 1998.

Zweig, Martin E. *Winning on Wall Street*. New York: Warner Books, 1994.

Index

293